MARRIAGE AND ITS OBSTACLES IN JEWISH LAW

Essays and Responsa

STUDIES IN PROGRESSIVE HALAKHAH, VOLUME VIII

Also in this Series

Walter Jacob and Moshe Zemer (eds.) DYNAMIC JEWISH LAW, Progressive Halakhah - Essence and Application

Walter Jacob and Moshe Zemer (eds.) RABBINIC - LAY RELATIONS IN JEWISH LAW

Walter Jacob and Moshe Zemer (eds.) CONVERSION TO JUDAISM IN JEWISH LAW - Essays and Responsa

Walter Jacob and Moshe Zemer (eds.) DEATH AND EUTHANASIA IN JEWISH LAW - Essays and Responsa

Walter Jacob and Moshe Zemer (eds.) THE FETUS AND FERTILITY IN JEWISH LAW - Essays and Responsa

Walter Jacob and Moshe Zemer (eds.) ISRAEL AND THE DIASPORA IN JEWISH LAW - Essays and Responsa

Walter Jacob and Moshe Zemer (eds.) AGING AND THE AGED IN JEWISH LAW - Essays and Responsa

MARRIAGE AND ITS OBSTACLES

IN JEWISH LAW

Essays and Responsa

Edited by
Walter Jacob and Moshe Zemer

Freehof Institute of Progressive Halakah
Rodef Shalom Press
Tel Aviv and Pittsburgh
1999

Published by the Rodef Shalom Press
4905 Fifth Avenue
Pittsburgh, PA 15213
U.S.A.

4905 Fifth Avenue
Pittsburgh, PA 15213
U.S.A.

4 Rehov Levitan
69204 Tel Aviv
Israel

Library of Congress Catalog Card Number 99-074145

Jacob, Walter 1930-

Zemer, Moshe 1932-

ISBN 0-929699-10

Dedicated

to

Daniel, Eslyn, and Bari

a happy family

CONTENTS

PREFACE

We continue to be grateful to the Rodef Shalom Congregation for supporting the Freehof Institute of Progressive *Halakhah* and its assistance in technical matters connected with the publication of this volume. Our special thanks to Nancy Berkowitz who has carefully copy edited and proof read this volume. We wish to thank Barbara Bailey for her efforts with the typescript for this volume as well as previous volumes.

INTRODUCTION

The Bible views marriage as a natural human relationship and so it devoted little time or attention to its details. Adam found a helpmate; the patriarch took wives from a close circle of relatives and added concubines. Various kinds of relationships were prohibited in the legal books, but the total material on the subject is limited.

The rabbinic period made up for this paucity of material as it discussed marriage at length and in an eminently practical manner with entire tractates of the Talmud devoted to the nature of the marriage bond (*kidushin*), the economics of marriage (*ketubot*), the discipline of sexual relations (*niddah*). This mass of the material rather than solving every conceivable problem, broadened the discussion and led to a whole range of subjects which the earlier Biblical writers had not even dreamed of. Many areas of this precious human relationship had only been partially covered and the widened discussions brought new matters into the discussion.

Neither the Bible nor the Talmud took monogamy for granted, we do and state that it has been a norm of Jewish life for more than a thousand years The story is not so simple or uncomplicated and the road has been long and difficult. Various impediments to marriage such as an adulterous relationships or remarriage with those of dubious descent played a major role in the rabbinic discussions. For centuries in the early rabbinic period efforts to maintain genealogies were made by leading families. Economic decline, persecution, and the vagaries of human life led to the abandonment of this effort. Our century sees many matters related to marriage in a different light. It is not only that our time is different, but our understanding of the past has changed.

Marriage with other groups was treated through a handful of summary prohibitions in the Pentateuch and then virtually ignored in the remaining Biblical literature. It obviously existed as we can see from the descriptions of the lives of the nobility and the common people. The prophets denounced the relationships with non-Israelites and Ezra sought to destroy them as they would weaken the devotion to Judaism. Neither effort succeeded and in the rabbinic period a new method of bringing Gentiles into the Jewish people provided a different approach to such marriages. These problems have been faced differently through the ages.

The essays of this volume and the responsa in the second half of the book deal with some of these issues. The issues are important and very much alive for Jews wherever they live - in the Diaspora or in Israel.

SAMUEL HOLDHEIM ON THE LEGAL CHARACTER OF JEWISH MARRIAGE: A CONTEMPORARY COMMENT ON HIS POSITION

David Ellenson

In 1 Samuel 10:11–12, the Jewish people are reported to have seen King Saul participating in the ecstasy of a band of prophets. The anomaly of this sight caused the people to exclaim incredulously to one another, *"Ha-im gam Sha'ul ba-n'vi'im*—Is Saul, too, among the prophets?" Inspired by their example, we today, gathered for a session of the Freehof Institute for Progressive Halakhah devoted to Samuel Holdheim (1806–1860) and his views on intermarriage, can likewise ask, *"Ha-im gam She'muel b-va'a'lei ha-halakhah*—Is Samuel, too, among the halakhists?"

Samuel Holdheim was the preeminent spokesman for radical Reform during the nineteenth century. He assessed the *halakhah* as a transitory element within Judaism and abjured law as an enduring dimension of the Jewish religion. Nevertheless, Holdheim, in his most famous work, *Über die Autonomie der Rabbinen und das Princip der jüdischen Ehe* (1843),[1] offered a serious and insightful analysis of *kinyan* as it related to *di'nei kiddushin* in Jewish law. We can see the reasoning he employed in this analysis as supplying a base for comprehending the stance he adopted regarding the question of Jewish-Christian intermarriage at the Brunswick Rabbinical Conference of 1844.

My presentation in this paper will delineate Holdheim's arguments on these matters and will take note of the critique Zacharias Frankel (1801–1875) lodged against his position. I shall place this debate within its historical context and conclude by offering my own thoughts on what the implications of Holdheim's stance on the matter of intermarriage might be for Liberal Jews today.

HOLDHEIM'S ANALYSIS OF *KINYAN* IN RELATION TO *DI'NEI KIDDUSHIN* AND FRANKEL'S RESPONSE

Holdheim's halakhic analysis of *di'nei kiddushin* focused on the nature of *kinyan* in Jewish matrimonial law. In offering his analysis, Holdheim set for himself the task of determining whether *kinyan* as it related to marriage was distinct from the mechanism of *kinyan* in other cases of acquisition.[2] In the first half of *Die Autonomie,* Holdheim noted that Jewish law used the term *kinyan* to refer to a variety of acts in which a person voluntarily obtains legal rights—both proprietary and contractual. *Kinyan,* for example, was the legal mechanism whereby one could acquire legal right to ownerless *(hefker)* or neglected *(yeiush)* property. *Kinyan* was also the means through which one acquired ownership over property through sale or gift. Holdheim further pointed out that *kinyan* referred to contractual or personal rights one party held in relation to another, such as servitude *(shi'bud)* or debt. Holdheim also noted that for *kinyan* to be legally valid and binding in Jewish law, in every instance the person or party that obtained legal rights had to affirm the acquisition by his or her own free will. Secondly, in cases where a previous person or party held legal rights, he or she had to consent freely to the transmission of those rights. If these conditions were met, *kinyan* could be effectuated. This was true of every mode of *kinyan* in Jewish law. As the act of *kinyan* was a standard part of virtually every act of acquisition in Jewish law, Holdheim argued that *kinyan* was a civil act.[3]

Holdheim went on, in light of these observations on the overarching nature of *kinyan,* to address the question of whether *kinyan* in connection with the institution of Jewish marriage also constituted a civil act. In other words, Holdheim sought to determine whether the act of marriage transformed the character of *kinyan* in such a way that the *kinyan* of marriage could be regarded as so qualitatively distinct from *kinyan* in other cases of legal acquisition that it no longer constituted a civil act. He ultimately concluded that the act of marriage did not accomplish this transformation. He maintained that Jewish law regarded the act of *kinyan* in relation to marriage as a civil act, just as it did the act of *kinyan* in any other instance of acquisition. As long as all the conditions of the acquisition were known to all involved in the transaction, *kinyan* was established, and a state of *kiddushin* (marriage) obtained between the husband and his wife. Holdheim claimed that the sentiments of love and trust that may well have existed between the man and woman were of no legal relevance in establishing a state of *kiddushin* between them as husband and wife. Even if these sentiments were lacking, the *kiddushin* between the man and the woman was valid and binding as long as the parties involved gave their consent and the husband gave his bride a coin worth at least a *perutah.*[4]

Holdheim buttressed his contention that the act of *kinyan* in marriage was a civil one no different from other acts of *kinyan* in Jewish law by comparing Jewish legal sources that dealt with the process of acquisition in the case of slaves and real estate with the stipulations put forth concerning the act of *kinyan* in regard to marriage. The Talmud, in the instance of slaves and real estate, asserted that legal title could be acquired in three ways: money, contract, and usucaption *(kesef, shtar, v'hazakah)*.[5] Holdheim then pointed out that a wife was acquired by her husband in a parallel fashion. As the Talmud states in *Kiddushin* 2a, "A woman is acquired in three ways: money, contract, and intercourse."[6] The first two modes of acquisition—money and contract—provided the normative means whereby title was established in Jewish law, and Holdheim stated that these modes of acquisition were absolutely identical whether the object of acquisition was a wife or anything else.

Interestingly, Holdheim observed that the third way— *bi'ah,* here meaning consensual intercourse—in which *kiddushin* was effectuated in Mishnaic law seemingly distinguished the act of *kinyan* in marriage from (and perhaps even elevated it above) the act of acquisition in other types of property transactions. He even conceded that the foundation of this mode of acquisition was the love and trust that existed between the couple. Furthermore, he acknowledged that in Jewish marriage law the bride and groom had each freely pledged to sanctify the union. Holdheim, however, contended that neither the sentiments of love and trust nor the sanctity involved in the couple's union distinguished *kinyan* in marriage from *kinyan* in regard to other contractual arrangements between two parties. Interestingly, he compared *bi'ah* as a mode of *kinyan* in marriage to the act of *akhilat ha-pei'rot* (the eating of fruits) as a means of establishing ownership in the case of a field. Just as *bi'ah* constituted an act sufficient to establish ownership in marriage, so *alkhilat ha-pei'rot* was an act sufficient to establish *hazakah (usucaptio)* in the case of a field. *Bi'ah,* from this point of view, was formally no different a mechanism for the acquisition of a wife than *alhi'lat ha-peirot* was for the acquisition of a field. Just as possession or investment of labor could give rise to title in the domain of the ordinary civil law of property, so too could intercourse give rise to possession in the case of a wife. *Bi'ah,* in Jewish law, like *kesef* and *shtar,* was a civil mode of acquisition.[7]

Holdheim further bolstered his argument that the act of *kinyan* in marriage was a civil act by citing two other Jewish precedents to support this position. He felt both confirmed his contention that *di'nei kiddushin* and the act of *kinyan* associated with it were marked by the same civil character as any other instance of *kinyan* in Jewish law. He first pointed out that Jewish law would not permit any type of *kinyan* to take place on either the Sabbath or the holidays. As these were designated as days of rest in *halakhah,* many forms of work were proscribed on them. In addition, no form of civil transaction was permitted. Yet, Holdheim noted that certain actions that would normally have been forbidden as violations of the interdiction against prescribed forms of labor on these days of rest were permitted if these actions were defined as religious ones. Hence, Jewish law ruled that *milah* (ritual circumcision) and *avodah* (Temple worship), *as religious acts,* superseded the Sabbath.[8] Marriage, however, though possessed of religious import and meaning, did not. Holdheim took this as a clear indication that marriage (and the act of *kinyan* associated with it) remained an act of civil law—*ein civilrechtlicher Act.*[9]

Holdheim immediately expanded and elaborated on the line of reasoning used to support this conclusion. We can summarize his argument as follows: inasmuch as the Talmud forbade *kinyan* of any type to take place on the Sabbath or Jewish holidays, the talmudic prohibition that specified that a marriage ceremony could not be held on these days of rest demonstrated that *kiddushin* and the act of *kinyan* associated with it were not defined primarily as religious acts. If Jewish law had regarded marriage as a religious and not a civil act, *kiddushin*—like *milah* and *avodah*—would have superseded the Sabbath, and *kinyan* could have taken place. In Holdheim's opinion, the failure of Jewish law to do so constituted a warrant for the position that the *kinyan* of marriage was not distinct in this way from the civil character with which *kinyan* was invested in other transactions. This led Holdheim inexorably to conclude that Judaism saw marriage as a civil-legal transaction, not a religious-moral act. Holdheim supplemented this argument by pointing out that the autonomy accorded the husband in biblical law to divorce the wife he had acquired through *kinyan* was identical to the right of any owner of any object to dispose of that object at will:[10] *kinyan* in Jewish matrimonial law was a civil, not a religious, deed.

Holdheim's analysis led him to conclude that marriage properly fell under the category of civil law, *di'nei mamanot,* and not Jewish religious law, *di'nei issura.* After all, *kinyan* in marriage constituted no less a commercial transaction than would *kinyan* in any other business matter. In making this assertion, Holdheim was able to contend that just as Jewish law—through the principle of *di'na d-malchuta di'na*—accorded state law sovereignty over Jewish law in civil matters, so too should state law have dominion over Jewish law in relation to marriage. By defining marriage as a civil act, Holdheim was able to argue that marriage came within the jurisdiction of the state and that civil law in this area superseded Jewish law; for, as Holdheim put it,

> That which is of an absolutely religious character and of a purely religious content in Mosaic legislation and in the later historical development of Judaism...and which refers to the relationship of man to God...has been commanded by God to the Jew for eternity. But whatever has reference to interhuman relationships of a political, legal, and civil character...must be totally deprived of its applicability everywhere and forever when Jews enter into relationships with other states.[11]

Holdheim's position met with swift and critical response. Samson Raphael Hirsch immediately published *Zweite Mitteilungen aus einem Briefwechsel über die neuste jüdische Literatur* and fulminated against Holdheim's abdication of rabbinic authority in this area and his unnecessary and unwarranted application of *di'na d-malchuta di'na* to Jewish matrimonial law.[12]

Another polemical work issued by Orthodox rabbis thundered,

> I ask you, Holdheim! Tell me, where has your heart gone? And if, according to your word, you would say, "All who are sanctified in marriage are sanctified according to the authority of the rabbis,"—"according to the authority of the rabbis" we have heard! "According to the authority of heretics and non-believers like you," we have not heard!...
>
> "According to the law of Moses and Israel," we have heard in connection with *kiddushin*. We have never heard, "According to the law of the king and the customs of the nations."[13]

Other Orthodox leaders joined in the chorus against Holdheim as well.[14] It was left to Zacharias Frankel, however, to produce the chief legal arguments against Holdheim's assessment of *kinyan* in relation to *di'nei kiddushin.*

Frankel had initially attacked Holdheim's position immediately after the publication of *Die Autonomie* and, again, shortly after the Brunswick Rabbinical Conference of 1844.[15] In these initial responses to Holdheim's work, Frankel was full of invective; he accused Holdheim of being a traitor to the Jewish religion.[16] Nevertheless, it was in an article published fifteen years later, *Grundlinien des Mosaisch-talmudischen Eherechts,* that Frankel explicitly advanced a strong argument against the interpretation of Jewish law Holdheim had put forth in this area.[17] Although Frankel did not mention Holdheim specifically, it is clear that his essay was designed to refute the claims Holdheim had made in *Die Autonomie* and offer a more elaborate response to him.

Like Holdheim, Frankel observed that the means whereby *kinyan* was established with regard to *kiddushin—Geld oder Geldeswerth, Urkunde, oder Beischlaf (kesef, shtar, u'bi'ah)*—were parallel to those modes whereby *kinyan* was effectuated in other civil matters.[18] Frankel contended, however, that the *kinyan* of marriage ceased to be akin to the *kinyan* of objects immediately after the act of *kiddushin* was performed. He argued that the *kinyan* of marriage was transformed as a result of the love and trust that obtained between the couple from a matter of acquisition into a matter of holiness and ethics.[19] Frankel pointed out that in Judaism the institution of marriage had developed in accordance with the principles of morality *(der Sittlichkeit),* and the act of acquisition *(Handlung)* itself had to be accompanied by the words, *"Du seiest mir geheiligt*—You are sanctified unto me."[20] The holiness accorded marriage in Jewish tradition led the rabbis to frown on intercourse as a proper mode for establishing *kiddushin.* Indeed, Frankel cited a passage in the *Mishneh Torah* of Maimonides, *Hilchot Issurei Bi'ah* 21:14 ("Any man who sanctifies his wife by means of intercourse...lashes are applied to him") as a warrant to support the view that the rabbis condemned *bi'ah* as *"Unsittlichkeit* - immoral."[21]

Holdheim, too, had stated that *kiddushin* involved an understanding that love and trust existed between the couple. He had argued, however, that these factors of sentiment were not legally actionable. They neither effectuated nor annulled the *kinyan.* Holdheim concluded that *kinyan* in connection with *di'nei kiddushin* was therefore no different from *kinyan* in other transactions in which rights of ownership were obtained.

Frankel considered this position incorrect and argued that the religious-moral character inherent in *kiddushin* had the effect of substantively differentiating the act of *kinyan* in connection with marriage from the act of *kinyan* as it related to other civil transactions. The recitation of the words, "You are sanctified to me," indicated that marriage was marked by more than a legal *(rechtlicher)* act. It had a religious *(religioeser)* dimension,[22] and this dimension meant that the *kinyan* of marriage could not be equated with *kinyan* in other transactions; it was sui generis.

Frankel further supported this contention on two other grounds. He noted that in the case of marriage, an act of infidelity on the wife's part required the husband to issue a *get* to his wife. The authority of the husband to do with his wife what he might wish in such an event was abrogated, and he had no license to forgive her. Jewish law provided no other option. Divorce was unavoidable. From this Frankel concluded that *kiddushin* and the act of *kinyan* associated with it could not be equated with other instances of *kinyan:* the wife was a person in her own right; she was not simply an inanimate piece of property over whom her husband could exercise total domination. If the wife were simply another piece of property, the husband's control over her would be absolute. If marriage were simply a civil act and his wife were simply akin to a piece of property, the husband could retain or dispose of his wife according to his will. The institution of marriage, however, was viewed from a religious-moral, not simply a legal, perspective; and the act of *kinyan* that established it had to be regarded as unique and therefore distinct from every other type of *kinyan.* The adulterous act of the wife was a "moral abomination - *sittlicher Abscheu.*" It violated both culture and modesty and represented a rupture in the moral order of society.[23]

Frankel, contra Holdheim, therefore refused to categorize laws of marriage as matters of *di'nei mamanot,* civil law. They were instead matters of religion. Frankel believed that this argument undermined Holdheim's position on the matter. Marriage was not simply a civil affair. Judaism could not surrender its right to regulate marriage through an unwarranted application of *di'na d-malchuta di'na* as Holdheim had proposed.

Frankel was not content to rest his case against Holdheim's stance. He continued by pointing out that a husband could not in every instance do with his wife as his heart desired. Indeed, the wife retained the right not to have intercourse with her husband if she so chose. Moreover, if she found her husband repulsive, Jewish law held that the rabbinic court had the power to compel the husband to issue his wife a divorce. Citing Maimonides, *Hilchot Ishut* 14:8, Frankel held that the wife was not a *"Kriegsgefangene* —captive."[24] Once more, Frankel held that in Jewish law the wife was a person possessed of rights, not an object subject to the caprice and whim of her husband.

The husband's control over his wife in the Jewish marriage relationship was circumscribed in other ways as well. Frankel observed that in other ancient cultures the husband could terminate his relationship with his wife at any time. She was identical to any other object he owned. He had no need to issue his wife a divorce should he desire to rid himself of her. Frankel observed that this situation did not obtain in Judaism. If the husband wished to terminate his relationship with his wife, he had to issue her a divorce and recite the words that allowed her to remarry.[25]

For Frankel, the phrase, *"Ha'rei at m'ku'de'shet li—Du seiest mir geheiligt,"* uttered by the husband when he betrothed his wife under the *huppah,* elevated the act of marriage in Jewish religious law, as well as the act of *kinyan* that accompanied it, to a level of holiness. The external acts associated with the process of marriage in Judaism might appear identical to those acts that accompany civil transactions, but *kedushah* was an integral part of the relationship established between the bride and the groom at the Jewish wedding ceremony. It transformed the mechanism of *kinyan* with regard to marriage from a civil to a religious act. Marriage, from the perspective of Judaism, was a religious affair; Frankel, unlike Holdheim, refused to reduce marriage to a civil matter.

In assessing Frankel's critique of the position Holdheim advanced, one must bear in mind that Frankel's essay was intended as more than a narrow, albeit interesting, disagreement with Holdheim about the character of *kinyan* in Jewish marriage law. Rather, Frankel's assault on Holdheim betrays a different perception about the character of Judaism in the modern world. To understand precisely what was at stake in this halakhic debate as well as to ferret out the meaning of this last statement, we need to place this entire argument in the historical context of the mid-1800s.

THE HISTORICAL CONTEXT FOR HOLDHEIM'S POSITION

The argument Holdheim advanced in *Über die Autonomie der Rabbinen und das Princip der jüdischen Ehe* was prompted by the continuing political struggle for Jewish emancipation that marked the Germany of his day. Holdheim's immediate target was Bruno Bauer. A Protestant theologian, Bauer published his *"Judenfrage"* in 1842 in the *Deutsche Jahrbucher* and reissued it as a pamphlet in 1843.[26] In it, he argued that the Jew, by his very nature, could not be emancipated. "As long as he is a Jew," he wrote, "his Jewishness must be stronger in him than his humanity, and keep him apart from non-Jews. He declares by this segregation that this, his Jewishness, is his true, highest nature, which has to have precedence over his humanity."[27] For this reason, "the Jews as such cannot amalgamate with the nations and cast their lot with them."[28] They must "always remain a foreign element."[29]

Bauer, in effect, argued that the "Jewish Question" in the modern political order could not be resolved because the Jew, by his very nature, placed fidelity to religion over allegiance to a state characterized by a putatively neutral public sphere. Emancipation could be granted the Jew in the modern political order only when the Jew was prepared to surrender the imperatives of his religion—when he was willing, for example, "to go to the Chamber of Deputies on the Sabbath and participate in public discussions."[30] In short, the condition modernity established as a prerequisite for Jewish emancipation and Jewish participation in the modern political order was for the Jewish people to agree voluntarily to surrender their particularity—their language, the initiatory rite of circumcision for their sons, and their observance of the dietary laws. Only then could the Jew become a full member of the nation. Until then, the nature of Judaism made full citizenship an impossibility for the Jew.[31]

Bauer pressed this point by devoting an entire section of his pamphlet to an analysis of the transactions of the Paris Sanhedrin.[32] He dismissed the distinction the delegates to the Sanhedrin had made between the political and the religious obligations Judaism imposed on its adherents as a lie and observed that many of the major addresses the delegates delivered to the Assembly were offered in Hebrew and only afterward translated into French. This was emblematic of the primacy the Jews accorded their own nation. Bauer wrote,

> It would be fine if the Jew openly declared, 'I want—since I wish to remain a Jew—to keep only that much of the Law which seems to be a purely religious element. Everything else which I recognize as anti-social I shall weed out and sacrifice.' But instead he pretends to himself, and wants to make others believe that in this distinction between political and religious commands he remains in accord with the Law, that the Law itself establishes this distinction.... Judaism cannot be helped, the Jews cannot be reconciled with the world, by the lie."[33]

Di'na d-malchuta di'na was at best an illusory remedy to the dilemma of the Jew. The nationalist component in Judaism could not be eliminated. The Jew *qua* Jew could not be made fit for participation in the modern political order.

Bauer's argument garnered a great deal of attention. Indeed, the most famous reaction to Bauer was issued by Karl Marx. In his response, Marx criticized Bauer for failing to take the implications of his argument to their logical conclusion. In singling out the particularity of Judaism as he had, Marx charged that Bauer neglected the particularity of the State itself and the role assigned to religion in it. He argued that present-day Jews and Christians could be free only when society was emancipated from religion altogether. The essential "species-being" of humanity demanded nothing less. There could be no distinction between political and private spheres. People could not be regarded as communal beings in the arena of politics while acting as private individuals in the realm of civil society.[34]

Holdheim disagreed, and his *Die Autonomie* was no less a response to Bauer than was the work of Marx. His book can thus be seen as an expression of classical nineteenth-century liberal political theory. It attempted to distinguish between public and private spheres and sought to carve out a position for particularistic religious commitments in the private realm. Indeed, Holdheim advanced the position that religion continued to possess a legitimate right to exist in the setting of the modern nation-state. Religion simply had to demonstrate that it could be confined to the private sphere and would not interfere with the performance of duties an individual citizen owed the modern nation-state in the public realm. Bauer, Holdheim contended, was wrong not to recognize that Judaism allowed for this no less than Christianity in the setting of the modern nation-state. The Jew's commitment to the Sabbath, for example, in no way served as an obstacle to the fulfillment of his civic duties. A Jewish soldier was no less obligated to serve in the military on the Sabbath than was his Christian counterpart to serve on Sunday. Nor would a Jewish bureaucrat neglect his duties as a citizen on the Sabbath. Indeed, the dictum of *di'na d-malchuta di'na* provided a religious sanction for these acts. Judaism, through this dictum, directed the Jew's actions in the political realm and made the Jew fit for life as a citizen in the modern political setting.[35]

The religiously sanctioned concept of *di'na d-malchuta di'na* allowed Holdheim, against Bauer, to assert that the obligation to observe the laws of the state sprang from meaningful religious warrants contained in Judaism itself. The doctrines of Judaism directed the Jews to an appropriate role in the emancipated world of nineteenth-century Germany.

Holdheim's argument on the nature of marriage in Judaism as well as his analysis of *kinyan* in relation to *di'nei kiddushin* was intended to further complement his brief on behalf of the suitability of Judaism in the present-day political order. His position was informed in large measure by instrumental considerations and was designed to advance the cause of Jewish political emancipation by demonstrating that Judaism recognized and affirmed a distinction between the domain of politics and the realm of religion. Holdheim's stance on this matter comported with the distinction he drew between the transitory national-ritual-legal dimensions of Judaism and the eternal ethical-religious sentiments he claimed informed its core.[36]

Contra Bauer, Holdheim, in asserting that Judaism did distinguish between civil and political spheres, was arguing that Jews, without abandoning their religion, were therefore fit for citizenship in the modern order. Holdheim, in Bauer's words, was prepared to "weed out and sacrifice" the "anti-social" elements in Judaism that were incompatible with that order. The distinction drawn in Judaism between religious and political commands was not, as Bauer had charged, an illusory principle. It was a vital component of Judaism, and it indicated that the teachings and ethos of Judaism were not incompatible with the contours of a contemporary secular order that attempted to confine religion to a private sphere. Holdheim's position on the nature of *kinyan* in Jewish matrimonial law was designed to support this stance. It is not surprising, in view of this, that Holdheim, one year later, at the famed Brunswick Rabbinical Conference, led the proponents of a measure that stated,

> Members of monotheistic religions in general are not forbidden to marry if the parents are permitted by the law of the state to bring up children from such wedlock in the Jewish religion.[37]

Indeed, his advocacy of this measure was totally consistent with the posture he adopted in his book of 1843. His actions on behalf of this resolution in 1844 reflect more than an alleged comment on and affirmation of sentiments expressed by the rabbis of the Paris Sanhedrin in 1807.[38] They bespeak a heartfelt longing for Jewish political emancipation and the articulation of a posture designed to accomplish this goal. Holdheim's views on *kinyan* in connection with *di'nei kiddushin* as well as the open stance he took with regard to intermarriage are paradigmatic of the efforts some Jews made to be deemed worthy of enfranchisement in the modern state.

Frankel's critique of Holdheim and Holdheim's assertion that marriage was a civil and not a religious act in Judaism can similarly be seen as a reflection of Frankel's dissent from the position that the complete emancipation of the Jew in the modern political order was contingent on assigning marriage to the civil realm. Or, to put it more precisely, nothing in Frankel's writings indicates that he was not an advocate of classical liberal political theory. Frankel also wanted the Jew to be a full participant in modern society, but, unlike Holdheim, he did not believe that, for such enfranchisement to take place, it was necessary to assign marriage to the public sphere as opposed to the private realm. Indeed, given Frankel's own views, not only was Holdheim's application of the principle of *di'na d-malchuta di'na* to Jewish laws of marriage unprecedented from a halakhic standpoint, but it also marked Holdheim, in Frankel's eyes, as an opportunist who would destroy the religious integrity of Judaism for "a mess of pottage." Frankel not only disagreed with Holdheim's characterization of

Jewish marriage as an exclusively civil act, but he could not, in effect, understand why Jewish participation in the modern political order depended on the assignment of Jewish marriage to the civil realm. Further research may shed light on the historical factors that caused Holdheim to disagree. For our purposes in this paper, it is enough to observe that the setting of the 1840s and the struggles for Jewish political emancipation that this decade witnessed provide a context for understanding some of the factors that motivated the positions Holdheim and Frankel adopted in their debate over the civil and religious nature of Jewish matrimonial law.

SOME CONTEMPORARY RAMIFICATIONS OF THE PRECEDING DISCUSSION

In light of all that has been presented, *ma'i nafka' minei*—what are we modern Reform Jews to learn from this? What are its policy implications for Jews in the modern West, in general, and in North America, in particular, who are confronted with the reality of massive numbers of intermarriages; and for rabbis who are called upon by many congregants to sanctify these unions through rabbinic officiation? How should contemporary Reform Rabbis charged with responsibility for the continuity of both Judaism and the Jewish people as well as the spiritual well-being of those whose lives we touch respond to Holdheim and the debates of intermarriage that wracked the leaders of our people 150 years ago?

These questions have no easy answers. Several thoughts do emerge, however. To begin with, it is clear that our situation is not Holdheim's. Our vector is distinct from his. As Franz Rosenzweig phrased it in his address at the opening of the Frankfurt Lehrhaus in 1921, Jews of Holdheim's generation were moving "from the center to the periphery." Judaism was integral to Holdheim's being. It was the *girsa d'yankuta*—the mother's milk—on which he was nourished. His was not the problem of Jewish particularity; his was the challenge of creating a Judaism fit for the modern condition. If we today view some of his positions as extreme and idiosyncratic, we can also appreciate the sincerity and good intentions that prompted them. We who stand here at this moment are in large measure his beneficiaries.

We need to acknowledge, however, as the preceding paragraph stated, that our situation is not his. Neither we nor our Jews move "from the center to the periphery." As Rosenzweig put it, the mark of the modern Jewish condition for the committed religious Jew is the "move from the periphery to the center." The conditions that led Holdheim to analyze *kinyan* and to take the stance that he did with regard to intermarriage no longer obtain. Ours is not a community that seeks civil emancipation; it is one that asks how to maintain community and meaning in the face of massive acculturation. Whether this different social context obviates Holdheim's contention that the *kinyan* of marriage is a civil and not a religious act is a matter that allows for honest disagreement, though I must admit that Holdheim's arguments leave me unconvinced. It seems obvious, nevertheless, that the social and political considerations that prompted Holdheim to offer such an assessment of Jewish matrimonial law are factors that demand some thought as we rabbis struggle with the question of officiation at intermarriages and as we strive to create an agenda for the present-day worldwide Jewish community that grapples with the issues surrounding such unions.

Secondly, the demographics that inform our situation today are radically different from those that informed Holdheim's. Holdheim's discussion was largely theoretical. Intermarriage between Jews and Christians in Germany was negligible, and the resolution passed at Brunswick affirming that the marriage of a Jew and an adherent of a monotheistic faith was not forbidden if the laws of the state permitted the children of such unions to be raised as Jews was entirely symbolic. Simply put, the laws of the state in which Holdheim lived permitted no such thing. Holdheim's consignment of marriage to the civil realm and the concomitant reduction of Judaism it entailed had few practical implications. It entailed fewer demographic implications. He could promote the position he did precisely because he believed that the advocacy of this position on a theoretical-symbolic level could have only positive consequences for the promotion of Jewish participation in the surrounding majority society. In our world such is not the case. Decisions we make in this area have real import for the future of the Jewish people. We do not have his luxury of an endogamous Jewish community.

Finally, I would turn to the social sciences for one last consideration. All of us who have read modern sociology know that the *Gemeinschaften* of yore are past. Jews and others no longer live in intimate communities that foster traditional associational patterns. Furthermore, the plausibility structures that formerly supported these patterns and provided religious warrants that justified in-marriage no longer have the power they once did among most Jews. In short, the integral Jewish community of the past is lost; and we rabbis, as the heirs to an ancient tradition but as the bearers of a modern religion, must rely on our powers of persuasion. The coercive legal authority that supported the dicta of our ancestors has been dismantled, and the pluralistic character of the modern world allows our people to choose their own course in life. Ours is largely a society of individual consumers, and if we fail to provide many of our congregants with the services they demand—make no mistake about it—a good portion of them will secure those goods elsewhere. How do we create community and maintain meaning in the face of this situation?

Advocates of rabbinic officiation at intermarriage in effect maintain that these twin goals of community and meaning can be obtained only if we grant normative status to this admittedly real situation of religious consumers and rampant intermarriage. In other words, in a world where Jews can and do intermarry despite rabbinic pleas to the contrary, the only way to maintain Jewish meaning and community is to adapt to the situation and *le'ehoz et ha-ra b-mi'u'to,* keep the damage to a minimum. Indeed, rabbinic officiation at intermarriage may well be a positive good from this perspective because it is a welcoming act that encourages and inclines both the Jewish and non-Jewish partners to join in the life of the Jewish community. Anecdotal, as well as statistical, information can be employed to both confirm and contradict this stance. The advocates of this posture, however, should recognize a structural parallel between their position on this issue and Holdheim's. Indeed, they may even go beyond Holdheim in one sense, for the normative weight Holdheim assigned to the demands of the modern world in constructing his position on Jewish marriage and intermarriage was implicit. The proponents of rabbinic officiation at intermarriages today actually assign explicit normative weight to the social-scientific realities we all recognize as true. Their position is informed by a judgment that the future of Judaism depends on this type of rabbinic response to the realities of the modern world. In so doing, they affirm a notion of Judaism as a voluntaristic enterprise and reject the polis-origins of a premodern religion that affirms a birth dogma or formal conversion as the only criterion for inclusion as a full participant in the rituals and life of the Jewish people.

Opponents of rabbinic officiation at intermarriage, while not denying these realities, refuse to cede normative authority to them. They, too, however—as was Frankel—are informed by a contemporary sociological judgment as real as that of those with whom they disagree. As Philip Rieff, the modern social scientist, phrases it in his many books and articles, culture is "a design of motives directing the self outward, toward those communal purposes in which alone the self can be realized and satisfied." Culture performs this task by "the power of its institutions to bind and loose men in the conduct of their affairs." The task confronting the rabbi and the committed Jew in the modern pluralistic situation is to ask whether Judaism can still so inform its adherents. Can an ancient religious faith adapt itself to the modern situation so as to still accomplish this powerful task? Can it contribute, in Rieff's words, in helping "unbelieving men [become] civilized?"[39]

Rieff is not optimistic about the prospects of religion accomplishing such a goal in the modern world. He is convinced, however, that a culture, if it is effectively to promote such a prospect, cannot be limited to a buffet table of information and significance available for individual choice. He writes, "Every culture must establish itself as a system of moralizing demands, images that mark the trail of each man's memory....In a word, culture is repressive."[40] Culture, he asserts, must involve limits.

Opponents of rabbinic officiation at intermarriages essentially agree with Rieff. They contend that Judaism must be a religion of norms and not only one of therapy if it is to survive and if the task of the Jewish people is to be fulfilled. "How are you," Rieff asks his reader, "on the trivial-old question of sabbath-keeping? Is any order worthy of the name without its strict sabbaths?" [41] "No is the answer," for, as Arnold Eisen, citing Rieff, puts it, "no is the word most indispensable to culture."[42]

Classical Judaism never sought "normality" for its people. Although it adapted to the demands of each era, it sought to do so while preserving its integrity and the identity of its people. This paper on Holdheim and the contemporary significance of his views on marriage and intermarriage has not attempted to provide a definitive answer that would resolve the debate swirling around his words. I cannot say absolutely whether his characterization of the nature of Jewish marriage law was wrong or right. As we ponder his words today, however, and consider their implications for our own position as rabbis on the issues surrounding intermarriage, I would assert that a striving for normalization—an attempt to adapt fully to the demands of a modern situation and to accord those demands normative weight in informing our decisions on these matters, as I believe Holdheim did—is not the Jewish way. We, as our rabbinic forbears, must try to extend and enliven Jewish culture while remaining faithful to our own history and its boundaries. For us, at our best, "normal" can have no other meaning.

Notes

1. Samuel Holdheim, *Über die Autonomie die Rabbinen und das Princip der jüdischen Ehe* (Schwerin, 1843).

2. For the *locus classicus* of his discussion on the nature of marriage as a civil act in Jewish matrimonial law, see Ibid., pp. 137–165.

3. Holdheim delineates the different modes of acquisition in Jewish law in ibid., pp. 85ff. For an excellent English language treatment of the details and complexities of *kinyan* in Jewish law, see *Encyclopaedia Judaica,* s.v., pp. 137–165.

4. Holdheim, *Die Autonomie,* pp. 139ff. See *Mishnah Kiddushin* 1:1.

5. Holdheim, *Die Autonomie,* pp. 86 and 137ff. On p. 86, Holdheim cites the famous passage in *Kiddushin* 26a that lists these three modes of acquisition and on the previous page in his footnote lists the various types of *kinyan* that exist in Jewish law, along with their Roman equivalents. For the Mishnaic sources that prescribe the same modes of acquisition for a wife as for Canaanite slaves and real property, see *Mishna Kiddushin* 1:1, 3, and 5. Judith Romney Wegner, a modern scholar, offers the following commentary on these sources in her outstanding book, *Chattel or Person? The Status of Women in the Mishnah* (Oxford, 1988), p. 42. Wegner writes, "The procedure for acquiring a wife (set forth in tractate Kiddushin) treats marriage as asserting a formal sale and purchase of a woman's sexual function—a commercial transaction in which a man pays for his bride's virginity just as for any other object of value." For a comprehensive English-language treatment of the many sources involved in the Jewish laws of matrimony and divorce, see Elliot N. Dorff and Arthur Rosett, *A Living Tree: The Roots and Growth of Jewish Law* (Albany, 1988), pp. 442—545.

6. *Encyclopaedia Judaica* (Jerusalem, 1972) p. 138.

7. Holdheim, *Die Autonomie,* pp. 86 and 137ff. Of course, as my friend and colleague Nomi Stolzenberg has pointed out to me, Holdheim's analogy here is quite problematic from a logical standpoint. For *hazakah* in relation to an ownerless field displays no contractual features. Absolute title to the field is established by possession of the property for an uninterrupted and specified period of time (three years—on this point see *Mishna Baba Batra* 3:1). There is no contractual element here, nor are there two persons involved as would be in the case of marriage. As stated in the body of the paper itself, *bi'ah* must be consensual if *kinyan* is to be established. It is impossible to imagine how one could speak of a field in these terms. In light of this point, it is significant that in *Baba Batra* 48b is a discussion where the betrothal of a woman is compared to the acquisition of a field, the sale of which is valid even if the sale occurs under coercion. The rabbis, however, ultimately reject this position. Consent remains a vital component of the marriage process.

I am aware of only two exceptions to this. The first is where a father designates the betrothal of his minor daughter without her consent. *Bi'ah* is not at all involved here. The second exception concerns the case of levirate marriage. In *Mishna Yebamot* 6:1 it is written that a state of marriage is established between the *yabam* (the brother of the deceased husband) and the *yabamah* (the widow) when intercourse takes place between them, even when the intercourse is unintentional (mistaken identity) or involuntary by either party. Here *bi'ah* is involved, but it is the only place in Jewish law where a marriage is established by nonconsensual intercourse. In sum, there are two instances in Jewish law where a woman may be married despite her lack of consent; in the case of a male, there is only one.

One more point of distinction is to be made concerning the analogy Holdheim drew between the *kinyan* of a wife and the *kinyan* of an ownerless field. In the case of a wife, *bi'ah* establishes the absolute right of the man to the woman only when the woman is unmarried. A married woman who willingly has intercourse with a man other than her husband is simply an adulteress. The consensual intercourse in which she has engaged with a man other than her husband does not effectuate *kinyan* in such a circumstance. *Hazakah* is distinct from *bi'ah,* then, on the grounds that the former establishes absolute, not relative, title. Even if the original owner of the property should return to claim title after three years, that person could not do so. *Bi'ah,* however, in contrast to *hazakah,* can be said to establish only a presumptive right. Even if the woman has honestly assumed that her first husband was dead, if the first husband is alive and there has been no divorce, then *bi'ah* could not establish *kinyan* between the "adulteress woman" and the man other than her presumably dead husband with whom she engaged in consensual intercourse.

8. Holdheim, *Die Autonomie,* pp. 107–108.

9. Ibid., p. 159.

10. Ibid., p. 138.

11. Ibid., pp. 49ff. The translation is taken from Jakob J. Petuchowski, "Abraham Geiger and Samuel Holdheim," *Leo Baeck Institute Year Book,* New York, Vol. 22 (1977), p. 143.

12. This work was published in Altona in 1844.

13. *Teshuvot B-anshei aven—Holdheim Vrei'a* (Frankfurt, 1846), p. 71.

14. Zvi Hirsch Chajes, Jacob Ettlinger, and others joined the chorus of protest against Holdheim and his followers. An account of the ire Holdheim aroused can be read in David Ellenson, "Traditional Reactions to Modern Jewish Reform," in D. Frank and O. Leaman, eds., *The Routledge History of Jewish Philosophy* (London, 1996).

15. Holdheim's response to Frankel's initial critique can be found in S. Holdheim, *Das Religioese und Politische im Judentum, mit besonderer Beziehung au gemischte Ehen* (Schwerin, 1845).

16. For Frankel's critique of Holdheim at this juncture, see Frankel's several articles on this issue in his *Zeitschrift fuer die religioesen Interessen des Judenthums, Heft* 5–8, 1844.

17. Z. Frankel, *"Grundlinien des mosaisch-talmudischen Eherechts,"* in *Jahresbericht des jüdisch-theologischen Seminar,* Breslau, January 27, 1860, pp. 1–17.

18. Ibid., pp. 11 and 25.

19. Ibid., p. 43.

20. Ibid., p. 25.

21. Ibid., p. 26. Frankel also cited the talmudic passage (*Kiddushin* 12b) on which Maimonides based his ruling. In that passage, Rav, a third-century rabbinic authority, sought to discourage betrothal through intercourse by imposing lashes on men who betrothed women in this way.

22. Ibid., p. 31.

23. Ibid., p. 44.

24. Ibid., p. 48.

25. Ibid., pp. 11ff. See especially pp. 44–45 and 47–48. One could, of course, look at the institution of divorce in Judaism from another perspective as well, for one could maintain that the divorce simply renders the women "unowned." In this way, the institution of divorce might be said to make the woman more rather than less akin to other forms of property.

26. Bruno Bauer, "The Jewish Problem," translated by Helen Lederer (Cincinnati, 1957).

27. Ibid., p. 22.

28. Ibid., p. 47.

29. Ibid., p. 55.

30. Ibid., p. 67.

31. Ibid., pp. 110ff.

32. Ibid., pp. 114ff.

33. Ibid., p. 122.

34. Karl Marx, *On the Jewish Question,* translated by Helen Lederer (Cincinnati, 1958).

35. Holdheim, *Die Autonomie,* pp. 96ff. See especially p. 100.

36. In making this argument, Holdheim was taking a stance in direct opposition to Bauer, who had branded the distinction made between political and religious commandments in Judaism "a lie." See note 31. On the distinction Holdheim drew between the "perishable" ritual and national elements within Judaism and the "eternally valid" religious teachings that constituted the essence of the Jewish religion, see David Philipson, *The Reform Movement in Judaism* (New York, 1967), pp. 252–53.

37. Gunther Plaut, *The Rise of Reform Judaism* (New York, 1963), p. 222.

38. Ibid., p. 220.

39. See Philip Rieff, *The Triumph of the Therapeutic* (New York, 1968), pp. 4–5. These quotations are taken from the manuscript of my friend Arnold Eisen's forthcoming book on Jewish practice and ritual in the modern world, *Rethinking Modern Judaism: Ritual, Commandment, Community,* to be published by the University of Chicago Press.

40. Rieff, *Triumph of the Therapeutic,* p. 11. Cited in Eisen, *Rethinking Modern Judaism.*

41. Philip Rieff, *Fellow Teachers* (New York, 1973), p. 136. Cited in Eisen, *Rethinking Modern Judaism.*

42. Eisen, *Rethinking Modern Judaism.*

LOVE AND MARRIAGE: REFORM JUDAISM AND KIDDUSHIN*

Peter S. Knobel

Professor Mark Washofsky of the Hebrew Union College Jewish Institute of Religion and Chair of the Central Conference of American Rabbis' Responsa Committee suggests that Reform decision makers can be divided into two opposite and often opposing camps on the basis of how they understand their relation to tradition. Each group bears a narrative that explains its view. He writes:

> We are children of the Enlightenment. We are the descendants of Jews whose world was altered irrevocably by the breakdown of traditional society. We are no longer what we were. For almost two centuries we have been enthusiastic participants in the world of liberal modernity. We are separated from the other world, the world of tradition and authority, by a gap of spirit and of intellect that is as deep as it is wide. We retain an affection for our tradition, but we are emphatically not of it. We do not justify ourselves according to its values, its teachings and its sacred texts. Our authority, instead, is modernity itself. As religion is an evolving consciousness, our gaze is fixed to the future and not to the past. Our hope, the thing for which we strive, is to construct a religion that is itself enlightened and rational, a religion that is morally and spiritually uplifting to the Jews of modernity, one that resonates with those whose world differs so profoundly from the world of the Jewish past.

Now the other, competing story, again roughly:

*I want to thank Rachel Adler for allowing me to see a copy of her book *Engendering Judaism: An Inclusive Theology and Ethics* (Philadelphia, 1998) and to cite it when it was still in manuscript form. All the quotations in this paper, however, are from the printed edition.

> We are Jews. We are the latest generation of that national, cultural and religious enterprise known as *Yisrael*. Our religion is therefore inextricably bound up with the historical religious experience of the Jewish people. We, too, stood at Sinai. We do not and cannot understand ourselves as separate and distinct from the ongoing tradition that, for millennia, we have called Torah. Yes, we are modern, able to look critically at our imperfect tradition. But we are not radically separated *from* tradition. We hold it, not at arm's length, but in a powerful embrace close to our heart. Thus, we seek to explain ourselves by constant recourse to our sacred sources; we justify our religious choices by means of argument that is constructed from, expressed through and energized by the texts of our tradition. Our discourse is not chiefly the discourse of science and philosophy, but rather that of Torah and text. We strive to build a religious life that, though it speaks to us as moderns, is unmistakably Jewish in form and content.

Each of these stories is an account of our religious reality, an attempt to place a general cast of meaning over and around the individual Jewish acts we perform. Each of them provides a satisfactory narrative rendition of a particular approach to Reform Judaism. And, when you get right down to it, the two of them are contradictory, incompatible, and irreconcilable.[1]

Although Professor Washofsky points out that very few individuals identify completely with either narrative, the conflicting narratives do reflect the growing gap in methodology and ideological unity within liberal Judaism.[2] In effect, each group speaks a different language, and therefore neither group speaks to the other but instead speaks past the other. As a result, it can be difficult, if not impossible, to achieve a unified stand on controversial issues.[3] But even among those who identify with the same narrative, there is always the possibility of disagreement.

This paper is the first of two that explore Reform Judaism and marriage. The goal of this paper is to demonstrate the transformation of marriage in Reform Judaism from its classical form as *kiddushin,*[4] rooted in property law,[5] into an egalitarian partnership, *Brit Ahuvim,* a Lovers' Covenant, a name Rachel Adler has coined. Dr. Adler makes explicit what has gradually been transpiring in Reform Judaism's understanding of marriage. Reform Judaism has reformulated the ceremony in both word and symbolic action to recognize that words and symbols that are identified with traditional Jewish marriage do not accurately reflect contemporary Progressive Jewish marriage. Progressive Judaism has spiritualized the term *kiddushin* and mutualized the act of *kinyan.*[6]

The second paper explores the implications of Reform Judaism's understanding of marriage for gay and lesbian Jews. The goal of the papers is to clarify the methodology of Reform halakhic decision making and its effects on Jewish marital law. In both papers I reach conclusions similar to those identified as the "the children of the Enlightenment," but methodologically I identify with "the Jews."[7]

A primary ethical and metahalakhic principle in Reform Judaism is the egalitarian principle. Rooting itself in the first creation narrative, humankind *(adam)* is created in the image of God; both male and female are identified as *adam.*[8] The *halakhah* must be changed to reflect commitment of male female equality.[9] If there is one principle agreed upon in Reform Judaism that is beyond compromise it is the egalitarian principle. In marriage it means that husband and wife have equal worth and equal responsibility. At least in theory, there are no predetermined role expectations or limitations.[10]

The *aggadah* (theology and ethics) are primary for liberal *halakhah;*[11] *halakhah* is also essential for liberal Judaism. Dr. Adler writes:

> *Halakhah* belongs to liberal Jews no less than to Orthodox Jews because the stories of Judaism belong to us all. A *halakhah* is communal praxis grounded in Jewish stories. Ethicists, theologians and lawyers who stress the centrality of narrative would argue that all normative systems rest upon stories....A praxis is more than the sum of various practices that constitute it. *A praxis is a holistic embodiment in action at a particular time of the values and commitments inherent in a particular story.* Orthodoxy cannot have monopoly on *halakhah,* because no form of Judaism can endure without one; there would be no way to live it out.[12]

In Judaism, sanctification is an act of separation that causes one to be in God's presence and/or to live in relation to God. *Imitateo dei* (the imitation of God) is a major mode of sanctification. It is a reciprocal process.

> You shall sanctify yourselves and be holy for I am the Eternal your God. You shall faithfully observe my laws. I the Eternal make you holy.[13]

In Reform Judaism, *kedusha* is primarily an ethical category but not exclusively so.[14] In Genesis 2–3, for example, God rests, blesses, and hallows the seventh day, thereby creating Shabbat. Each week the Jew does the same thing to create Shabbat. Without human action Shabbat does not come. The time remains in the category of *chol* (ordinary) rather than *kadosh* (holy). If the Jew does not do what God does, Shabbat does not come. It remains only *in potentia.* The Torah itself provides the primary rationale for Shabbat observance as a reminder of Creation and Redemption.

These theological concepts have important ethical implications; and in relation to marriage, Creation and Redemption are the basic themes of the *Sheva Berachot* (Seven Wedding Blessings). In Leviticus 19:1ff., our imitation of God as the means to achieve holiness is described in great detail. An analysis of the passage demonstrates that the emphasis is overwhelmingly on ethical behavior, but there are also acts that distinguish a Jewish society from others. The hermeneutic of Reform Judaism is an ethical critique of *kedusha* (holiness), but to identify the holy only with the ethical is a grievous error. Holiness means living a life in relation to and in the presence of God. Marriage is the sanctified relationship par excellence that sets the parameters of all others. "*Kedusha* is acquired through fulfilling the *mitzvot.*"[15]

Reform Judaism is its quasi-halakhic guide to Jewish living. In *Gates of Mitzvah*[16] Rabbi Herbert Bronstein asserts that marriage is a *mitzvah* incumbent upon every Jew:

> It is a *mitzvah* for a Jew to marry and to live together with his/her spouse in a manner worthy of the traditional Hebrew designation for marriage, *kiddushin.*[17]

It is the meaning of the term *kiddushin* that is essential to our understanding of Jewish marriage. Only when we understand the values that define the word will we be able to ask the appropriate halakhic questions. One of the best descriptions of the meaning of marriage as *kiddushin* in Reform Judaism is found in an essay in *Gates of Mitzvah.* The essay is both definitional and emblematic. It does not define the *halakhah* of marriage, but it describes the theology and ethics that must be represented by the *halakhah.*[18]

Nothing clarifies the Jewish attitude toward marriage quite as well as the traditional name for the wedding ceremony, *Kiddushin,* derived from the Hebrew *kadosh*—holy. As we come to understand the deeper meaning of *kadosh,* we may begin to appreciate why Jewish tradition reserved the word *Kiddushin* for marriage.

In the outlook of Judaism, all existence is derived originally from God and is, therefore, potentially holy. Time and space, God-given, are sacred but can also be desecrated by idolatry— the worship of things or of self. In consequence, we set special times and places aside for respect, for reverence, so that they may be kept apart from the realm of the profane, from exploitation for material gain and utilitarian usage....

Humanity lives, however, not only in the dimensions of time and space, but also, from birth, in the dimension of relationship. And while all relationships, like all time and space, should be considered essentially sacred, certain relationships are especially exalted. In Judaism the Holy of Holies of all relationships, to which the poetic genius of the Hebraic spirit turned most often for the paradigm of the covenant between God and Israel, was and is the covenant between husband and wife (see, for example, Hosea 1 and 2). A sacred entity comes into being in Jewish marriage. As in the *Kiddush* of Shabbat we set apart a period of time as holy, in *Kiddushin* husband and wife set each other apart. Jewish tradition considered the woman who married as *mekudeshet*—"made holy," set aside and apart for her husband, consecrated and thus inviolate. In the view of Reform, this is mutual; both husband and wife are consecrated to each other.[19] They create a sacred entity in the act of *Kiddushin* consecration.

In the Jewish marriage service, in the very act of consecrating a particular relationship as holy, the potential sanctity of all relationships is asserted. Husband and wife represent the bond between God and humanity, the ideal toward which all human relationships should strive. *Kiddushin* is the rooting of the human

> in the realm of the sacred, with the goal that all our relationships become holy, bearing the blossom and fruit of life.

Rabbi Bronstein's analysis of the *Sheva Berachot* makes clear that they define the ultimate meaning of the ceremony and represent the primary values of Jewish marriage. Jewish marriage is a recapitulation of creation and an anticipation of redemption. Marriage is to relationships what Shabbat is to time. The process of sanctification has ritual aspects that lead to behavioral consequences. Both Shabbat and marriage entail positive and negative commandments.

> Traditional Jewish worship was designed around the three overarching biblical motifs of Creation, Redemption (Exodus), and Revelation (Sinai). The entire round of Jewish observance is suffused by these same three themes. For *Kiddushin,* the act of marriage, the rabbis of our classic period chose the theme of Creation around which to design the celebratory blessings. These are known in our tradition as the *Sheva Berachot,* the Seven Blessings of Praise.[20]
>
> Indeed, the *Sheva Berachot* contain in brief compass the entire sweep of the Jewish conception of existence, from the miraculous glory of the original panoply of Creation to the sublime perfection of Creation in the Messianic Completion. Both the evocation of Paradise and the affirmation of the messianic celebration are comprised in a seven-versed poem on the theme of Creation....
>
> Further, the purpose of Jewish existence is the partnership with God in the maintenance, the harmonization of Creation. And every good marriage is considered to be a *tikkun,* a "putting in order," for each good marriage lifts existence to a state of higher harmony....
>
> And yet, while certainly expressing an ethos of pleasure in life, the *Sheva Berachot* do not encourage the couple to relinquish

> social obligations or, through self-isolating privatism, to endeavor escape from the ills of the world. The text of the blessings also evokes the messianic hope....As the couple begins to create their own world, they know that together they must bring something to the perfection of God's Creation, so that the time may soon come when God, as it were, will rejoice with His bride, the people of Israel.

I have quoted this essay at great length because it sets the stage for a Reform understanding of marriage. It is the spiritualization of *kedusha,* which affects our halakhic concept of marriage.[21] Reform Judaism takes theology seriously, and when its liturgical formulae and ritual actions do not accurately reflect its ethicotheological underpinnings the formulae and ritual actions are changed or reinterpreted.[22]

The primary metaphor for marriage, which dominates Jewish theology, is *brit.* The marriage metaphor is used to describe the covenant between God and the Jewish people. The wedding took place at Sinai with the Torah as the *ketubah.* It is this theme of covenant that dominates the thinking of Eugene Borowitz as Reform Judaism's leading contemporary thinker. He has described marriage as the most appropriate ethical context for sexual relations because it is the best vehicle for expressing intimacy and perpetuating the Jewish people and because every Jewish marriage is a reflection of the covenantal marriage between God and the Jewish people.[23]

> The Jewish community has found no more central and significant form for the individual Jew to live in...than the personal covenant of marriage. In its exclusiveness and fidelity it has been the chief analogy to the oneness of the relationship with God as the source of personal worth and development. In marriage's intermixture of love and obligation the Jew has seen the model of faith in God permeating the heart and thence all one's actions. Through

> children, Jews have found the greatest personal joy while carrying out the ancient Jewish pledge to endure through history for God's sake.[24]

Contemporary Jewish marriage is ideally an I-Thou relationship between the lovers. For Buber, the Eternal Thou (God) is present in every I-Thou relationship, and the Rabbis believed that God was present in proper moments of sexual intimacy between wife and husband. Borowitz struggles theologically with an understanding of relationship with God, who is superior and more powerful than humankind, and how the relation to that deity is modeled in the marriage. Borowitz ultimately maintains that human dignity depends on autonomy and freedom.[25] He writes:

> We have an old-new model for such open, unsettled but mutually dignifying relations, namely "covenant," now less a contract spelled from on high than a loving effort to live in reciprocal respect. As the pain of trying to create egalitarian marriages indicates, we cannot know early on what forms and processes most people will find appropriate to such relationships. We can, however, accept covenantal relationship as a central ethical challenge of our time and pragmatically learn how we might sanctify ourselves by living it.[26]

Borowitz realizes that marriage is undergoing significant change. Central to the covenant of marriage as Borowitz describes it is its egalitarian nature. This, he indicates, represents a substantial shift from the past. The intimacy of the relationship and egalitarianism are reflected in contemporary readings of Song of Songs. One of the most frequently invoked wedding texts is from Song of Song *Ani ledodi vedodi li,* "I am my beloved's and my beloved is mine." The book seen as a whole is a description of an ideal, mutual, loving relationship in which both lovers initiate sex. The woman's voice in the relationship is as prominent as the man's. The rabbinic interpretation of Song of Songs as an allegory about the relationship between God and Israel only heightens the religious meaning of sexual intimacy. Love is the dominant emotion. The lovers freely choose one another.

Feminist readings suggest that it provides a model for a loving relationship in which neither partner is dominant. The feminist theologian Judith Plaskow writes:

> Unabashed by their desire, the man and the woman in these poems delight in their own embodiment and the beauty surrounding them, each seeking the other out to inaugurate their meeting, each rejoicing in the love with our dominion that is also the love of God.[27]

The relationships of Jonathan and David and of Ruth and Naomi are marked by covenantal promises. Jonathan and David's is described as *brit* and is marked by a ceremonial gift.[28] Although neither relationship is a marriage, it illustrates the transfer of primary loyalty from the family of origin to another family. Each has elements of risk and sacrifice. Fidelity is its primary characteristic. The absence of a sexual component distinguishes it from marriage. The love and friendship it represents is paradigmatic for the ideal marriage.

Human love is also the love of God. Proper marriage has deep spiritual dimension. The *shekhinah* is present in the couple's sexual intercourse. This is further reflected in the text from Hosea (2:21–22)[29] "I will espouse you forever. I will espouse you with righteousness and justice and loving kindness and compassion. I will espouse you in faithfulness and you shall know God."[30] The bride and groom might recite it together or it might be chanted after the rings have been exchanged.

A primary principle of Reform Judaism is the equal rights of men and women. It is rooted in our theological understanding of creation that "God created Adam in God's image, male and female God created them." Man and woman were created at the same time, and both are equally created in the divine image.[31] This metaprinciple governs the way in which we interpret *halakhah.*[32] Marriage takes place between two equals that choose to marry one another. Each individual has reached the age of majority and commits her/himself to the other person. This is a far cry from the traditional concept of *kiddushin,* whereby a woman moves from the authority of her father to the authority of her husband. Judith Plaskow, reflecting what is clearly the progressive Jewish ideal, writes:

> Marriage will not be about the transfer of women or the sanctification of potential disorder through the firm establishment of women in the patriarchal family, but the decision of two adults to make their lives together, which includes sharing their sexuality.[33]

Rachel Adler sees the debate over women's equality as reflected in the fourth blessing of the *Sheva Berachot.*[34] She translates,

> Blessed are You, Adonai our God, ruler of the universe, who has shaped humanity in your image *(ahser yatzar et ha-adam b'talmo),* patterned after your image and likeness *(b'tzelem demut tavnito),* and enabled them to perpetuate this image out of their own being *(v'hitkin lo mimenu binyan adei-ad).* Blessed are You, Adonai, shaper of humanity *(yotzer ha-adam).*

She points out that Philip Birnbaum translates the phrase *v'hitkin mimenu binyan adai ad* as "who hast created man in Thy image and didst forever form woman out of his frame to be beside him."[35] Her elaborate discussion makes clear that the theological argument has halakhic implications. Women as equal partners are not secondary creations. They are part of the original male-female *Adam* and not the rib or the tail of Adam.

It is the *Sheva Berachot* that express the essence of marriage, and it to this text that we must look if we are to understand marriage. As Adler says, it is these blessings that make it "respectable" and reframe *kiddushin* as acquisition as an archetype of redemptive union."[36] God is creator, and humankind shares the divine image with God, and, like Him, they are capable of creation. The couple's love participates in the perfection of the Garden of Eden and the first marriage of Adam and Eve, whose *mesadder kiddushin* was God; and its joy anticipates the messianic fulfillment promised by the prophets. Its symbols are a cup of blessing and the *chuppah,* the marital chamber that symbolizes the intimacy they will share and the sanctuary they will build. For the home is the replacement for the sanctuary. It is *mikdash meat,* the Temple writ small.

In Reform Judaism the symbolic act of *kinyan* (acquisition) has become a mutual exchange rather than a unilateral exchange. Such an exchange in the traditional *halakhah* invalidates the transaction. *Birkat Erusin* (the betrothal blessing) has either been eliminated or severely truncated because there is no longer the assumption of virginity before marriage. Specific reference to the *arayot* (forbidden sexual relationships) is eliminated in every progressive version of the current wedding ceremony.[37]

A brief look at *Birkat Erusin* will further our understanding of how we have separated ourselves from the traditional understanding of marriage. The traditional blessing, "Blessed is Adonai our God, ruler of the universe, who has sanctified us with Your commandments and commanded us concerning the forbidden sexual relations/'nakedness' *(arayaot)."* You have forbidden us the merely espoused *(arusot)* and permitted us those who have been fully wed to us *(nesuot)* by means of the bridal chamber and the holy setting aside *(huppah vekiddushin)*. Blessed are You who sanctifies Israel by means of the bridal chamber and the (holy) setting aside *(huppah vekiddushin)*.[38]

It was eliminated in earlier versions of the CCAR *Rabbi's Manual,* but it was reintroduced in *Maaglei Tzedek* in an egalitarian form. "We praise you, Adonai our God, Ruler of the universe, who hallows us with *mitzvot* and consecrates this marriage. We praise you, Adonai our God, who sanctifies our people Israel through *kiddushin,* the sacred rite of marriage at the *chuppah. (Vehitir lanu et hanesuim vehanesuot lanu al yedi huppah vekiddushin)."*[39]

The text in *Forms of Prayer,* the *siddur* of the Reform Synagogues of Great Britain, is "Blessed are You, Lord our God, King of the universe, who makes us holy through doing His commands, and who makes His people Israel holy by the ceremony of *chuppah* and the sanctity of marriage."[40] The text of the Union of Liberal and Progressive Synagogues is, "We praise you, Eternal God, Sovereign of the universe. You teach us the ways of holiness, and by Your laws Jewish marriage is sanctified" *(Mekadeish amo Yisrael al yedei chuppah vekiddushin)*.

The *ketubah* has been replaced by a marriage certificate or by an egalitarian document that eliminates most if not all the halakhic language. The text of a traditional *ketubah* is primarily an economic document that stipulates a man's obligation to his wife during the marriage and in case he dies or divorces her. The document is not mutual and is rarely used in Reform weddings. In fact, ethically, it ought not be used.[41]

As will be clear from even a cursory reading of the text below, the traditional *ketubah* is a one-sided document that deals with economic rights of women, who must be protected from the disproportional power of men in patriarchal marriage. Although some will argue that the *ketubah* represents an improvement in the status of women, Judith Hauptman points out that the main change that takes place between the biblical and the rabbinic view of marriage is "from the purchase of a woman from her father to a kind of 'social contract' entered into by a man and a woman, albeit with him dominant and her subordinate. The critical difference between her old status in marriage as chattellike and her new status as 'second-class citizen' is that she acquired, in exchange for sexual and other service to her husband, a wider array of rights and protections."[42]

> On the_____day of the week______the day of the [Hebrew] month of___the year____after the creation of the world, according to the manner in which we count here in the community of_____, the bridegroom,_____son of____, said to this virgin______, daughter of_______, Be my wife according to the law of Moses and Israel and I will work, honor, feed and support you in the custom of Jewish men who work, honor, feed and support their wives faithfully. I will give the settlement of virgins, two hundred silver zuzzim, which is due you according to Torah law, as well as your food, clothing,

necessities of life and conjugal needs, according to universal custom.

Miss______agreed and became his wife. The dowry that she brought from her father's house, was in silver, gold, jewelry clothing, home furnishing or bedding. Mr_______our bridegroom, accepts [this] as being worth one hundred silver pieces. Our bridegroom, Mr______, agreed, and of his own accord added an additional one hundred silver pieces paralleling the above. The entire amount is two hundred silver pieces.

Mr_____, our bridegroom, made this declaration: The obligation of this marriage contract, this dowry and this additional amount I accept upon myself and my heirs after me. It can be paid from the entire best part of the property and possessions that I own under all the heavens, whether I own [this property] already or will own it in the future. [It includes] both mortgageable property and non-mortgageable property. All of it shall be mortgageable and bound as security to pay this marriage contract, this dowry and this additional amount. It can be taken from me, even from the shirt on my back, during my lifetime and after my lifetime, from this day and forever.

This obligation of this marriage contract, this dowry and this additional amount was accepted by Mr________, our bridegroom, according to all the strictest usage of all marriage contracts and additional amounts that are customary for daughters of Israel, according to the ordinances of our sages of blessed memory. It shall not be a mere speculation or a sample document....

We have made a kinyan from Mr______, son of_____, our bridegroom, to Miss_____, daughter of____, this virgin, regarding everything written and stated above, with an article that is fit for such a kinyan. Everything is valid and confirmed.

_________, son of_______, witness
_________, son of_______, witness[43]

When one of the many individualized or standardized progressive *ketubot* are used, the bride and the groom sign the *ketubah,* and both men and women can serve as witnesses. The promises are always mutual; they affirm the quality of the relationship as well as a commitment to Jewish life.[44] In North America, civil divorce, at least, has been substituted for the *get,* and most Reform rabbis will remarry people who have not obtained a *get.*[45] The almost exclusive recognition of civil divorce is due to the lack of power a woman has to initiate divorce proceedings and the many abuses that occur when men refuse to give their wives a *get* or they extract extraordinary conditions. In Reform Judaism we have abandoned the category of *aguna* on ethical grounds.

Jewish marriage is an agreement, a *brit,* between two Jewish adults who love each other and want to share faithfully every aspect of their lives. It is the individuals who enter into the contract by signing the *ketubah* in addition to the two witnesses and the officiating rabbi. They exchange rings and make a declaration of sanctification, and they share a cup of wine over which the seven blessings describing marriage are recited.

In the *halakhah,* only a woman's status is changed completely. She becomes permitted sexually to her husband and forbidden to all other men. Her husband's status, on the other hand, hardly changes. He is still permitted to most of the women to whom he was previously permitted, except for certain relatives of the bride. Although monogamy is the norm in Orthodox Judaism, in countries where it is standard for men to have more than one wife it is still potentially and maybe actually permissible. In addition, a married man that "commits adultery" with an unmarried woman is still not subject to the same penalty as a woman that commits the same offense. If a woman commits adultery, her husband is required to divorce her and she loses the monetary settlement of the *ketubah*.

In an extended analysis of the Jewish wedding ceremony, Rachel Adler points out that two different visions of the relationship of husband and wife are presented: possession and covenantal partner:

> By the time of the Mishnah...a wedding has become a religious event of cosmic significance. Taking a woman to wife is categorized as a unique kind of acquisition, blending characteristics of both purchase and the religious act of setting goods aside for sacred donation, *hekedesh*. The ceremony of taking acquires a new rabbinic name reflecting its sanctification: *kiddushin*.[46]

The ceremony is about normalizing the place of women. It represents a view of women that Reform Judaism rejects. The maintenance of the ceremony of *kiddushin,* even in its egalitarianized form, is insufficient to symbolize the radical nature of the change that Reform Judaism has made in the status of women. A new ceremony would mean that women were more than honorary men, but that they were full partners whose gender is acknowledged as being part of the original creation of humankind:

> Mishnah cannot make women into men. But it can provide for a world in which it is normal for women to be subject to men—father or husband—and a system to regularize the transfer of women from the hand of the father to that of the husband. The regulation of the transfer of women from the Mishnah's way of effecting the sanctification—that is, special handling—of what, for the moment, disturbs and disorders the orderly world. The work of sanctification becomes necessary in particular at the point of

> danger or disorder so as to preserve the normal mode of creation so that maleness may encompass all, even at the critical point of transfer.[47]

We can reinterpret a ritual, or we can create a new ritual to symbolize the newly understood reality. This is the choice that Rachel Adler's description of marriage as *Brit Ahuvim* poses to us. Most Reform Jews would already understand their marriage to be an egalitarian covenantal partnership.[48] The double *kinyan* is understood to accomplish this, but it already changes the halakhic paradigm, because a double *kinyan* invalidates the transaction. Further, a man cannot bestow himself on a woman; he must declare "you are mine" and not "I am yours."[49]

A woman cannot initiate a marriage. I would have thought, if she [the wife] gives him [the husband] money and betroths him, it would be a valid *kiddushin:* therefore Scripture wrote, "When a man taketh," but not, "When a woman taketh," nor can it result from mutual exchange:[50]

> It is the woman who must be acquired, because only the woman undergoes a status change. She will belong exclusively to that man. The man will not belong to the woman because, in relationships, men are subjects but never objects, unless they are slaves. Hence, a man can validly declare, "Be espoused to half of me," because he may divide himself among as many women as he chooses, but if he declares "I hereby espouse half of you," no *kiddushin* has been effected, because unlike a slave who may be owned fractionally by several masters, a woman can only be espoused as the exclusive acquisition of one man.[51]

Rachel Adler also rejects mutual *kinyan* for the additional reason that it is a continuation of the commodification of people.[52] She argues that this does not reflect contemporary egalitarian Jewish marriage. She takes seriously the ritual of marriage as a statement of the *halakhah* as well as of theology and ethics. She proposes, therefore, to call marriage what it has become, *Brit Ahuvim,* a Lovers' Covenant, and to create the covenant as a partnership, creating a ritual that reflects the way partnerships are created in the *halakhah.*

She points to three elements in the creation of a partnership:[53]

1. A partnership deed
2. A statement of personal undertaking in which partners commit themselves to certain acts on behalf of the partnership
3. A *kinyan* or symbolic act of acquisition of the partnership

Her *brit* document contains the following elements: (1) a pledge of sexual exclusivity; (2) a commitment to the rights and duties of a familial relationship; (3) an assumption of joint responsibility for children; (4) a pledge to live a holy life as a Jewish family; (5) a pledge to fulfill communal responsibilities; (6) a pledge that either spouse will protect the dignity and comfort of the other in his or her dying.[54]

The text *Brit Ahuvim,* a Lovers' Covenant, should be contrasted with the text of the traditional *ketubah* cited above:

> On____(day of the week) the____day of ____(month) ____ according to Jewish reckoning (____month____day____year according to secular reckoning) in the city of ____,____ (state or region),____(country), ____(Hebrew name) daughter/son of____and____, whose surname is ____and____(Hebrew name) daughter/son of ____and____, whose surname is ____, confirm

in the presence of witnesses a lovers' covenant between them and declare a partnership to establish a household among the people of Israel.

The agreement in which ______ and ______ are entering is a holy covenant like the ancient covenant of our people, made in faithfulness and peace to stand forever. It is a covenant of protection and hope like the covenant God swore to Noah and his descendants saying,

> When the bow is in the clouds, I will see it and remember the everlasting covenant between God and all living creatures, all flesh that is on earth. That, God said to Noah, "shall be a sign of the covenant I have established between me and all flesh" (Gen. 16–17).

It is a covenant of distinction like the covenant God made with Israel saying,

> You shall be My people and I shall be your God (Jer. 30:22).

It is a covenant of devotion, joining hearts like the covenant David and Jonathan made, as it is said,

> As Jonathan's soul was bound up with the soul of David. Jonathan made a covenant with David because he loved him as himself (1 Sam. 11:3).

It is a covenant of mutual loving kindness like the wedding covenant between God and Zion as it is said,

> I will espouse you forever. I will espouse you with righteousness and justice and loving kindness and compassion. I will espouse you in faithfulness and you shall know God (Hos. 2:21–22).

Provisions of the Covenant

The following are the provisions of the lovers' covenant into which______, (Hebrew name) daughter/son of _______ and

______ and _________, (Hebrew name) daughter/son of ______ and ______, now enter:

1. _____ and ______ declare that they have chosen each other as companions as our rabbis teach:

> *Get yourself a companion.* This teaches that a person should get a companion to eat with, to drink with, to study Bible with, to study Mishnah with, to sleep with, to confide all one's secrets, secrets of Torah and secrets of worldly things *(Avot d'Rabbi Natan* 8).

2. ____ and ____ declare that they are setting themselves apart for each other and will take no other lover.

3. ____ and _____ hereby assume all the rights and obligations that apply to family members to attend, care, and provide for one another [and for any children with which they may be blessed and for _________ _________ child/children of______________].

4. _____ and _____ commit themselves to a life of kindness and righteousness as a Jewish family and to work together toward the communal task of mending the world.

5. _____ and _____ pledge that one will help the other at the time of dying by carrying out the last rational requests of the dying partner, protecting him/her from indignity or abandonment, and by tender, faithful presence with the beloved until the end, fulfilling what has been written:

> Set me as a seal upon your arm, for love is stronger than death (Song of Songs 8:6).

To this covenant we affix our signatures:

The Partners:

____

____

Witnessed this day ________ of Parashat______(Hebrew date)

The witnesses:

____________________[55]

____

One may quarrel with some of the formulations and provisions, but it is a far-reaching revision of marital *halakhah*. It does not tinker around the edges but moves the whole enterprise from property to partnership law. Adler's proposal, whether it is accepted in detail or not, is a way of normalizing liberal Jewish marriage in a halakhic framework. She suggests that the *kinyan* be a symbolic pooling resources where each partner places an object of value in the bag and the bag is held together. Since rings are metonymically not incidental to the wedding ceremony but in fact are understood to constitute marriage, she suggests that the couple put the rings in the bag.

The ceremony she proposes takes place under a *chuppah,* begins with *Mi addir,* and is followed by an officiant's speech explaining the ceremony and its difference from *kiddushin* as well as speaking personally about the couple. This is followed by the blessing over the wine, which is then shared among those who are under the *chuppah.* The *brit* document is read. The *kinyan* takes place. The partners place objects in the bag and then lift the bag and recite a blessing. The *Sheva Berachot* are recited, a glass is broken, and the couple departs for *Yichud.*[56]

The rewriting of the ceremony in such a dramatic way would, in fact, make it clear that in Reform Judaism we have reformulated our concept of marriage. It would have implications for the dissolution of marriage as well.

Many Reform rabbis have rejected the necessity of the *get* because, just as only the man has power to execute a marriage, only the man can initiate divorce. Adler raises the question of whether this nontraditional form of marriage would require a *get*. Whereas for the sake of consistency we would insist on a ceremony that indicates that the partnership has been dissolved, that ceremony would obviously be different from a *get*. The *Seder Predah* ceremony created by the Central Conference of American Rabbis might suffice. At least in North America, acceptable *gittin* are issued only by the Orthodox, and although some of us suggest a *get* to preserve the marriageability of the divorced and to protect unborn children against the accusation of *mamzerut,* we in Reform have eliminated the category of *mamzerut,* will marry a *kohen* and a divorcee,[57] and have our own standards for conversion, all of which are unacceptable to the Orthodox. It is clear to me that we should evolve our *halakhah* according to our theological and ethical standards. We should stand on solid ground, but we must reject Orthodoxy as the standard by which we determine what is halakhic.

If ethical categories are determinative for our halakhic conceptualization and effectuation of marriage, we should expect that in the future, as society's understanding of intimate relationships and sexual identity continue to undergo transformation, we will make other changes.

Radical transformation can take place within a halakhic framework. In the paper "Reform Judaism and Same Sex Marriages: A Halakhic Inquiry," I will outline in greater detail the halakhic categories that justify change based on the authority of the contemporary *posek/et* to alter the decisions of previous generations, and the use of extrahalakhic material to change the *halakhah*.

Notes

1. Mark Washofsky, "Reinforcing Our Jewish Identity: Issues of Personal Status," Central Conference of American Rabbis *Yearbook*, 1994.

2. At the end of the twentieth century, the old ideology of the Enlightenment and Rationalism, which were the underpinnings of modernity, have run their course. They have been replaced by Post-Modernism. But, in fact, there is no clear dominant ideology in liberal Judaism beyond autonomy of the individual, which has been translated, often in the name of justice, into support for the individual right to choose one's life style options and then to normalize this as Jewishly acceptable. Society as a whole has undergone a revolution in relations between men and women, in its understanding of sexual identity, and in relations between Jews and non-Jews. As we have rediscovered particularism, we have not fully explored how it affects our decision making. Having spent six months on sabbatical in England, I have learned first hand that the attitude of Progressive Jews, who are a minority in the Jewish community, are more conservative about making controversial changes in Jewish law, especially in matters of personal status. The issue of our relation to *Klal Yisrael* and the effect of our decisions on other liberal Jewish communities, especially Israel, dominates these discussions. In North America we are freer to find our own course because we represent the majority of the North American Jewish community. In a world of instant communication, what happens in one community has an immediate impact on another community. On the other hand, the realities of each community are different, and what might be appropriate in one place may not be in another. One community will frequently make a decision that only later will become acceptable elsewhere.

3. "We discovered we were no longer talking *to* or even arguing *with* each other, rather we were conducting a series of parallel monologues in place of the dialogue that has served us so well in the past one." CCAR *Responsum* 5756.8, "On Homosexual Marriage," p. 1. This statement illustrates the difficulty that this issue poses, but in a deeper sense it poses a dilemma for Reform Jewish decision making. The Responsa Committee, for example, can formulate a decision precisely at the same time as another committee; in this case the Ad Hoc Committee on Human Sexuality, is working on the same issue. Their respective methodologies and conclusions can be similar or disparate. Such a situation provides a plurality of responses. One can either decry the lack of a unitary position or one can applaud the respect for diversity. But this can also lead to organizational paralysis. In a time when neither methodology nor ideology can be understood as a given, decision making becomes much more complex.

4. A central thesis of my argument is that *kiddushin* is understood as a legal process in which a partnership is sealed using symbolism drawn from property law. The meaning of the transaction is understood through the medium of the *Sheva Berachot.* Rachel Adler in *Engendering Judaism,* pp. 169–207, makes an important proposal to change the ceremony using partnership law not property law. This will be discussed in detail below. Central to my argument is that we have created a new legal institution that has similarities to the old and uses a ceremony to effectuate it that is drawn from the old paradigm. The similarity of name and ceremony has prevented us from recognizing the changes that Reform Judaism has made.

5. It is clear that the Rabbinic tradition and Orthodox authorities such as Maurice Lamm in *The Jewish Way in Love and Marriage* (San Francisco, 1980) are uncomfortable with the concept of a woman as property, but they have largely failed to change the *halakhah* to redress the unequal distribution of power and to permit women to initiate divorce so that they do not have to remain married against their will. In addition, during the wedding ceremony the woman is a passive rather than an active participant, making it clear she is a "second class citizen."

6. This does not mean that our understanding of marriage is merely spiritual, not halakhic. Although a considerable amount of current liturgical creativity is in relation to marriage, it only reflects the fact that the marriage paradigm is undergoing a significant shift. The ceremony is a legal act whose language is performative. Its speech acts to create a new reality, i.e., two unrelated individuals become a married couple. These acts have legal and economic consequences and must be terminated by a legal process. Our spiritualization of *kiddushin* reflects a changed halakhic, not merely aggadic, understanding.

7. It is for others to judge whether I have been successful in using the language of tradition and texts.

8. Gen. 1:27, 5:1–2.

9. Societal change constitutes *shinnui haittim,* change in the times. New information justifies a change in the *halakhah.*

10. I say "in theory" because women who work still carry a disproportionate share of family responsibilities. Marriage as an institution is still in a state of flux.

11. Peter S. Knobel, "Suicide Assisted Suicide, Active Euthanasia: An Halachic Inquiry," in *Death and Euthanasia in Jewish Law,* edited by Walter Jacob and Moshe Zemer (Pittsburgh, 1995), pp. 28–34.

12. Adler, *Engendering Judaism,* pp. 25–26.

13. Lev. 20:7–8.

14. We do not believe that God commands the unethical. If a particular law is deemed unjust we therefore exercise our authority using the principle *Ein lo la-dayyan ella mah she-einav ro'ot.* See Joel Roth, *The Halakhic Process* (New York, 1986), pp. 85ff. We also would apply the concept attached to some of the laws in Leviticus and Deuteronomy that anything that oppresses or exploits another is prohibited because we were strangers and slaves in Egypt. A hermeneutic of justice strictly and carefully applied is part of the Reform halakhic process.

15. See Max Kadushin, *Worship and Ethics* (New York, 1964), p. 223.

16. Simeon Maslin (Ed.), *Gates of Mitzvah* (New York, 1979), citing Herbert Bronstein, p. 123. This slim but important volume is a guide to Reform Jewish religious living created by the Central Conference of American Rabbis. It is designed to list and briefly describe the essential deeds, *mitzvot,* that constitute an observant Jewish life. The footnotes and the essays were written to clarify the meaning of the *mitzvot* in a Reform context. In Reform Judaism, *taamei hamitzvot,* i.e., providing the rationale for a *mitzvah,* is an important aspect of the halakhic process. It is used to defend or refine the meaning of an ancient practice or as a means to change that practice so that it conforms to contemporary understanding. In addressing an essentially minimally observant community, the rational becomes part of the deed. This is especially important when societal change or new knowledge requires a break with the past. Rabbi Maslin reminds us that the burden of proof remains on the one that wishes to changes a practice rather than on the one that wishes to maintain a practice. This is a fundamental principle of the approach of Reform Judaism to the *halakhah* for those in the Reform movement that claim that Reform Judaism is a halakhic movement.

17. Maslin, *Gates of Mitzvah,* pp. 123–24. The concept that marriage is the norm is problematic for those concerned about our sensitivity to single people and also for those that believe marriage is an outmoded or incorrigibly patriarchal institution. Marriage is understood as a *mitzvah* only for those that are physically and psychologically able. Reform Judaism reaffirms even in the face of criticism and the high divorce rate that marriage is a Jewish norm, and, in a similar vein, that procreation is a *mitzvah.* The assertion of norms or ideals that some cannot or will not abide by may cause pain, but this in and of itself is insufficient to cause us to abandon it.

18. *Halakhah* is the crystallization of *aggadah.* This is clearest in Reform Judaism, in which the tradition of *taamet mitzvah* is taken for granted as providing the rationale for observance. Reform has tended to reject or reformulate that which it cannot justify ethically, psychologically, or aesthetically.

19. The issue of mutual *kinyan* is discussed in detail below.

20. Certain specific aspects of the *Sheva Berachot* are analyzed below, p. 158. In Reform Judaism it is the *Sheva Berachot* and not *Birkat Erusin* and *kinyan* that have provided understanding of marriage.

21. The *Sheva Berachot* soften the most objectionable aspects of the *kiddushin* as ceremony of *kinyan* acquisition. It seems clear that the rabbis used the blessings to transform the meaning of the event and to distinguish it from other economic transactions. Reform Judaism makes explicit what is implicit in the *Sheva Berachot.*

22. The double ring ceremony and substitution of either a marriage certificate or an egalitarian *ketubah* for the traditional one are among the most obvious examples in the wedding ceremony.

23. Maslin, *Gates of Mitzvah.*

24. Eugene Borowitz, *Exploring Jewish Ethics,* as cited in Laura Levitt, *Jewish and Feminist: The Ambivalent Search for Home,* p. 75.

25. Eugene Borowitz, *Renewing the Covenant* (Philadelphia, 1991), Passim.

26. Eugene Borowitz, *Exploring Jewish Ethics,* as cited in Levitt, *Jewish and Feminist,* p. 79.

27. Judith Plaskow, "Toward a New Theology of Sexuality," in Christie Balka and Andy Rose (Eds.), *Twice Blessed: On Being Gay and Lesbian* (Boston, 1984), p. 144.

28. See Ruth 1 and 1 Sam. 18.

29. For discussion of this text, see Adler, *Engendering Judaism,* p. 156–67. The culmination of the passage is, according to her, nothing less than a prophecy of "a time when marriage will not be a relationship of master to subordinate, owner to property or omnipotent giver to extractive dependent." In a striking parallel to the hopes of contemporary ecofeminists, the prophesied resolution of the war between the sexes is to usher in a new covenant of universal harmony, pp. 165–66.

30. This text is often added or substituted for *Harei at mekedushet li be taba'at zo kedat Moshe ve Yisrael.* David Polish (Ed.), *Maaglei Tzedek, Rabbi's Manual,* (New York, 1988), p. 54. See Adler's discussion, *Engendering Judaism,* pp. 165–66.

31. See Adler's discussion of the translation of Blessing No. 4, p. 158.

32. I have deliberately used the term *halakhah* rather than *the halakhah* to indicate that *halakhah* is not monolithic, and that although some would deny that Reform is a halakhic movement, a good case can be made for a Reform *Halakhah.*

33. Judith Plaskow, *Standing at Sinai Again* (San Francisco, 1990), p. 145.

34. Adler, *Engendering Judaism,* pp. 183–87.

35. Adler, *Engendering Judaism,* citing Philip Birnbaum (Ed.), *Siddur* (New York, 1949).

36. Ibid., p. 181.

37. The elimination of the *arayot* may simply reflect an ambivalent aesthetic appropriateness of the language in the wedding ceremony and male orientation of the table of consanguinity. However, the category of incest and adultery remain significant. The question of the *arayot* needs to be explored in detail.

38. Adler, *Engendering Judaism,* p. 177.

39. Polish, *Maaglei Tzedek, Rabbi's Manual.*

40. The Assembly of Rabbis of the Reform Synagogues of Great Britain (Eds.), *Forms of Prayer for Jewish Worship,* 1. Daily, Sabbath, and Occasional Prayers, 7th Ed. (Oxford, 1977), p. 281.

41. Some will argue that, for the sake of *Klal Yisrael,* we ought to use the *ketubah.* As Moshe Feinstein has pointed out in *Resp. Igerot Moshe,* EHE, 1:76–77, Reform weddings are *safek kiddushin* at best because there is a prima facie assumption that no kosher witnesses were present. Although his decision allows a woman married by a Reform rabbi to remarry without a *get* (Jewish divorce) and may be considered a leniency, our decision must not be based on trying to satisfy the halakic requirements of other movements unless it can be done in a way that maintains the ethical nature of *kedusha.* The use of the traditional *ketubah* calls into question the *kedusha* of our marriage ceremony.

42. Judith Hauptman, *Rereading the Rabbis: A Woman's Voice* (Boulder, 1998), p. 60.

43. Levitt, *Jewish and Feminist,* pp. 32–33.

44. For new type of covenantal document, see below, Rachel Adler's *Brit Ahuvim.*

45. A rethinking of Reform halakhah requires a rethinking of Jewish divorce. How ought a marriage be dissolved? The traditional *get* is unacceptable. A new ceremony, *Seder Peredah,* has not gained wide acceptance. One fundamental question remains unresolved, and that is the question of remarriage of a divorced woman without a *get* outside Reform Judaism. What are our ethical obligations as well as our relation to *Klal Yisrael?* If we reject the traditional concept of *kiddushin* as unethical, how do we encourage women and men to participate in such practices. Adler, *Engendering Judaism,* pp. 203–212.

46. Ibid., p. 172.

47. Jacob Neusner, *A History of the Mishnaic Law of Women: The Mishnaic System of Women,* Part 5, (Leiden, 1980), p. 268.

48. I suspect that most Orthodox Jews would understand their relationship similarly. In this situation there is a cognitive dissonance between what is done ritually and what is believed theologically. Orthodox feminists, however, have begun to offer an increasingly insistent critique of Jewish marriage law.

49. *Kid.* 4b.

50. *Kid.* 3a, 6b.

51. Adler, *Engendering Judaism,* p. 176.

52. Ibid. Adler strives for an ethical consistency while looking for a proper halakhic paradigm for marriage. Her solution is very much in keeping with the founders of Reform Judaism, who justified their changes on the basis of traditional texts. She acknowledges that marriage is legal and not only spiritual and therefore must have a legal framework for its initiation and termination.

53. Ibid., p. 193.

54. Ibid., p. 194.

55. Ibid., pp. 214–15.

56. Ibid., pp. 197–98.

57. Reform Judaism, in fact, has rejected the concept that *kohanim* have special privileges or restrictions.

THE SLOW ROAD TO MONOGAMY

Walter Jacob

Monogamy is considered the only acceptable form of marriage in Western civilization; it treats men and women equally and provides the fullest opportunity for mutual development. Thousands of years ago the prophets of Israel used poetic imagery of God and Israel in a monogamous relationship and expressed this as their ideal; yet the path of Judaism in that direction has not been easy. Few of our thinkers through the ages have dealt with this issue; none has made it a matter of primary concern. The *halakhah* has moved in the direction of monogamy but, as we shall see, only slowly.

Sexual boundaries are one thing; monogamy quite another. Every religion has set boundaries for the sexual expressions of its adherents, as this has always been an area of human conflict.[1] The Bible did so initially through the family tales of Genesis and, subsequently, through legislation. These stories also represented the beginnings of the slow road to monogamy, an elusive ideal since its first presentation in the tale of the Garden of Eden.

The Genesis stories built families on the basis of polygamy, concubinage, and slave wives. They incidentally dealt with forbidden incestuous relationships. The family was oriented toward its masculine head, as the long genealogical lists make especially clear. Women played crucial but subsidiary roles, at least on the official level.

The legal literature of the Torah presented clearer definitions of marriage and placed major restrictions on sexual unions. The subsequent Jewish legal literature clarified those limits but only incidentally moved toward monogamy; it was a form of marriage that many favored, so some steps were taken in that direction. This paper will begin with a brief discussion of restrictions on sexuality and then concentrate on the major obstacles to monogamy.

SEXUAL PROHIBITIONS

The sexual prohibitions of the Torah were limited to sexual relations with animals (bestiality),[2] between men (homosexuality),[3] with a series of close relatives (incest),[4] and with someone already married (adultery).[5]

Although the unfaithful wife was a frequent image of the prophetic literature, and the Book of Proverbs made recommendations about marriage, there was no discussion of legal marriage in the Bible after the Torah. Issues surrounding sexuality and marriage were important to the scholars of the Talmud, as we can see from four very large tractates *(Kiddushin, Ketubot, Niddah,* and *Yebamot)* that dealt almost exclusively with these subjects, as well as *Gittin,* which treated divorce. These matters were often considered extensively in other tractates as well. The rabbinic literature extended the detailed prohibitions of consanguinity to ascending and descending familial lines or through logical extension.[6] It also defined the relationships that were recognized as marriages.

The tractate *Kiddushin* described three ways of creating a legally effective marriage. The most common was a deed witnessed by two competent individuals and handed by the groom to the bride. This has remained an essential part of weddings through the ages.[7] The document was a contract stipulating specific obligations for both bride and groom, and grounds for divorce existed when these obligations were ignored or violated.

The minimum financial commitment made by the groom (200 *zuzim*) was considerable; it did not have to be paid at the time of the marriage but was due if the marriage was dissolved or the groom died.[8] The obligations of the husband included providing sexual satisfaction on a regular basis, which depended on the nature of his work,[9] as well as a home and maintenance according to his means. Should these diminish, however, the bride's living standards could not decline without her consent.[10] The groom also had to provide medical care, ransom, and funeral expenses.[11]

The bride had to be willing to engage in sexual relations unless she was unclean or had another good reason to refuse; she, or the servants she brought into the marriage, was responsible for the ordinary house work, consisting of grinding flour, baking, cooking, knitting, washing, nursing an infant, and mixing the husband's drink. The bride was personally responsible for making her husband's bed and for washing his face, hands, and feet.[12]

Since these provisions were so specific, they provided a framework for marriage, protected the wife, and began the road toward monogamy. The fact that an amount had been listed in the *ketubah,* either as *matan* or *mohar,* placed a considerable financial obligation upon the man. Multiple wives increased that obligation and, in case of infractions of the agreement on his part, could bankrupt him. The introduction of the *ketubah* undoubtedly limited polygamy to the wealthy even more than in earlier periods.

A marriage also took effect if an item of value was transferred between the bride and groom in the presence of two competent witnesses. This remains a part of the modern wedding in the form of presenting a ring or another object of value while the formula *harei at mekudeshet*... is recited.[13]

In addition, marriage could and can still be effected through intercourse *(biah)* when preceded by a statement indicating the wish to take this woman as a wife or if two witnesses have seen the couple leaving for a private place. Marriage is assumed, as intercourse was taken for granted. The later marriage ceremony seeks to combine all three elements. This, too, should be taken as a step toward monogamy, as it made marriage a formal, public, legal act, less likely to be disputed.

The Bible had established marriage through sexual relations,[14] and the rabbinic literature felt it necessary to include this along with the other two methods, although the authorities objected strenuously to marriage through sexual union alone. The general rabbinic opinion was that all sexual unions were to be taken seriously unless there was definite evidence to the contrary[15]—a situation, probably, often far from the minds of those engaged in the act.

On the other hand, the reality that the sexual drive was difficult to control led some scholars to suggest that if the urge was too strong, the individual should put on a dark garment, go to a neighboring community, and find a woman.[16] In addition, the Talmud made it possible for those away on trading trips to take wives on a temporary basis, as brief as a single day. They could, of course, also take wives on a permanent basis in the community of their destination if they visited there often. This, too, was a bow to reality. There was no numerical limit, but four was suggested.[17] The fact that these statements survived in the texts suggests that marriage and sexuality were approached with a high sense of reality, but also that the struggle toward monogamy had only begun.

PROHIBITED MARRIAGES

Major categories of individuals who could not be married were listed in the Bible;[18] in addition were the prohibitions against marriage with neighboring nations, with which we shall not concern ourselves here. The list of consanguineous relationships as expanded by the later rabbinic literature was generally accepted, and the questions that arose in the later rabbinic literature tended to be around the edges of this legislation. This, too, should be viewed as a step toward monogamy, since such relationships within the family circle, if permitted, could easily multiply. The prohibited marriages were castigated but rarely annulled. The rabbis in every period refrained from taking this step, possibly because of potential problems with offspring, although some exceptions are found in the literature.[19] This failure to annul, of course, weakened the prohibitions against these marriages, but not enough to make them a serious problem.

ADULTERY AND MARRIAGE

The literature takes adultery very seriously; it was a break in the fundamental basis of marriage. In the biblical period the death penalty was prescribed; later, flogging.[20] In addition, the promises made in the *ketubah* were invoked, and the guilty party paid heavily. Every effort was made to keep the individuals who had been engaged in an adulterous relationship from getting married; such marriages were prohibited.[21] This, of course, is part of an effort to limit adultery within the Jewish community; and, among those groups that had already established monogamy, to strengthen it. There were exceptions in which the authorities bowed to the reality that the individuals involved would simply live together without the blessings of Judaism and the official community. Rather than see this occur, they decided to accept such a marriage, if it had already taken place, presumably through an officiant who was unaware of the adultery.[22] We may see this as a way of maintaining some control over the sexual lives of the community and vaguely as a step toward monogamy as it sought to provide a way back into the community for those who had trespassed.

POLYGAMY

The major obstacle to a monogamous union was polygamy, which was very much part of the Bible. The lives of the Patriarchs indicated that polygamy was well established and was taken for granted. The obvious problems of the status of each wife and the status of the offspring were raised in a realistic manner in Genesis and, later, within the royal families of Israel and Judea. Polygamy, of course, was possible only for the wealthy. It waxed and waned in Jewish life; Epstein indicated that it virtually ceased at the end of the biblical period but resumed in Hellenistic times.[23] Some groups, such as the Zadokites of Damascus[24] and, later, the Karaites,[25] legislated monogamy. Most talmudic scholars, however, accepted polygamy.[26] Although the ideal of monogamous marriage existed, it was not pursued with vigor.

Imperial Rome sought to eliminate polygamy throughout the empire, but as one can see from repeated decrees by Theodosius (379–395), Justinian (527–565), and Leo the Philosopher (886–912), with only limited success.[27] According to Epstein, matters changed through popular pressure in the Gaonic period (700–110), when clauses protecting the first wife were inserted into the *ketubah*. This method was used particularly by wealthy families to protect the status of their women. Such examples existed in *ketubot* found in the Cairo Geniza and were cited in Gaonic responsa. They stated that

> he may not marry or take during the bride's lifetime and while she is with him another wife, slave-wife, or concubine except with her consent, and if he does...he shall from this moment be under obligation to pay her the *ketubah* in full, and release her by a bill of divorcement by which she shall be free to remarry.[28]

We can conclude that polygamy continued to be accepted in Jewish life when tolerated by the surrounding society. This meant that it was practiced to some extent in the Near East throughout history.

In Christian Europe the decree *(herem)* ascribed to Rabbenu Gershom (960–1040), prohibited polygamy in Ashkenazic lands; this may have been due to a slow internal development[29] or have brought Jewish practice into line with the surrounding society. Falk and, earlier, Frankel, showed that the decree was in any case part of a long series of steps taken in this direction.[30] The medieval legal discussions of polygamy did not deal with the nature of marriage or the status of women; they mainly treated the exceptions to monogamy that might be allowed in case of childlessness or the *yibbum* (levirate marriage to the widow of a deceased brother). Although the *herem* of Rabbenu Gershom prohibited the individual from marrying an additional wife, special permission for exceptions could be provided by one hundred rabbis from three districts—in other words, in extraordinary circumstances, which will be discussed later. These rulings, along with the nature of the contemporary discussion, indicated that monogamy was established as the practical road of Ashkenazic Jewry; Asher ben Yehiel (1250–1328) considered monogamy binding in his code. From the contemporary responsa of Solomon ben Aderet (1235–1310), we can see that it was not accepted in Spain or in Provence.[31]

Polygamy was therefore almost eliminated in northern Europe, although it continued in the Muslim-dominated lands of the Mediterranean. When we view polygamy in Islamic society, we find it taken for granted, with virtually no statements about the ideal of monogamy; no efforts to eliminate polygamy were successful in Muslim-dominated societies.

EXCEPTIONS FROM THE *HEREM* OF RABBENU GERSHOM

Despite the force of Rabbenu Gershom's decree, it was not seen as an absolute ban on polygamy in Ashkenazic lands or in the border areas where some communities followed Sephardic customs. Exceptions were permitted, albeit seldom. The fact that other ways of dealing with the exceptional circumstances outlined below were not used, however, indicated a reluctance to move decisively in this direction. Other remedies could have been found for every instance in which polygamy was invoked, but this was not done.

The various discussions of the *herem* dealt with four instances in which polygamy could be permitted even in lands where it was normally not practiced: levirate marriages, a wife's barrenness, a wife's insanity, and special instances of a wife's improper conduct.

Let us begin with the levirate marriage, which represented a major area of concern through the ages; *yibbum* was intended to ensure that a deceased brother's lineage would continue. The widow could be released from her obligation to her brother-in-law through the ceremony of *halitzah.*[32] In Sephardic lands, naturally, *yibbum* continued to be practiced and so led to numerous cases of polygamy; it was also condoned in northern Europe, although there *halitzah* became the norm. This question was never completely resolved.[33]

According to the *Mishnah,* which after all based itself on the biblical command "be fruitful and multiply,"[34] a woman had to be divorced or a second wife taken if she remained barren after ten years. After some initial discussion such exceptions were not permitted in northern Europe on these grounds.[35]

A wife's insanity or her conversion to Christianity, both of which made divorce impossible, led to the suspension of the *herem.* It was similarly not enforced when the conduct of the wife demanded a divorce according to talmudic law but she was unwilling to accept it.[36] In northern Europe the authorities were reluctant to make any exceptions to the *herem* after the first generation, nevertheless such bans did take place. In Sephardic lands nothing changed.

CONCUBINAGE

Polygamy was not the only obstacle to a monogamous marriage. The taking of two or more wives could also occur through concubinage *(pilegshut).* Concubines were women of lower status than the main wife, if there was one. Concubinage occurred frequently in the biblical period, most often among the kings of Israel.[37] We, of course, find it already among the wives of the Patriarch Jacob, so that Rachel and Leah were first-rank wives whereas their servants had an inferior status. We know little about the status of subsidiary wives in the biblical period.[38] The Genesis tales demonstrated that when secondary wives produced children, these progeny were on an equal footing with those of the primary wives. According to Epstein, concubinage died out in the late biblical period but was reintroduced in Hellenistic and Roman times. The Romans had curbed polygamy but permitted concubinage until the time of Constantine (326 C.E.).[39]

The Talmud made an effort to regularize the concubine, and in the Babylonian Talmud she was seen as possessing neither *kiddushin* nor *ketubah;* according to the Palestinian Talmud, however, a concubine had *kiddushin* but no *ketubah;* in other words, it opted for partial protection of the woman.[40] It was the Babylonian definition that most later authorities followed:[41] they denied married status to the concubine and so denigrated this relationship. Rashi (1040–1105), Ribash (1326–1408), and others, followed the Jerusalem Talmud. The two definitions may refer to two levels of concubinage or may reflect errors in the original Talmudic text.[42] The sources agree that we were dealing with an individual of intermediate status that did not have all the rights of a married wife but on the other hand was not to be considered a prostitute. Among Medieval authorities, Maimonides (1135–1204) protested vigorously against concubinage and sought to eliminate it by claiming that it was a right limited to royalty and not permitted to ordinary Jews.[43] He did not engage in a discussion of monogamy or an ideal state of marriage but treated it as a practical matter. He considered the woman involved in this relationship a prostitute *(zona);* both she and her lover were to be whipped.[44] Jacob b. Asher (d. 1340) and Joseph Caro (1488–1575) later prohibited concubinage.[45] Concubines were permitted, however, by many Spanish and Provençal authorities such as Abraham ben David of Posquières (1125–1198), Solomon b. Adret (c. 1235–c.1310), Asher ben Jehiel (c. 1250–1327), and Menachem b. Solomon Meiri (1249–1316), although they disagreed on the status of the concubine. Nahmanides (1194–1270) accepted concubines, but he warned against the moral evil involved and discussed this on a moral plane.[46] After this intense period of discussion in the early Middle Ages, the debate failed to proceed much further.

Concubines were accepted, albeit reluctantly, in the Middle Ages among both Sephardic and Ashkenazic Jews and were often considered outside the *herem* of R. Gershom.[47] Moses Isserles (1520–1572) permitted concubines as long as they were careful about *mikveh*. To him, the ideal of ritual cleanliness loomed more important than monogamy.[48] Most authorities cited here based their prohibition and cautions on the deuteronomic law prohibiting prostitution in Israel.[49]

The general mood of the rabbinic authorities was to limit concubinage or accept it *bediavady*. The *herem* of R. Gershom was interpreted to include concubines in the Ashkenazic community but was not absolutely enforced, so concubinage in various forms continued until the beginning of the nineteenth century. Although the practice of concubinage became infrequent in the Mediterranean basin after the sixteenth century, it was discussed in the codes and by an occasional responsum. A curious exception was presented in the eighteenth century by Jacob Emden, who favored the institution as a way of increasing the population of the Jewish community.[50]

Sexual relationships with gentile slaves and servants were, of course, prohibited; some responsa dealt with these matters.[51]

We can see in the discussions of concubinage and polygamy a slow movement toward monogamy, first in Ashkenazic lands and then in the Mediterranean basin. It was driven more by popular consent than by rabbinic leadership. Absolutes were avoided and so was radical change. If this had been a major matter of principle, no such division in family life between the Ashkenazic and Sephardic communities would have developed. The distinction was tolerated, unlike the views of various other sectarian groups within Judaism. The Ashkenazic discussions of this question were known in the Sephardic community, but they brought about no change.

INFORMAL "RELATIONSHIPS" AND RULINGS ON VIRGINITY

Casual sexual relationships, of course, have always been a danger to monogamy. Proverbs warned against prostitutes. The Bible prohibited prostitution and made it punishable by death;[52] the rabbinic tradition changed this to whipping.

Casual sexual relationships were problematic in a polygamous or a monogamous society. Every effort was made to keep young women from such relationships. Precautions were taken to ensure their virginity through a strict regime of chaperonage, and the rules continued after engagement, although the standards were stricter in Galilee and Babylonia than in Judea,[53] and men and women were to be punished equally. The traditional authorities also did their best to protect the female from false charges and erroneous assumptions about her lack of virginity; anyone wishing to bring charges against a bride found it extremely difficult. The biblical text made provision for an accusation of nonvirginity brought by the groom after the wedding night. The parents would proceed with the defense of their daughter. If, indeed, she was not a virgin, she was liable for the death penalty. If she had been accused erroneously, her husband was fined a hundred pieces of silver and forfeited the right of ever divorcing her.

All this was discussed further in the Talmud and later literature.[54] One authority, however, indicated that if such an accusation was brought before him, the young man was to be whipped, as the accusation indicated that he himself had engaged in illicit intercourse earlier. Another limited such a challenge to a man previously married, since he possessed legitimate experience.[55] Furthermore, after a girl is more than twelve years and six months old *(bogeret),* the hymen may disappear naturally and no sign of virginity remain. Should she have lost her virginity by accident, her *ketubah* was reduced by 100 *zuzim,* a large sum; no such reduction was made if she claimed rape after betrothal. It was generally made almost impossible for a groom to file a complaint of nonvirginity.[56]

A *ketubah* normally assumed that the bride was a virgin, unless it was known that she was a widow or divorced, and the rabbis have not concerned themselves with the possibility that this was not so.[57] The rabbinate did not seem to hesitate to use the term "virgin" in the *ketubah* even when it was in doubt. The Gaonim composed a special *berakhah* to be recited by the groom on his wedding night if his wife was a virgin.[58] The recital of such a blessing if the wife was not a virgin would be *levatalah.* The ritual was eliminated in post-Gaonic times.

THE SLOW ROAD TO MONOGAMY

In an effort to encourage marriage and long-term family relationships, the rabbinic authorities, through a strict system of chaperonage that applied to women of all ages, married and single, did their best to discourage casual sex or even the vaguest suspicion of it.[59] There are numerous discussions about the details in the rabbinic literature. These rules were effective, but there were infringements in every age, as thousands of responsa attest.

Discussions in the responsa inevitably dealt with women, and with men only when the accusations were false. Monogamy was enforced in one direction only; and although many moral statements were addressed to men, they were not followed by legal enactments.

THE EMANCIPATION AND MODERN TIMES

In the period of the Emancipation, monogamy was taken for granted throughout the Western world. The most decisive statement was given in response to a question of Napoleon in 1807. The assembled dignitaries could confidently state monogamy was firmly established, and this statement confirmed that fact.[60]

None of the numerous synods and conferences held in Europe or North America that led to the establishment of the Reform and Conservative movements felt it necessary to discuss monogamy. They dealt with related matters frequently as they dealt with the marriage ceremony, divorce, and various status questions.[61] Many Reform thinkers have treated the status of women and their rights; these works have included discussions of marriage and the role of men and women in marriage, and each has assumed monogamy and made it the basis of its discussion.[62] Discussion of monogamy in the Reform and Conservative responsa literature has been very limited.

The State of Israel has eliminated polygamy even among its Sephardic citizens; immigrants from lands where polygamy continued were forced to choose one wife while providing maintenance for any others.[63] In 1950, this mainly affected mmigrants from Yemen and a few other lands.

CONCLUSION

We have traced the slow movement of Judaism toward monogamy. Two decisive developments were the introduction of the *ketubah* in the talmudic period and the ban attributed to Rabbenu Gershom in the Middle Ages. Each of these steps represented a major shift, but the second was clearly driven as much by external as internal forces, so it did not spread to the Sephardic community. One must also note the absence of strong leadership, either halakhic or philosophical, in this direction. Female status questions were of little importance to Jewish thinkers until modern times and the advent of the liberal Jewish movements.

In the last decades of the twentieth century, some of the issues discussed in this paper have disappeared, but monogamy remains problematic, especially in the face of a new development: we may have attained it in one sense, but not in another, as we now have frequent consecutive marriages. With divorce frequent, half of Jewish adults will have more than one spouse during their lifetimes, and a fair number will have more than two. This will be due not to death as in previous periods, but to divorce. This means that although monogamy exists, the urge toward polygamy and polyandry has taken a different turn. It differs from previous situations and presents a different threat to monogamy and even more to the family as the most significant unit in Jewish life. This means that when we speak of monogamy, we are no longer talking of a lifelong commitment, but of one that is more time bound. We have only begun to deal with these new conditions and with the changes in basic assumptions to which they are bound to lead.

These factors, in addition to the movement toward women's equality and the separation of sexual activity and reproduction, have led to a system of monogamy brought about by personal wishes rather than by religious, economic, or social forces. In a period when new technologies and new freedom from a wide variety of constraints have made virtually anything and any "life style" possible, monogamy is doing reasonably well. Discussions on an ethical and philosophical level have begun. We are no longer limited to practical halakhah. Halakhists have also added a moral tone when they deal with these matters. The road in this direction has been long and difficult and much still lies ahead.

Notes

1. As we can see in the tale of Abraham and Pharaoh (Gen. 13:10–20) or David and Bathsheba (2 Sam. 11).

2. Exod. 22:28; Lev. 18:23, 20:15–16; Deut. 17:21.

3. Lev. 18:22, 29:13.

4. Lev. 18:20; Deut. 27.

5. Exod. 20:13; the law went further and prohibited coveting, Exod. 20:14.

6. *Yeb.* 21a; *J. Yeb.* 2.4; *Yad, Hil. Ishut* 1.6; *Shulhan Arukh, Even Haezer* 25:24.

7. *Kid.* 9a; *Shulhan Arukh, Even Haezer* 32.1–4.

8. *Ket.* 54a.

9. *Ket.* 62b.

10. *Ket.* 48a; 61a.

11. *Ket.* 46b, 51a, 52a.

12. *Ket.* 61a, 63b.

13. *Kid.* 2a, b; *Shulhan Arukh, Even Haezer* 27:1.

14. Gen. 4:1 "knowing."

15. *Kid.* 9b; *Yeb.* 107a; *Ket.* 73a; *Git.* 81b; *Shulhan Arukh, Even Haezer* 33:1.

16. *Moed Katan* 17a; *Tos.* to *Kid.* 40a.

17. *Yeb.* 44a, 65a; S.D. Goitein, *A Mediterranean Society,* Vol. 3 (Berkeley, 1978), p. 206f.

18. For a full list see Moses Mielziner, *The Jewish Law of Marriage and Divorce* (Cincinnati, 1884), pp. 33ff.

19. R. Asher decided that the rabbinic authorities had the power to annul marriages that violated rabbinic law. He justified this as a fence around the law. Divorce could therefore be forced; Sher, *Responsa* 43.8, cited in A. H. Freiman, *Seder Kiddushin Venisuin* (Jerusalem, 1964), p. 71. Some others followed him, but this was not the normal path.

20. Death penalty Lev. 20:10; Deut 22:22; Mak. 7a.

21. The Bible provided the death penalty for both parties (Lev. 20:10; Deut. 22:24), and this was continued into Mishnaic times and discussed in the Talmud (*Mat.* 27:27, 35; *San.* 6.3; *San.* 50b ff). Like all capital punishment, this became theoretical because of the reluctance of the rabbis to invoke it. They made it so difficult that it was virtually annulled (*San.* 40b–41a). Instead, the adulterers were whipped (Whipping, *Shulhan Arukh, Even Haezer* 11; *Yad Hil. Issurei Biah* 1.8).

In later times a man was to divorce his adulterous wife, and this could be done even against her will (Meir of Rothenberg, *Responsa* 245). The adulterer could not marry her (*Yeb.* 24b; *Shulhan Arukh, Even Haezer* 11.1).

22. If the marriage had taken place *(bediavad)* it was recognized, and the parties were not forced to divorce (*Shulhan Arukh, Even Haezer* 11.2; *Otzar Haposkim, Even Haezer* 11.1, 44).

23. L.M. Epstein, *Marriage Laws in the Bible and Talmud* (Cambridge, Mass., 1942), pp. 3–33.

24. L. Ginzberg, *Eine unbekannte jüdische Sekte* (New York, 1922), pp. 24–25.

25. A. Neubauer, *Geschichte des Karäertums* (Leipzig, 1866), p. 46.

26. *Suk.* 27a; *Yeb.* 15a, b; 44a; Justin Martyr, *Dialogue* 134, 141; in some instances the second wives were in different cities (*Yeb.* 37b; *Yoma* 18b). Earlier, Josephus, *Antiquities* 18 (1, 2). As polygamy was less common in the Land of Israel, it could be grounds for the first wife's suit for divorce, but not in Babylonia (*Yeb.* 65a).

27. J. Starr, *The Jews in the Byzantine Empire* (Athens, 1939), p. 144.

28. L. Epstein, *Jewish Marriage Contract* (New York, 1927), p. 272; J. Mann, *Texts and Studies* (Cincinnati, 1931–38), Vol. 2, p. 177; Goitein, *A Mediterranean Society,* (Berkley, 1991), Vol. 3, p. 147.

29. The decree itself was lost long ago, but it was cited by many early sources. M. Güdemann, *Geschichte des Erziehungwesens* (Vienna, 1888), Vol. 3, pp. 115–119.

30. Z.W. Falk, *Jewish Matrimonial Law in the Middle Ages* (Oxford, 1966), pp. 1, 24–34.

31. Neuman, *The Jews of Spain,* Vol. 2, pp. 52ff; Solomon ben Aderet, *Responsa* 1 (812, 1205); 3 (446); 4 (180, 257, 280).

32. Both *yibbum* and *halitzah* are based on Deut. 25:5–10.

33. *Shulhan Arukh, Even Haezer* 1.10; Caro and Isserles differ; the commentaries cite numerous responsa on each side; *Sefer Hassidim* 284; Jacob Weil, *Responsa* 188.

34. Gen. 1.28; 9.1, 7; *M. Yeb.* 6.6.

35. *Tur Even Haezer* 1.1, *Bet Yosef,* and other commentaries; Solomon Luria, *Responsa* 65.

36. R. Joel Tam or earlier, according to L. Finkelstein, *Jewish Self-Government in the Middle Ages* (New York, 1924), Vol. 2, Chap. 2. *Shulhan Arukh, Even Haezer* 1.10 and commentaries; *Otzar Haposkim, Even Haezer* 1.10 (61).

37. 2 Sam. 3:7, 21:8ff, 5:13; 1 Kings 11:3; 1 Chron. 11:21.

38. L. Epstein, "The Institution of Concubinage among Jews." *Proceedings of the American Academy for Jewish Research,* New York, Vol. 6, pp. 153ff, deals with the various types of subsidiary wives in the ancient period.

39. F. Schulz, *Classical Roman Law,* (Oxford, 1951), p. 137.

40. *San.* 21a; *J. Ket.* 5.2, 29b.

41. Caro to *Yad, Melachim* 4.4; de Boton to *Yad, Melachim;* Radbaz, *Responsa* Vol. 5 (225), Vol. 7 (33); Adret, *Responsa* Vol. 4 (314).

42. G. Ellinson, *Nisu-in Shelo Kedat Mosheh VeYisra-el,* pp. 40ff.

43. *Yad Hil. Melachim* 4.4.

44. *Yad Hil. Ishut* 1.4.

45. *Tur* and *Shulhan Arukh, Even Haezer* 26.1.

46. *Responsa* 284; commentary to Gen. 25:6.

47. *Tseida Laderekh* 3 (1, 2); Aderet, *Responsa* Vol. 1 (1205); Vol. 5 (314); Rabbenu Nissim, *Responsa* 68; Asher, *Responsa* 37.1; Meir of Padua, *Responsa* 19; *Shulhan Arukh, Even Haezer* 13.7; *Otsar Haposkim, Even Haezer* 26.3ff.

48. Isserles to *Shulhan Arukh, Even Haezer* 26.1.

49. Deut. 23, 19ff; Lev. 19:29, 21:9.

50. Jacob Emden, *Sheelot Ya-avets* 2 (16).

51. *M. Temurah* 6.2; *Bet Yoseph* to *Tur Even Haezer,* start of *Kiddushin; Yad, Hil. Issurei Biah* 12.13.

52. Lev. 21:7–9; Deut. 22:20–22; Jubilees 20:4.

53. *M. Ket.* 1.4, 5; *Ket.* 7b; 12a; *J. Kid.* 64b.

54. Deut. 22:13–19; *Ket.* 10a, 46a.

55. *Ket.* 10a.

56. *Ket.* 10a, b; 36a; *Yad Hil. Ishut; Shulhan Arukh, Even Haezer* 39.

57. *Nahalat Shiva* (Warsaw, 1884), 12–15; Benzion Schereschewsky, *Dinei Mishpachah* (Jerusalem, 1984), p. 99.

58. B. Lewis, *Otzar Hagaonim,* Vol. 8; *Ket.* pp. 14–15; Lawrence A. Hoffman, *The Canonization of the Synagogue Service* (New York, 1991), p. 136.

59. *Ned.* 20a; *Git.* 81a; *Ket.* 27b ff; *A. Z.* 36b; *San* 21b; *Kid.* 80b; *J. Kid.* 66b; *Shulhan Arukh, Even Haezer* 22.4 and commentaries; *Yad Hil. Issurei Biah* 21.27; *Arukh Hashulkhan, Even Haezer* 119.25–28.

60. For a summary of the conferences see Central Conference of American Rabbis *Yearbook* (Cincinnati, 1890), Vol. 1, pp. 80ff; Softon D. Temkin, *The New World of Reform* (Bridgeport, 1974), pp. 51ff.; Walter Jacob (ed.), *The Changing World of Reform Judaism—The Pittsburgh Platform in Retrospect* (Pittsburgh, 1985), pp. 91ff.

61. "Resolutions of Past Conferences," Central Conference of American Rabbis *Yearbook* (Cincinnati, 1891), Vol. 1, pp 80–125.

62. Works by Samuel Cohon, Eugene Borowitz, Roland Gittelson, Solomon B. Freehof, and Emil Fackenheim.

63. Schereshevsky, *Dinei Mishpachah* (Jerusalem, 1984), pp. 72ff, 213; Paltiel Dyban, *Dinei Niisuin Vegerushin* (Tel Aviv, 1956), p. 153.

SEPARATING THE ADULT FROM ADULTERY

Daniel Schiff

"*Lo Tinaf*—You shall not commit adultery."[1] These two simple Hebrew words comprise the only sexual transgression to be mentioned in the Ten Commandments themselves.[2] Of all the many sexual prohibitions recorded in the written Torah, adultery alone came to occupy this place of enormous prominence. It is hardly surprising that this is so, for in the Jewish mind set adultery, unlike other sexual violations, represents the shattering of a precious covenant of commitment and devotion. Not by accident does the seventh commandment appear directly opposite the second commandment on the tablets of the Decalogue: just as idolatry signifies a destructive spurning of the covenant with God, so adultery signifies the rupturing of the most fundamental covenant in human life. In fact, as the *Mechilta* saw it, there is an integral connection between the two: "someone who betrays his spouse will eventually betray God himself."[3] Given this kind of observation, there can be little wonder that Judaism came to hold adultery as a desecration of great magnitude.

Viewed through the perspective of history, the conspicuous location of the interdiction against adultery within the Ten Commandments ensured that adultery would occupy a most significant place in the moral teachings of both Jewish and Western civilization. Indeed, the adultery prohibition, the guard at the gates of marital fidelity, came to be seen as critical to the very functioning of society itself. For it was, after all, obedience to this most basic of laws that provided the family—the fundamental unit seen to be mandated by God—with ensured boundaries within which it was possible for a secure environment to flourish.

Moral thinking, however, is never static, and although the passing centuries saw the prohibition against adultery continue to be etched in stone, the fate that awaited the adulterer underwent a profound transition. In the biblical period, an individual acknowledged as guilty of adultery faced either threat of death or some of the severest punishments available in life.[4] Three millennia later, it has become possible for a modern Jew, while remaining within the Jewish community, to commit adultery and still pursue a successful career, further intimate relationships, and maintain positions of leadership. Attitudes to adultery have plainly changed to such an extent for most Jews that it is inconceivable that any responsible formulation of Jewish public policy could advocate a return to speaking of adultery as a capital crime. The issue, then, with which contemporary Judaism must grapple, is the manner in which Jewish public policy on adultery ought to be formulated in a society that regrets but does little to discourage adultery and in which Jewish law can no longer mandate the imposition of its will. If the historical understanding of the resounding implications of adultery, engraved at the heart of the Ten Commandments, continues to hold true within our current ethos, how might a progressive *halakhah* respond appropriately to adultery using the available tools of the Jewish legal system?

THE CONTEMPORARY PARAMETERS OF ADULTERY

A coherent reply to these questions requires some analysis of the extent and nature of present-day adultery. Today, an adulterous relationship is generally—though not always Jewishly[5]— defined as a voluntary sexual relationship between two parties, at least one of whom is married to someone else.[6] A sexual encounter of this kind constitutes adultery if it happens just once in a lifetime or if it takes the form of a continuing interaction.

Reliable statistics on adultery indicate that although the popular mythology of the rampant nature of such behavior is vastly exaggerated, adultery is by no means a rare occurrence. It is, in fact, cogent to assume from the available data that around one marriage in five will be subject to adultery at some point in its duration.[7] This is certainly a statistic large enough to foster societal implications that cannot be ignored. There is, moreover, no reason to suspect that the figures are any different for the vast majority of the Jewish community that is thoroughly integrated into modern society.[8]

Although the numbers might be relatively straightforward, the picture of adultery is made complex by the reality that not all forms of adultery are alike: we can discern at least five qualitatively different types of adultery. First is what might be called "technical" adultery. In an act of technical adultery, the parties involved may not even think of their behavior as being adulterous. An example that occurs frequently is that of the couple that has been separated for some time in anticipation of a divorce where one spouse decides to have a sexual relationship with someone other than his or her married partner. Whereas the parties concerned might well consider the marriage to be effectively "over," insofar as the marriage has not been ended by a legal divorce, any sexual relationship must technically be defined as an act of adultery. From a Jewish perspective, of course, technical adultery represents a critical halakhic issue, because if no *get* has been exchanged, any new marriage that might be contracted inevitably results in what is halakhically regarded as an adulterous union. The Reform movement's late nineteenth-century decision to rely on civil divorce to effect Jewish divorce without need of a *get* has created innumerable cases of such technical adultery from the point of view of traditional *halakhah.*[9] Another instance of technical adultery that used to be encountered regularly within Jewish law would arise when a *get* received by a woman from her first husband and assumed to be valid, turned out—through some imperfection—to be invalid. Although the parties' adultery was produced by an unfortunate technicality, not infrequently a mistake on the part of the *beit din*—the halakhic consequences were just as serious as if the adultery had been fully intentional.

Second is what might be described as "circumstantial" adultery. Circumstantial adultery takes place under extraordinary conditions, most often in cases of the serious physical or mental impairment of a spouse. In such situations the married partner committing the adultery will usually be very conscious of it, but the other partner will often be incapable of such awareness. A spouse in a long-term coma, for instance, is no longer sexually available, may live for many years, and, for a variety of reasons, divorce may be undesirable. If the spouse of the comatose patient finds a committed partner with whom a sexual relationship is shared, adultery will be the result, though it is an adultery that arguably might warrant a moral response different from that given to other categories.

Third is what might be referred to as "unknowing" adultery. Unknowing adultery can result from a deliberate intent to mislead, such as when a single individual has sex with a person that claims to be single but is, in fact, married. Whereas the married individual's adultery is clear, the single person has been deceitfully induced into an act of unwitting adultery. The law, however, also considers cases of unknowing adultery that are entirely accidental. This situation might arise when an individual *(X)* has sexual relations—presumably in the dark—with somebody *(Y)* that *X* believes to be his/her spouse. In actuality, *Y* turns out to be somebody other than the spouse.[10] Although it is possible that *Y* might have planned the deception deliberately, it is also feasible —albeit remotely—that *Y* simply ended up in the wrong place, also believing him/herself to be together with his/her spouse.

Fourth is "consenting" adultery. When consenting adultery is committed—in contrast to unknowing adultery—the married partners involved are fully aware of the adultery, since they actually agree to it. Partner-swapping, or the practice of so-called "open marriage," illustrates this form of adultery, in which the spouse of the adulterer has fully acquiesced.

Fifth is what might be termed "classic" adultery. This is the form of adultery most widely embarked upon and also the one most usually thought of when the term "adultery" is mentioned. Classic adultery may or may not be kept secret from the adulterer's marital partner, but it is the kind of adultery that—if the partner were to be aware of it—would be seen on some level as a betrayal of the marital bond.[11] Classic adultery can, of course, also include sex for money, so that prostitution, where one of the parties is married, is classic adultery.

The deep concern of Jewish tradition with all manner of adultery meant that the traditional halakhic approach never differentiated between varying kinds of adultery and did not, therefore, address the possibility that diverse consequences might be appropriate to the divergent forms of adultery: adultery was adultery. Whereas classic adultery consequently represented the primary preoccupation of the proscriptions against adultery, other varieties of adultery received much the same treatment. The provisions of the Torah itself make it clear that it was classic adultery that Judaism most particularly abhorred.[12] While, then, the other types of adultery await contemporary Jewish evaluation to determine whether they ought to be addressed differently, this exploration will focus on potential modern Jewish legal proposals to deal with the foremost problem of classic adultery.

CLASSIC ADULTERY FROM A TRADITIONAL PERSPECTIVE

It is impossible, of course, to formulate an appropriate contemporary halakhic response to classic adultery without first appreciating and evaluating the thrust of the halakhic tradition on the subject. The Jewish legal tradition on the matter, rooted as it is in the practices, attitudes, and commandments of biblical Israel, provides an early, sharp differentiation between the Israelite approach to adultery and that of surrounding Near Eastern societies such as the Babylonian, Assyrian, and Hittite. In these other ancient communities adultery was perceived primarily as a wrong done to the husband by a wife, who was his property. The husband, consequently, had full rights to determine the fate of his adulterous wife and to wreak vengeance upon the adulterer. Thus, though judicial process was involved, the injured husband whose "property rights" had been trampled could determine—and personally implement—the fate of the guilty; his options ranged from extending forgiveness to demanding death, with a number of horrible punishments in between.[13]

Some of the thinking that set the stage for these adultery laws of the neighboring peoples was also evident in Israelite society. Thus, in ancient Israel—as in the surrounding cultures—the wife at times was treated as property, although—as we shall see— unlike elsewhere, the husband's property rights were demonstrably less than absolute.[14] One clear outcome of this "property mind set," however, was the acceptance of male polygamy, a practice that remained "on the books" until the *herem* of Rabbeinu Gershom in the eleventh century.[15] Beyond the "property" designation, a wife in ancient Israel also came to be seen as an "extension" of her husband[16] insofar as it was her responsibility to "build up" and continue his name by bearing his children.[17] As a result, clarity on the matter of paternity was of considerable societal importance, since it assured husbands that their names and status[18] would be transmitted to offspring that were indeed theirs.

These two factors—polygamy, combined with the desire to obviate any possible doubts over paternity—led in Israelite society, as it did elsewhere, to a set of adultery restrictions considerably different for men than for women. According to the tradition, a married woman was forbidden to have sexual relations with anybody except her husband.[19] A married man, on the other hand, was forbidden to have sexual relations with any married or engaged woman, but since the Torah permitted both multiple wives and concubines, sex with a single woman—though frowned upon—was not considered adultery.[20] Hence, a single woman could never be an adulteress, a single or married man was an adulterer only if he had sexual relations with a married woman, and a married woman was an adulteress if she had sex with either a single or a married man. "In other words, the wife owed faithfulness to her own marriage; the husband owed faithfulness to another man's marriage."[21]

The pivotal issue that decisively differentiated Israelite adultery laws from the surrounding societies, however, arose from the fact that in Israel the crime of adultery was seen to be committed not just against one's spouse, but—most significantly—against God. The Torah directly alludes to this in the case of Joseph, who—while fending off the attempted adulterous advances of Potiphar's wife—declares, "He [Potiphar] has withheld nothing from me except yourself, since you are his wife. How then could I do this most wicked thing and sin before God?"[22] Evidence of the same theme is found in Avimelech's avoidance of an adulterous relationship with Sarah. God says to Avimelech in a dream: "I kept you from sinning against me."[23] Inasmuch, then, as God was seen to be party to a marriage,[24] a betrayal of the marital bond represented not only a painful breach of promise to one's spouse, but to God as well. No longer a crime against a fellow human being alone, adultery became a repudiation of God as well.

The implication of this reality for the Israelite legal code was dramatic. Like the laws of other societies of the time, the Torah advocated that the adulterer and the adulteress be put to death.[25] Unlike those laws, however—which placed the ultimate decision as to the nature of the punishment in the hands of the injured husband, who could opt for forgiveness—Israelite law mandated communal rather than private action. This was because a husband was seen to have no prerogative to forgive or to judge as to the appropriate punitive measures for a crime that—besides victimizing him—was also viewed as a moral transgression against God. Whether the husband called for action or not, the adultery nevertheless demanded redress, and the courts had to act in accordance with their procedures.[26] The Book of Proverbs expresses this demand for a societally imposed penalty with poetic clarity: "Can a man rake embers into his bosom without burning his clothes? Can a man walk on live coals without scorching his feet? It is the same with one who sleeps with his fellow's wife; none who touches her will go unpunished."[27] Thus, in biblical Israel, mandatory punishment for adultery served to weaken the "property rights" claim the husband had over his wife by denying him an autonomous decision over what would be her fate or that of her lover. Rather, it affirmed the place of adultery as a violation of God's will, a transgression of a divine ethic that human beings had no right to forgive.

The fact that the transgression against God demanded accountability did not, however, imply that the stated punishment remained immutable. Whereas the legal language of the tradition expressed an unrelenting demand for the death of both the adulterer and the adulteress that broached no exceptions, in practice this ultimate penalty was almost always ameliorated. In all likelihood it was rare in biblical times for the death penalty actually to be carried out for the crime of adultery,[28] and the Bible itself records no specific cases. Some biblical references clearly suggest that although capital punishment was demanded for the adulterer, the punishment for the adulteress—already in those days—was divorce.[29]

In the rabbinic period the status of adultery as a transgression against God cemented an unyielding attitude to the crime as a sin of fundamental seriousness. Not only did the two versions of the Ten Commandments explicitly prohibit it for Jews, but the rabbis declared its proscription to be one of the seven fundamental Noahide laws, applicable to all humanity.[30] The rabbis affirmed the universality of the principle with their statement that any man "clings to his wife, but not to his neighbor's wife."[31] They regarded adultery as so heinous that they included it in one of the three kinds of odious acts for which—if given the choice between committing them or being killed—one should prefer death rather than engaging in them.[32] Indeed, the Talmud alludes to adultery as *"Ha-Aveirah,"* conveying the sense of it being "The Sin" par excellence,[33] and the rabbis warned that "all who descend into *Gehenna* subsequently reascend, excepting three who do not reascend: He who commits adultery with a married woman, publicly shames his neighbor, or fastens an evil epithet upon his neighbor."[34] Plainly, the aggadic responses of the rabbis reveal that they viewed adultery as a matter of the utmost gravity.

Their halakhic enactments, moreover, were in keeping with this outlook, even though they took steps to circumvent the harshest potential sanction of capital punishment. The rabbis created regulatory fences around the death penalty concerning *eidut, hatra'ah,* and other matters that—in the case of adultery—made it virtually unthinkable that capital punishment could ever have been implemented.[35] As one scholar wrote, it is evident from their actions that "capital punishment for adultery was meant by the rabbis to be and remain a theoretical teaching, but was not favored as a practical penal guide for the courts."[36]

Despite this, the rabbis were not about to let adultery go unpunished. Their approach was to enhance the biblical "defilement" provisions,[37] according to which a married woman that had sexual relations with a man other than her husband was considered defiled and, hence, prohibited to her husband. The rabbis supplemented this prohibition with their interpretation that the Torah's dual use of the word "defiled" was meant to demand a permanent separation not only from the paramour, but from the husband as well:

> Mishnah: Just as she is prohibited to the husband *[asurah le-ba'alah]*, so is she prohibited to the paramour *[asurah le-vo'alah]*; as it is said: "Defiled...and is defiled" [Num. 5:14, 29]. This is the statement of Rabbi Akiva. Rabbi Josiah said: "Thus did Zechariah ben Ha-Katzav use to expound: Rabbi said: 'The word "defiled' occurs twice in the scriptural portion, one referring [to her being prohibited] to her husband and the other to the paramour."[38]

As a consequence, in a case of proven adultery, the adulteress was to be divorced from her husband, forbidden to her paramour, and probably would have faced a bleak future, with little prospect of finding a new partner. Moreover, whereas capital punishment had been possible only on the testimony of two unimpeachable witnesses, defilement separation of the parties could be called for on the basis of a single witness, even if that witness was the self-incriminating adulteress or the aggrieved husband. Two witnesses, however, remained the standard if the *beit din* were to demand a divorce.[39]

The "forced separation" penalty enshrined within the traditional *halakhah* implied a blatant inequality between men and women that remains a systemic feature to this day. Since the adulterer was not subject to the same defilement as the adulteress, he was not required to divorce his wife, although his adultery was certainly grounds upon which his wife could expect successfully to petition the *beit din* to impel her husband toward giving her a *get*. In a way this inequality could be seen as having been protective of the aggrieved wife in centuries past: if divorce had been enforced, she would not only have suffered the adultery of her husband, but would also then have been required to relinquish her marriage, with significant attendant economic and social implications, as well.

Under a law based on equality, she would thereby have suffered doubly, whereas—under the actual law—though a man whose wife committed adultery had to endure her loss, in all probability he still possessed sufficient status and resources to rebuild his life. Hence, the aggrieved wife—unlike an aggrieved husband—could opt to continue her marriage, or she could petition the court to rule that her husband provide her with a *get*. Nevertheless, the corollary of this unequal application was that a husband guilty of adultery, as a result of the way the law developed, might suffer no more than stern societal disapproval. There is good reason to believe that the law was more concerned with deterrence than with punishment,[40] and, consequently, in the case of adultery, only one party needed to be deterred for the act to be prevented. Still, the lack of a punishment for the guilty husband inevitably must be seen as diluting the standing of the crime as a moral sin against family and God.

The other serious consequence of adultery that remains a feature of traditional *halakhah* and has significant impact on both adulterer and adulteress is that any offspring of an adulterous union was considered a *mamzer*.[41] The rabbis discerned that the child of a relationship forbidden by the Torah and punishable by *karet* or death is restricted from marrying anybody except another *mamzer* and that this blemish was passed on till the tenth generation, which was understood to imply "for all time."[42] Maimonides provides a lucid account of his understanding of the reason behind this law:

> In order to deter people from illicit unions, a bastard is forbidden to marry a daughter of Israel; so that the adulterous man and adulterous woman should know that by committing their act they attach to their descendants a stigma that can never be effaced. The children born of adultery being, moreover, always despised

> to every way of life and in every nation, the seed of Israel is regarded as too noble to mix with bastards.[43]

According to Maimonides, then, deterrence from illicit unions, particularly adultery, is the primary aim of the indelible status of *mamzerut*. This communal stigmatization of the child of adultery—along with its progeny—must surely have acted as a powerful impediment to adultery in much the same way as the death penalty previously had.

The thirteenth-century *Sefer HaChinukh* further develops Maimonides' secondary concern about the "seed of Israel" being mixed with that of bastards:

> At the root of the precept lies the reason that the engendering of a bastard is very evil, occurring in uncleanness, abominable thought, and sinful counsel. And there is no doubt that the nature of the father is hidden (latent) in the son....[44]

In other words, the taint of the sin—in this case, adultery—committed by the parents is somehow transferred to the child and, as a result, the child must be kept away from general Jewish society to protect the community from the spread of evil. Although the stated intent here is the need to quarantine immorality, the core purpose of the idea remains the same: to place the illicit union so far beyond the pale of decency that it becomes impossible even to contemplate.

Mamzerut, combined with the enforced separation of the adulteress from her husband and paramour, has remained, for two millennia, the very serious consequence of adultery within traditional *halakhah*. In the State of Israel, where the traditional *halakhah* has legal authority for Jews over matters of status, the *mamzerut* sanction remains potent. In all communities governed by the traditional *halakhah,* these sanctions retain the potential to be applied and continue, therefore, to serve as a deterrent. Indeed, through the centuries, the clear traditional halakhic condemnation of adultery has never wavered. *Sefer HaChinukh* provides a vivid articulation of the attitude toward adultery that persevered through the generations. From concerns over paternity, the author moves to an explanation of why adultery is tantamount to the breaking of many of the Ten Commandments:

> And so did He wish that about a human child it should always be known whose it is, and they should not become intermingled with one another.
>
> Quite a few other harmful results will also be found to follow from adultery: for it will be the cause of transgression of several obligations which God imposed on us. Thus, He commanded us about honoring parents, and they will not be recognized by the children where there was adultery. There will be a further disaster about what we were equally commanded, not to be conjugally intimate with a sister and with many other women [relatives]: All will be uprooted, overturned, on account of adultery, for people will not recognize their female relatives. And this apart from the fact that there is in adultery with a married woman an aspect of theft, which is something that, clearly, the intelligence should spurn. Moreover, it is a cause of the loss of human life: for it is a known fact about human nature that people grow jealous over the adulterous relations of their wives with others, and they settle accounts with the adulterer even to the death. And there are so many other misfortunes in addition to these.[45]

The conclusion could hardly be clearer: the tradition saw adultery as a tragedy of epic proportions that deserved stern condemnation and serious sanctions in an attempt both to minimize its occurrence and to punish its participants for their sins against fellow human beings and against God.

CLASSIC ADULTERY FROM A MODERN JEWISH PERSPECTIVE

With this unequivocal traditional position as an inheritance, it would seem reasonable to expect that, of all the modern branches of Judaism, Reform Judaism would have had a particular interest in expressing itself on the subject of adultery. Post-Enlightenment Orthodox Judaism, of course, saw no need to deviate from the traditional halakhic approach to the issue.[46] But Reform Judaism—particularly in America—declaratively shed any sense of full adherence to the halakhic past and, instead, elevated the ethical as the critical concern of a revitalized Judaism: The Pittsburgh Platform clearly stated that "today we accept as binding only the moral laws"; and the Columbus Platform emphasized that "in Judaism religion and morality blend into an indissoluble unity...." The road to Godliness and holiness in Reform Judaism was paved with ethics.

In addition to ethics, American Reform Jews have given great prominence to the Ten Commandments as the chief cornerstone of Jewish adherence. It was no less a figure than Isaac Mayer Wise, who—echoing an idea promoted in the pioneering days of American Reform—attested that the Ten Commandments were literally revealed and transmitted by God to Moses on Sinai; all the rest of the Torah represented human expansion.[47] It is small wonder that, ever since Wise, many Reform Jews have followed in his footsteps, venerating the Ten Commandments as the divinely ordained foundation of the Jewish contribution to the world.[48]

It is curious, then, that through more than a century of concentration on the ethical in Judaism and of upholding the Decalogue as the singularly most inspired contribution of Jewish history, so little Reform attention has focused on the significance and the application of the Seventh Commandment. It is all the more mystifying when we recall that at one of the earliest conferences of Reform rabbis, in Philadelphia in 1869, an unwavering rejection of adultery was explicitly stated within the context of decisions that otherwise brought about profound revisions to the laws of marriage. Indeed, the rabbis suggested that, in the wedding ceremony itself, a direct reference ought to be made to the importance of marital fidelity:

> For the traditional benedictions, *Birkat Erusin,* there shall be substituted such a benediction as sets forth the full moral grandeur of marriage, emphasizes the Biblical idea of the union of husband and wife into one personality... and designates purity in wedlock as a divine command.[49]

Given the strength of this initial Reform outlook and the continued ethical orientation of the movement, the almost complete silence on the subject of adultery through the following decades is truly striking.

Part of the explanation for this near-total muteness may lie in another nineteenth-century action of the developing Reform movement: the "abolition" of *mamzerut*. The early Reformers saw *Mamzerut's* affixing of an undeserved, restricting, tainted status on the children of forbidden relationships as deeply at odds with the fundamental ethical outlook of Judaism. They felt strongly that "whilst the intention behind the concept of *mamzerut* was to combat immorality, its effect was to create another immoral situation."[50]

Reform Judaism consequently determined to do away with this "immorality" by ceasing to recognize that any individual could be designated as a *mamzer*. The obvious outcome of this dispensation was that the "immorality" of *mamzerut* was effectively defeated, but a potent combatant against the "immorality" of adultery was also removed from the operational field. Hence, while the uninterrupted Orthodox monitoring of *mamzerut* continued to contribute to the active discussion of adultery in the world of traditional halakhic adjudication, such issues were effectively removed from the Reform Jewish realm.

Still, insofar as the progressive Jewish world never deemed adultery to be anything less than a very serious matter, one could well have expected that even if Reform rabbis were not being buffeted by specific problematic cases, they might well have raised a call for gender equality in this area. After all, the rabbis assembled in Philadelphia in 1869 acted swiftly to equalize various parts of the marriage service, and later Reform rabbis took further path-breaking steps toward gender even-handedness. Given the clear inequities involved in the traditional approach to adultery,[51] one might reasonably have anticipated explicit reform of these traditional imbalances. In fact, one could contend for two reasons that the adultery laws were particularly conspicuous candidates for such treatment: first, a balanced approach to the punishment of adultery for both men and women would serve to strengthen the claim of Judaism that serious sanctions had to be applied to all adulterers in the light of their sin against God. Second, the Talmud itself had established a precedent for acting to bring about a uniform approach to adultery for men and women. The rabbinic explanation for why the biblical test of the "bitter waters" for the suspected adulteress[52] was brought to a halt was seen to be motivated by this very aim:

> *Mishnah:* When adulterers multiplied, the ceremony of the bitter water was discontinued and it was R. Yochanan ben Zakkai who discontinued it....
> *Gemara:* When adulterers multiplied: Our rabbis taught: "And the husband shall be free from iniquity" (Num. 5:31). At a time when the husband is free from iniquity, the water proves his wife; but when the man is not free from iniquity, the water does not prove his wife.... Come and hear: "I will not punish your daughters when they commit whoredom, nor your brides when they commit adultery" (Hos. 4:14). And should you say that his sin with a married woman [prevents the water from proving his wife] but not if it is with an unmarried woman, come and hear: "For they themselves go aside with whores and with harlots" (Hos. 4:14)...R. Eleazar said: "The prophet said to Israel: If you are scrupulous with yourselves, the water will prove your wives; otherwise the water will not prove your wives."[53]

The rabbis plainly admonish men that they cannot expect their wives to be subject to legal scrutiny when they themselves are guilty of adulterous behavior. The sages even insert a clear protest against those men that use the cloak of polygamy to whore with unmarried women while these very same husbands demand that their wives be rigorously checked for any hint of adultery. The pretext for doing away with the test of "bitter waters" is the idea that it is improper to make women undergo a difficult scrutiny for adultery under conditions where men are similarly guilty of adultery and licentiousness. This talmudic ruling could well have formed a solid foundation for a modern extension of the same principle: that it is unfitting to apply onerous penalties to women for adultery in circumstances in which men are similarly guilty but are either not halakhically acknowledged as adulterers or are not punished in the same way. A declaration that sexual relationships between married men and single women are to be Jewishly regarded as adultery and that married men should be subject to the same penalties for adultery as married women could well have been grounded in this sure textual foundation.

Beyond these two reasons one could even have fashioned a credible halakhic case that a sexual relationship between a married man and a single woman ought to be considered adultery. After all, an individual who so much as engages in an "appurtenance" of one of the three transgressions that demanded that a Jew forfeit his life rather than commit them, was considered to have transgressed.[54] One could surely have built a respectable case that—at least from the time the ban on polygamy came into effect—a sexual relationship between a married man and a single woman represented a condemnable appurtenance of adultery. But no such case was forthcoming. With one Israeli exception,[55] even the compelling demand of equality failed to terminate the silence surrounding adultery. As a result, virtually all progressive Jews remain without explicit guarantees of the equal application of precepts of adultery for men and for women.

Even if the challenge of equality were overlooked and *mamzerut* were absent as a spur, the vast twentieth-century changes in the ethics of marriage and sexuality should have supplied ample material to evoke multiple questions on adultery within Reform Judaism. the fact that, through more than one hundred years, the sum total of progressive *pesikah* on adultery amounts to only two *teshuvot,* is remarkable. The first of these *sh'eilot,* not posed until 1986, is itself instructive as regards the development of the thinking of Reform Jews about adultery since 1869:

> One of the partners in a marriage has engaged in an adulterous relationship, and the marriage has terminated in acrimonious

> divorce. Subsequently, the adulterous party has asked the rabbi to officiate at the marriage to "the other person." Should the rabbi comply with the request?[56]

The inquiry implies that the "acrimonious divorce" was a result of the adulterous relationship and this is thus a clear case of classic adultery. But it implies even more. It also conveys the sense that a legitimate conundrum exists, and that, indeed, there might be compelling reasons why the rabbi ought to comply with the request. No branch of Judaism had, up until this point, gone on record as relinquishing the traditional halakhic prohibition of marriage to the paramour. As a result, the question itself demonstrates that the attitude of later twentieth-century progressive Jews toward adultery had so relaxed that the "adulterous party" saw no need to "test the waters" by first asking if such a relationship—entered into civilly—would *b'diavad* be acceptable. The questioner evinces no hesitation in directly requesting a rabbinic blessing of this relationship begun in adultery. In any prior period of Jewish history, the notion of parading one's adultery before a rabbi and asking such a question not only would have been the cause of profound embarrassment, but also would have been unthinkable. In 1986, contemporary attitudes combined with the reality that the couple could easily step outside the community and marry under non-Jewish auspices required the rabbis to furnish an answer.

There can be little doubt that, in the context of this particular *teshuvah,* the "adulterous party" would have been well satisfied with the answer provided. For, after a review of the traditional prohibitions against formalizing a relationship with the paramour, Rabbi Walter Jacob ruled as follows:

> Despite these strictures the reality of the situation, which usually led the adulterous parties to live together and possibly to marry, brought rabbinic recognition of this status. Tradition gives its grudging consent by stating that if, nevertheless, the adulterous parties marry, they are not compelled to divorce (*Shulhan Arukh Even Haezer* 11.2ff. and commentaries, 159.3; *Otzar Haposqim Even Haezer* 11.1, 44).
>
> A rabbi may, in this instance, find herself in a difficult position as she is duty bound to strengthen family life and defend the sanctity of marriage. If she, however, refuses to marry this couple, they may simply opt to live together, as is frequent in our time; that will not help their situation or the general attitude towards family life. Therefore, the rabbi should officiate at such a marriage, while at the same time discussing her own hesitation in keeping the tradition. She may insist on some special counseling before the ceremony. She should insist that it be a simple ceremony and one which places special emphasis on the seriousness and sanctity of marriage.[57]

Although it is true, as Rabbi Jacob observes, that traditionally the parties were "not compelled to divorce," this was only in cases where two unimpeachable witnesses were unavailable. If, however, witnesses could be produced to attest to a reasonable certainty of adultery, the *beit din* would move to compel the divorce.[58] Nor, of course, should the rabbis' reticence to demand a divorce, when the probability of adultery was high but such witnesses were unavailable, be construed as anything more than what Rabbi Jacob appropriately terms "rabbinic recognition" that nothing could be done from a legal standpoint. It most assuredly did not indicate rabbinic approval of this relationship remaining intact, much less any notion that such a relationship could possibly be the beneficiary of Jewish sanction or blessing.

Nevertheless, though such approval was never previously forthcoming in Jewish history, Rabbi Jacob grants it. To be sure, his assent is given without any suggestion that this relationship should be regarded as a *simchah;* Jacob's equivocal reaction to this union is clearly seen in his advice that the ceremony be "simple," with a "special emphasis on seriousness." Nevertheless, we should not overlook the revolutionary nature of this *teshuvah:* it represents the first time that any rabbinic authority states a Jewish legal position that explicitly acts to remove the paramour prohibition from the traditional adultery provisions. Not only does it circumvent this penalty, but, in its place, it provides a consent for rabbinic officiation at the marriage of the adulterer and the paramour. This consent, of course, could well be construed as rewarding the adulterous parties with the communally sanctioned togetherness and stamp of Judaism's official imprimatur that they so fervently desire.

Before turning to Rabbi Jacob's second *teshuvah,* it is worth noting that, outside the responsa genre, very few Jews with a liberal orientation have even written *en passant* on the subject of adultery. Among the several who have done so, one or two have addressed the other traditional relationship prohibition, not at issue in either Jacob *teshuvah:* the *Mishnah*'s ruling that the adulteress not only was forbidden from being together with the paramour *(asurah le-vo'alah),* but also was primarily forbidden from being together with her husband *(asurah le-ba'alah)* and ought to be divorced from him. Although in modernity the partners to a marriage in which adultery has occurred are frequently eager to divorce, the question arises as to whether—in the name of penalizing the adulterous party for a sin against God and family— progressive Judaism ought to continue the tradition of insisting on such a divorce if the couple is unwilling to part. Rabbi Eugene Borowitz, a leading progressive

Jewish thinker, is of the view that such a demand would be intolerable:

> And shall we agree to the law that after adultery a husband may never take his wife back, ignoring every human consideration as to what brought the act about? Here the law speaks with implacable, impersonal rigor. In the name of community standards of sanctity it calls for depriving the people in the relationship of the right to a positive decision as to what might now best become of it. I do not see that it is a fatal mitigation of the seriousness of adultery to suggest that our modern understanding of persons requires us to introduce more compassion in dealing with a transgressor in this area than the Halacha did.[59]

Borowitz is not alone in holding such a view. Progressive halakhic decision makers within the Conservative rabbinate have advocated that not only should the couple be permitted to stay together, but the community should do everything in its power to encourage a process of *teshuvah* on the part of the guilty party, a reconciliation of the couple, and a continuation of the marriage, thereby following the example of the prophet Hosea rather than the rulings of the rabbis.[60] Indeed, there is every reason to believe that this position would be the one taken by the majority of progressive thinkers.

When these three highly significant revisions—the cancellation of *mamzerut,* Rabbi Jacob's decision to allow the Jewish marriage of the adulterer and the paramour, and the widespread desire to salvage marriages that have suffered adultery—are considered in conjunction, they lead to an extraordinary result: the effective elimination of all the major traditional sanctions against adultery, at least for Reform Jews. There can be no doubt that, without setting out purposefully to reach this outcome, the determination to respond with compassion and acceptance to the *mamzer* and to both the instigators and victims of adultery has ended up bringing about the annulment of all substantive penalties for adultery within Reform Judaism.

Seen in this light, it becomes rather important to evaluate whether Rabbi Jacob's response to the question asked of him represents the most cogent position available from the perspective of public policy. After all, when contemplating what might be considered feasible contemporary sanctions for adultery, progressive rabbis would be very hard pressed to rekindle any respect for the *mamzer* status within the progressive community. Indeed, there is general agreement among liberal halakhic thinkers that the situation of the *mamzer* is so ethically untenable that the traditional *halakhah* as well should have deactivated the status. Furthermore, in contemporary society the consequences of divorce are far less serious for couples—and particularly for the economic status of women—than they were in the past. As a result, mandatory separation would nowadays probably be regarded as less of a penalty to a marriage that has been subject to adultery than being asked to stay together in an attempt to save the damaged partnership. Thus, the restraint on adultery that the prospect of forced divorce once represented has lost any real effectiveness, not least because couples that want to try to make their marriages work are apt to be viewed as heroic rather than sinful. As regards the traditional sanctions for adultery, then, the question of granting permission for the Jewish marriage of the adulterer to the paramour remains the only historic penalty that potentially could still be employed gainfully within the contemporary progressive community.

Rabbi Jacob, in making a choice between what he regards as two undesirable options, favors allowing for rabbinic officiation at the marriage of the adulterous couple in preference to the specter of the couple living together. Indeed, Rabbi Jacob views the mere possibility that "they may simply opt to live together" as enough of a threat to the "general attitude towards family life" to make rabbinic officiation worthwhile. Rabbi Jacob does not explain, however, how rabbinic officiation at the marriage of a couple that has committed adultery might serve the interests of this "general attitude towards family life," beyond displaying a clear commitment to the institution of marriage. One could, of course, argue that in a climate in which marriage is still widely seen as a desideratum, requiring such a couple to live together, rather than consenting to their marriage, might be an eloquent articulation of society's disapproval of their prior desecration of family life. Is it not conceivable that—in support of family life—Jewish society could express its thorough disapproval of couples living together and could make this disapproval crystal clear by depicting living together as the only available choice of those who have engaged in undesirable behavior?

Moreover, even if Rabbi Jacob is correct, and it is in fact more desirable for such a couple to regularize their relationship through marriage, this does not at all necessitate a rabbi or Judaism being involved. Civil marriage is certainly a possibility that, having been extensively discussed in the traditional responsa over the last several centuries, is an accepted category within Jewish law.[61] Indeed, given the circumstances of a couple that has committed classic adultery, civil marriage might be said to possess the double attraction of providing a societally recognized formalization of their status while yet according the relationship no Jewish standing. If the community sees it to be undesirable to give an adulterous relationship the sense of having attained Jewish blessing—a sense that is most likely conveyed each time a rabbi acts as *m'sader(et) kiddushin* at a wedding—civil marriage may provide a solution to the problem.

Indeed, in the broader world of liberal *halakhah,* Israeli Progressive Judaism, American Conservative Judaism, and British Reform Judaism are all on record as continuing to oppose dignifying such relationships with *kiddushin.* Whether the couple lives together or enters into a civil marriage is, of course, beyond the control of these rabbinic authorities, but the possibility that the couple might make either choice has not propelled these groups to offer Jewish marriage as an alternative. The traditional paramour prohibition, apparently, is still seen to be worthwhile, though none of these groups provides explicit indication of why it is considered deserving of preservation. Since, however, they are unlikely to see the adulterous parties as being personally "tainted," we might well assume that the paramour interdiction is maintained as a punitive disincentive to adultery, with much the same reasoning as that offered by Maimonides for the institution of *mamzerut.* The position of the British Reform Movement is particularly noteworthy because, although all three groups advocate that individual cases be handled on their merits by properly constituted *batei din,* the British rabbis explicitly draw a distinction between instances of technical adultery, after which they are prepared to conduct the marriage of the adulterer and paramour, and classic adultery, after which they are not.[62] Plainly, then, in cases of classic adultery, the ban on marrying the paramour does not represent some relic of the halakhic past, but remains a decisive element of the present.

Although the position of these three groups demonstrates that penalties for adultery are not unheard of within progressive halakhic structures, the question nevertheless remains whether they go far enough. For though the paramour prohibition might well be a significant factor when the adulterer and the paramour really want to be together, it is not unusual for the adulterous party to have no interest in marrying the paramour—particularly if the paramour is a prostitute—and for the prohibition, therefore, to be inoperative as a discouragement to adultery. In such circumstances none of the traditional sanctions against adultery could be said to have sufficient impact on a progressive Jew to act as a meaningful barrier to adultery.

But if the traditional sanctions carry little contemporary weight, are there modern penalties that might prove to be more potent tools? Post-Enlightenment progressive Jewish communities are characterized by voluntary affiliation and therefore are unaccustomed to applying sanctions that are of real moment. Nonetheless, at least three measures have been employed in different circumstances to send a strong message of disapproval of certain actions. Barring an individual from congregational membership is probably the strongest available penalty. On the basis of the notion that it is counterproductive to distance the sinner from *teshuvah* resources, however, this punishment would probably be seen as an inappropriate penalty for the adulterer, who is arguably more in need of the synagogue's guidance toward *teshuvah* than many others.

Two other possible sanctions exist, though, either of which could more suitably be applied in the case of the adulterer. The first proposes making the adulterous individual ineligible for synagogue honors. The second advocates excluding or removing the person from leadership positions in the congregation. Both these penalties have previously been recommended within Reform congregations for serious transgressions. In a 1962 responsum, for example, Rabbi Solomon Freehof, discussed, *inter alia,* the eighteenth-century case of a man that had "embezzled the money of the *Chazan* and [run] away with the *Chazan's* wife." Although the man had publicly confessed his guilt, he had made no attempt at restitution. Freehof concluded that such a "notoriously evil man" should not, within the modern Reform setting, "be allowed to shame the congregation by being called up to the Torah."[63] An instance of the "leadership" penalty appears in a 1995 responsum that ruled that a Board Trustee that had been found, beyond doubt, to have cheated another member of the congregation and "owes him a significant sum of money," should leave office, unless he is prepared "to do *teshuvah,* to admit his wrong and to make restitution to his accuser."[64]

Could such penalties be used for cases of proven adultery? Rabbi Freehof's responsum does not clarify whether his ban on *aliyot* relates more to the theft of the money or to the "theft" of the wife or both. But, turning to Rabbi Jacob's second *teshuvah* related to the issue of adultery, it is plain that Rabbi Jacob views these kinds of penalties as absolutely appropriate. In 1989, a question arose about a woman in her forties who was participating in an adult *Bar/Bat Mitzvah* program. With the course of study nearing its end and the ceremony fast approaching, it emerged that the woman was involved in an adulterous relationship. "Is it possible," the *sho'el* asked, "to have her participate in the *Bat Mitzvah* ceremony under these circumstances?" [65] Rabbi Jacob replied as follows:

It is good that this woman has taken this course of study and hopefully it will bring her closer to Judaism not only in the formal ritual sense, but to a deeper understanding of the commandments. The ceremony itself bespeaks a willingness on the part of the children to accept and live by the commandments of Judaism. This, rather than the brief *haftorah* portion and the family festivities are the primary aim of *Bar/Bat Mitzvah*. It is to be taken very seriously.

For an adult that acceptance has occurred long ago and an adult *Bar/Bat Mitzvah* marks a completion of a course of study and a rededication to the mitzvot rather than a change to the pattern of life. This woman can hardly rededicate herself to *mitzvot* and also commit adultery. She should *not* participate in this ceremony.

We must also ask whether we should give an *aliyah* to a known public adulterer. There are some who would argue that being called to the *Torah* is a *mitzvah,* not an honor, and as a *mitzvah* one can not withhold it from anyone. Solomon B. Freehof has demonstrated that the tradition disagreed on this issue with some authorities arguing in each direction. He felt that we should not deprive an individual of the *mitzvah* of reading from the *Torah* unless the person was "notoriously evil" or the honor of the congregation was at stake. He made this decision as he considered this act as a *mitzvah.* In our modern congregations, especially the larger ones, the *aliyah* is an honor as it is impossible to involve the entire congregation in the *Torah* service even over a period of several years. Individuals are honored for communal leadership, or family and life cycle events through an *aliyah.* This honor should be restricted to those individuals who exemplify Jewish ideals and Jewish morality or at the minimum do not publicly reject a major commandment. I am sure that the woman in question will understand such a decision and finish the course in the spirit which led her to enroll in it. At some later time when the pattern of her life has changed, she should be called to the Torah. This will recognize her study and also her efforts to resolve her marital problems.[66]

Rabbi Jacob is clearly of the view that, when the facts of adultery are not in dispute, it is proper that here, in fact, be some public consequences for adulterous acts. He regards the incongruity inherent in the instance of an adulterer who unrepentantly transgresses the *Torah* being called to recite blessings over the *Torah* as being beyond problematic. Transgressions of such dimensions, Rabbi Jacob conveys, call forth proportionate sanctions in return.

Indeed, though Rabbi Jacob does not address the issue, it is worth considering the implications of not employing such sanctions. For, insofar as Reform Judaism allows substantial public penalties like exclusion from *aliyot* or removal from office to be applied to pecuniary impropriety but not to adultery, the unavoidable message sent to the community must be that progressive halakhic thinking regards financial theft as far more serious than covenental betrayal.[67] If, then, progressive Judaism continues to regard adultery with the gravity that—since 1869—it has never disavowed, the question becomes rather: How could such penalties *not* be used for cases of proven adultery? If these penalties are used in other circumstances—but not for adultery—the potential adulterer could easily conclude that, having dismantled all previous penalties without enacting any replacements, progressive Judaism is now less than resolute in its opposition to adultery. Conversely, by using some of the sanctions at its disposal to deal with classic adultery, progressive Judaism would convey the significant idea that adultery remains one of the weightiest transgressions a Jew can commit and that, consequently, it may not be dismissed lightly.

The prospect of sanctions, of course, immediately raises numerous questions related to due process and justice: Would witnesses be required to attest to the reality of the adultery? If so, how many witnesses would be required? Who would determine whether a case of adultery was proved? Would this not create a "witch-hunt" atmosphere akin to that that sometimes existed in bygone generations? How could an equal application of such rulings be ensured?

Such questions could well be answered in the same spirit as that shown by the rabbis in their approach to capital punishment. Just as the extensive talmudic discussion of capital punishment for adultery was "meant by the rabbis to be and remain a theoretical teaching, but was not favored as a practical penal guide,"[68] so contemporary rabbinic authorities might be well served by proclaiming modern penalties, even without intending to use them as practical penal measures. Although they may, very occasionally, be forced, in the name of *kavod ha-tzibbur,* to take action in those cases of classic adultery that are flagrant and where the facts are undisputed by any of the parties involved, such cases are never the subject of controversy over questions of witnesses, witch-hunts, or judicial wisdom. Under normal circumstances, however, appropriate adultery sanctions could be openly and firmly stated, without any need to pursue adulterers or zealously to ensure that justice is seen to be done.

But if the sanctions are not enforced and adulterers are not carefully tracked, then why have penalties at all? The reason, quite simply, is that any good legal system not only has the function of regulating behavior through the efficient employment of punitive disincentives, but also has a vitally important educational function. This is especially true of *halakhah.* Time and again the *Torah,* in both its written and oral forms, threatens dire punishments that it never intends to be carried out.[69] The aim, rather, is to convey an unambiguous message about the values of Jewish society and the critical interest of the body politic in embracing certain behaviors and rejecting others. Overblown punishments are threatened to communicate just how menacing a particular infraction is seen to be to the welfare of Jewish civilization. Once the punishment has been stated, enforcement methods become a lesser issue; breaking the law and inviting the predetermined wrath of society—even if empirically that wrath almost never comes—is sufficiently distasteful to most people to make the educational arm of the law powerful, indeed. Although it is true, then, that the particular penalties mentioned may not, in and of themselves, be convincing deterrents to adulterous behavior, if the societal message of disapproval of adultery that inheres in them makes some reconsider their actions, such sanctions would fulfill a most useful purpose. In practice, of course, liberal Jewish communities should opt to require a sincere process of *teshuvah* as their primary vehicle toward rehabilitation from adultery. But this will not address those cases in which the guilty party refuses to do *teshuvah,* nor does it obviate the vital significance of accountability that clearly stated penalties could convey to society as a whole.[70]

If such sanctions are to be valuable educational tools, however, then those charged with teaching them have to be credible role models. It is for precisely this reason that rabbinic adultery is such a serious matter, for whereas rabbis are not considered "holier" than other Jews, their role as educational specialists in Jewish law gives their actions increased weight in response to the law. When a rabbi commits classic adultery, consequently, the primary outcome, as always, is a heinous disloyalty to God and spouse. But additionally, and just as importantly, by demonstrating that a teacher of the law believes that potential penalties and community standards can be ignored with impunity, the rabbi also personally acts to undermine the educational impact of the law itself. Beyond the issues of abuse of power that are frequently involved,[71] rabbinic adultery is damaging because it sends the message that the person who ought to be in the best position to know that adultery is a fundamental transgression is plainly insufficiently awed by the law to avoid such behavior. For thus torpedoing the educational force of the law, it is appropriate for rabbis who are guilty of classic adultery to face more demanding penalties than others. This is true only, however, if penalties of some nature are proposed for all; for if penalties that have strong educational impact are seen to be undesirable for the crime of adultery generally, it would be an unfair inconsistency—and a truly unequal application of progressive *halakhah*—to punish rabbis severely for a transgression that, when committed by others, lacks even theoretical consequences.

It is a fundamental tenet of civilization, of course, that if society is to be elevated to its fullest potential, clear signals concerning "the right and the good" path, leading to agreed upon boundaries of behavior, are essential for all. It is, furthermore, a truism that Jewish civilization has always viewed strong families founded in secure marriages as the sine qua non for the transmission of society's visions, as well as for the healthy raising of the next generation. Moreover, today's realities suggest that in a considerable number of liberal Jewish households, although adultery may not always be a direct cause of marital breakdown, it is too often the act that precedes irrevocable marital fracture. If these truths are all indeed evident, it follows that any responsible halakhic approach has a duty to rule with the utmost clarity on which types of behavior it regards as conducive—and which non-conducive—to the well-being of marriage and of society. Following this, it must formulate a public policy that has the goal of strongly encouraging conformity and compliance with these expressed ideals. A very real probability exists that among the tools used to attain this goal there will need to be some clearly articulated disincentives for those who might otherwise be only too willing to engage in undesirable behaviors. The fact that these deterrents might find their greatest effect through repeated enunciation rather than actual activation will not diminish their vital role in plainly transmitting the critical core interests of society.

Thousands of years ago the Ten Commandments were chiseled into the foundation stones of Judaism. No Jew since has taken issue with their significance. The Decalogue started out prohibiting adultery because adultery tore at the very fabric of Judaism's divine vision of society, founded on committed relationships of *kiddushin.* Centuries later, the same Jewish vision lives on among its contemporary inheritors. Both liberal and traditional forms of *halakhah,* therefore, carry a mandate to do everything possible to safeguard the sanctity of marital relationships within the context of every new generation. This mandate, unchanged by the passing millennia, conveys a message that is as relevant today as ever and that is once again worthy of revitalized attention.

Notes

1. Exod. 20:14 and Deut. 5:18.

2. Indeed, adultery is referred to not only directly in the Seventh Commandment, but obliquely as well in the Tenth Commandment's reference to coveting one' neighbor's wife.

3. A. C. Feuer, *Aseres HaDibros* (New York, 1981), p. 56.

4. See *infra* at p. 10ff.

4. See *infra* at p. 8.

6. *The American Heritage Dictionary of the English Language* (Third Edition) defines adultery as "voluntary sexual intercourse between a married person and a partner other than the lawful spouse."

7. There is good reason why adultery is often regarded as much more widespread than it really is. Andrew Greeley, "Marital Infidelity," *Society* (May/June 1994), pp. 9–13, observes that most well-known data reported before 1990 vastly overstated the extent of adultery. Thus, Kinsey asserted that about 50 percent of the men and 25 percent of the women in his samples had committed adultery. Shere Hite in *The Hite Report* averred that 72 percent of married men were adulterous. The June 1977 issue of *Marriage and Divorce* stated that "70 percent of all Americans engage in an affair sometime during their marital life." More recently, the *Janus Report on Sexual Behavior in America* put the infidelity figures at around 33 percent of married men and 25 percent of married women. But, as Greeley observes, "All these statistics have one characteristic in common: they are not based on national probability samples...."

Hence, the statistically more acceptable numbers are less dramatic. According to Greeley, the authoritative 1991 *General Social Survey,* based on a national probability sample, reveals that 21 percent of men and 11 percent of women have had sex with someone other than their spouse during marriage. If prostitution is excluded from the statistics, however, and only those who are in the work force are counted, the gender gap disappears: "Fifteen per cent of working women and men who have never paid for sex report that they have had sex with someone other than their spouse." Theorists hypothesize that the opportunities for women to find partners for adultery increase when they enter the work force. It is clear, though, that if 21 percent of men have committed adultery of some type (including prostitution), then—unless the 11 percent of women who have committed adultery are all married to the male adulterers—the figure of one in five marriages being touched by adultery may well be conservative. It is, of course, also possible that although the researchers use all available tools to compensate for those who are apt to answer untruthfully, a degree of underreporting may nevertheless be a factor.

Greeley also suggests the possibility that infidelity rates may be slightly on the rise. He bases this estimation on the fact that adultery rates among younger people seem to be a little higher than for older age groups.

8. Indeed, the 1994 University of Chicago survey, *The Social Organization of Sexuality,* reports that Jews—on average—had the most partners (lifetime) of any religious grouping. It would stretch credibility to maintain that fewer of these partners represent adulterous liaisons than for the rest of the population. See *Time Magazine,* October 17, 1994.

9. This decision of the Reform movement was first articulated at the 1869 Philadelphia conference. The original text can be found in David Philipson, *The Reform Movement in Judaism,* (New York, 1931), p. 484, n. 38.

10. Such confusion is clearly referred to in *M. Yevamot* 3:10.

11. There are those who maintain that classic adultery is not so much a betrayal as a symptom of a marriage that, even though the parties may not be fully aware of the fact, is already in trouble. Although this may be true, it hardly lessens the transgression involved in classic adultery. After all, stealing might be viewed as a symptom of unabated poverty, but it is a crime nevertheless.

12. The context of Lev. 20:10, for example, substantiates this point.

13. Louis M. Epstein, *Sex Laws and Customs in Judaism* (New York, 1967), pp. 194–96.

14. See *infra.* at p. 10.

15. Shlomo Eidelberg (Ed.), *The Responsa of HARAGMAH* (New York, 1955), p. 19.

16. The foundation of this idea is in Gen. 2:24. Indeed, the *Tur* comments on this verse, "Let him cling to his wife and to none other, because man and wife are in reality one flesh, as they were at the beginning of Creation."

17. This notion is made most explicit within the institution of levirate marriage. Deut. 25:5ff. requires that the wife bear children by her deceased husband's brother "so that his name not be blotted out from Israel."

18. As *Kohen, Levi,* or *Israel.*

19. *Yevamot* 95a.

20. Ibid.

21. Epstein, *Sex Laws and Customs,* p. 194.

22. Gen. 39:9.

23. Gen. 20:6.

24. See, for example, *Pirkei de Rabbi Eliezer,* 12.

25. Lev. 20:10 and Deut. 22:22.

26. Ibid.

27. Prov. 6:27–29.

28. Epstein, *Sex Laws and Customs,* p. 199.

29. Hos. 2:4ff. and Jer. 3:8. It is possible that the deuteronomic legislation evidenced in Deut. 22:22 and 24:1ff. was enacted as an attempt to include the wife in the more serious penalty. See Anthony Philips, *Ancient Israel's Criminal Law* (New York, 1970), pp. 110–112.

30. *Sanhedrin* 56a-b, based in Gen. 2:16; Maimonides, *Hilchot Melakhim,* 9:5.

31. *Sanhedrin* 58a, based in Gen. 2:24.

32. *Sanhedrin* 74a; *Yoma* 82a.

33. *Avodah Zarah* 3a.

34. *Bava Metzia* 58b.

35. *Sanhedrin* 40b–41a. *Yad, Sanhedrin* 12:1–2. *Eidut* raises the issues of the witnesses' suitability and credibility; *hatra'ah* relates to a specific set of warnings that had to be provided to the guilty party before the commission of the crime if capital punishment were to be considered.

36. Epstein, *Laws and Customs,* p. 209.

37. See Num. 5:29, Jere. 3:1.

38. *Sotah* 27b. See also *Yevamot* 24b.

39. Maimonides, *Hilchot Ishut,* 24:17, 18. See also Benzion Schereschewsky, *Dinei HaMishpacha* (Jerusalem, 1984), pp. 409–410.

40. See *infra* at p. 15 for the reasons given by Maimonides for *mamzerut.* Arguably the very same reasons provide the fundamental motivation behind the strong rabbinic prohibition of the wife's continuing relationship with either the husband or the paramour.

41. Based on Deut. 23:3 but made explicit by the rabbis in *Kiddushin* 3:12 and *Yevamot* 4:13. See also Maimonides, *Hilchot Issurei Bi'ah* 15:1.

42. Ibid. See also *M. Yevamot* 8:3, *Yevamot* 45b, and Maimonides, *Hilchot Issurei Bi'ah* 15:33.

43. *Moreh Nevukhim,* III.49. This translation from Shlomo Pines, *The Guide of the Perplexed* (Chicago, 1963), Vol. 2, p. 611.

44. *Sefer HaChinukh, Mitzvah* 560.

45. Ibid., 34.

46. See, for example, Maurice Lamm, *The Jewish Way in Love and Marriage* (San Francisco, 1980), pp. 42–48.

47. Michael A. Meyer, *Response to Modernity* (Oxford, 1988), pp. 229, 240–41.

48. The *Encyclopaedia Judaica* gives testimony to the continuation of this belief when it observes that it is a practice peculiar to Reform Judaism that in "many Reform congregations, the solemn recital of the Ten Commandments is part of the confirmation ceremony which is generally celebrated on Shavuot...." *Encyclopaedia Judaica* (Jerusalem, 1972), Vol. 5, p. 1447. Since Shavuot is the festival of revelation, the symbolism, of course, is powerful.

49. Philipson, *The Reform Movement*, pp. 483–84, n. 38. See also Michael A. Meyer, *Modernity*, p. 257, where Meyer maintains that the Philadelphia rabbis' concerns about "extramarital relations" were owed to the fact that adultery was as "seemingly prevalent among some Jewish men as among non-Jews."

50. Jonathan A. Romain, *Faith and Practice* (London, 1991), pp. 189–91.

51. One example is the lack of recognition—even after Rabbeinu Gershom's *takkanah* outlawing polygamy—of a married man's intercourse with a single woman as constituting an adulterous act. Traditionalists have attempted to justify this inequality on rational grounds, such as that expressed by Mendell Lewittes, *Jewish Marriage—Rabbinic Law, Legend, and Custom* (Northvale, 1994), pp. 15–16:

> It seems to me that there is a more profound rationale for this distinction between the man and the woman, reflecting the different intensity of emotional involvements in the sexual act. No matter what feminists might say, hormones and emotions interact. For the woman, since a single act of sexual intercourse may lead to pregnancy, it expresses a profound emotional attachment to the male partner. For her, accepting a partner other than her husband indicates a weakening of her attachment to him and portends a breakdown of the family bond. As for the man, the sexual act does not necessarily indicate a serious emotional attachment to his paramour; it may be for him a casual relationship, a fleeting submission to a carnal urge....

It is unlikely that most liberal Jews would see this reasoning as persuasive grounds to maintain the legal inequality.

Another illustration of inequity is the above-stated requirement that an adulterous wife be divorced, which was never applied to adulterous husbands.

52. The test of the "bitter waters" to which the *sotah*, the suspected "errant woman" was subjected is described in great detail in Num. 5:12–31, and is the focus of extensive rabbinic deliberation, largely in tractate *Sotah*. The purpose of the test—in which the woman had bitter waters administered by a priest, who monitored her for specific signs—was to provide a "divine proof" of the guilt or innocence of a woman who was thought to have committed adultery. While first im-

pressions might convey the sense that this test was nothing more than a demeaning social tool in which the *halakhah* became involved in the public degradation of women by their jealous husbands, further insight suggests other possibilities. Rachel Biale, *Women and Jewish Law—An Exploration of Women's Issues in Halakhic Sources* (New York, 1984), pp. 186–87, proposes that the ease with which the test would have been passed may well have been designed—in the vast majority of cases—to prove women's innocence. This was particularly important since "suspicion of adultery in a close-knit community would be almost impossible to dispel, and could easily lead to ostracism and perhaps violent revenge." According to Biale, seen in this light, "the ordeal is changed from a measure threatening women to a mechanism for their protection." Whether Biale's explanation as to the motivation for the test itself is plausible, the concern for fair treatment that brought about the cessation of the test is beyond doubt.

53. *Sotah* 47a–b.

54. Hyam Maccoby in his "*Halakhah* and Sex Ethics," in W. Jacob and M. Zemer, *Dynamic Jewish Law* (Pittsburgh, 1991), p. 138, clearly expressed this notion when he wrote: "But the doctrine of *abrizaihu,* on this interpretation, also requires martyrdom for lesser offenses that are in some way connected with adultery: for example, the offense of embracing and fondling another man's wife, which is regarded as Biblically forbidden (on pain of *malkut*) by Lev. 18:6."

55. The only Jewish statement on gender equality in matters of adultery was made by *Maram,* the Israel Council of Progressive Rabbis, in 1983. In a document setting forth its decisions on marriage, *Hehachlatot Maram B'Nosei Nissuin—Rishum V'Arichat T'kasim,* at section 14A, *Maram* declared: "The approach of *Maram* in the matter of adultery is founded in equality...." This ruling, however, applies only to those who come under the aegis of the Israel Movement for Progressive Judaism, which—at most—numbers several thousand people.

56. Walter Jacob, *Contemporary American Reform Responsa* (New York, 1987), p. 286.

57. Ibid., pp. 286–87.

58. *Shulhan Arukh Even Haezer* 11.2.

59. Eugene B. Borowitz, *Exploring Jewish Ethics—Papers on Covenant Responsibility* (Detroit, 1990), p. 266.

60. Elliot N. Dorff, "This Is My Beloved, This Is My Friend—A Jewish Pastoral Letter on Human Sexuality" for and with the Commission on Human Sexuality of the Rabbinical Assembly, April 11, 1994, p. 11; Michael Gold, *Does God Belong in the Bedroom?* (Philadelphia, 1992), pp. 51–53.

61. For a good summary see Benzion Schereschewsky, "Civil Marriage," in Menachem Elon, *The Principles of Jewish Law* (Jerusalem, 1974), pp. 371–74.

62. Romain, *Faith and Practice,* p. 48.

63. Solomon B. Freehof, "Unworthy Man Called to Torah," in Walter Jacob (ed.), *American Reform Responsa* (New York, 1983), pp. 101–106.

64. Unpublished *teshuvah* of the Central Conference of American Rabbis Responsa Committee, 5754.17.

65. Walter Jacob, "Adult Bar/Bat Mitzvah and Adultery," in *Central Conference of American Rabbis Yearbook,* Vol. 99 (New York, 1990), p. 239.

66. Ibid.

67. The argument that is sometimes advanced, that the different treatment of pecuniary and sexual transgressions represents an appropriate differentiation between the public and the private realms, makes no sense from a Jewish perspective. Although Judaism obviously acknowledges significant and critical differences between the two spheres, appropriate sanctions for transgression have always been administered by the rabbis with the tools at their disposal, no matter in which sphere the transgression took place. Moreover, the creation of neat divisions between the private and public domains is no easy matter, and adultery, particularly, extends into both areas, since it is seen as a transgression against the spouse *and* against God or society. Judaism could hardly tolerate an effective disregard of adultery simply on the basis that it is carried on behind closed doors.

68. Epstein, *Sex Laws and Customs,* p. 209.

69. According to Deuteronomy 21:18-21, for example, the *ben sorer u'moreh,* the "stubborn and rebellious son," was to be stoned to death. But in a frank *baraitha* recorded in *Sanhedrin* 71a, the rabbis declared: "There never has been a 'stubborn and rebellious son,' and never will be. Why then was the law written? That you may study it and receive reward...." In other words, the law was intended to be a spur to education, and the proposed death penalty was designed to focus profound attention on the transgression and its gravity.

70. If sanctions were ever actually applied they need not, of course, be in place forever. They could be applied for a limited period or until *teshuvah* had been satisfactorily effected. In this context one ought to remember that *teshuvah* is a process without specific length that can be considered complete only when "recognition of the sinful act, sincere remorse, confession, restitution, and resolve" have been addressed. It goes well beyond simply saying, "I am sorry." See Arthur Gross Schaeffer, "Teshuva and Rabbinic Sexual Misconduct," *CCAR Journal: A Reform Jewish Quarterly* (Summer/Fall 1995), pp. 75–80.

71. See Rachel Adler, "A Stumbling Block before the Blind: Sexual Exploitation in Pastoral Counseling," *CCAR Journal* (Spring 1993), pp. 13–43.

TRADITIONAL AND PROGRESSIVE REMEDIES FOR IMPEDIMENTS TO MARRIAGE

Moshe Zemer

Many halakhic impediments to marriage stem from biblical and talmudic rulings as well as medieval codification. Notwithstanding these prohibitions, rabbinical sages through the centuries have found halakhic ways of permitting these prima facie forbidden unions.

This paper will study approaches to this problem in various periods: rabbinic decisions found in the Talmud and the responsa literature, nineteenth-century Reform resolutions, and twentieth-century Reform responsa.

The rabbinical decisions from the Talmud and the traditional responsa may demonstrate the use of radical techniques, including legal fiction, to remove halakhic impediments to marriage. I shall compare these decisions with attempts Progressive Judaism has made to resolve these problems.

SOLUTIONS IN TRADITIONAL RABBINIC LITERATURE

One of the earliest lenient decisions was rendered by Hillel the Elder, President of the Sanhedrin, 30 B.C.E.–10 C.E. The women of Alexandria were considered adulterous because, after their betrothal, they had been taken away by other men. The Sages of their community were about to rule that their children were *mamzerim.*

Hillel interpreted the mothers' *ketubot* tendentiously, as if they contained a rabbinic condition that invalidated the mothers' first betrothal. Thus, according to Hillel, the women were not married to their first husbands when taken by the fathers of their children. These women were therefore not adulterous, and their children were not *mamzerim* (BT Baba Metzia I04a). Through the legal fiction of reinterpreting five words in the ketubah: ("When you come under the marriage canopy, be my wife"), Hillel effectively annulled the betrothal of the Alexandrian women because they had not completed the requirement of their first marriage by entering the *huppah* with their betrothed.[1]

MARRYING A SLAVE

Maimonides (1135–1204) ruled in the *Mishneh Torah* about a Jewish man who married a slave women after having been suspected of having sexual relations with her: "If a man was suspected of having intercourse with a slave girl who was later emancipated he may not marry her" (Laws of Divorce 10:14).[2]

The elders of a twelfth-century Egyptian Jewish community asked Maimonides what action they should take in a case like this regarding a young man of their community who had purchased a Gentile female slave and was living with her.

Instead of applying his own halakhic verdict, Maimonides responded that "a *beit din* should force him either to send her away or to emancipate and marry her." He justifies this action, relying on three talmudic decrees, without explaining their relevance to his *teshuvah:* 1. *Takkanat hashavim* (the "Regulation for the Penitent");[3] 2. "It is better for him to eat the gravy and not the fat itself."[4] 3. "It is a time to act for God; they have violated Your Torah."[5]

The Rambam did not explain these three Talmudic *takkanot* (provisions or regulations). In a recent study I proposed that Maimonides was sanctioning the lesser of two evils, and this justified his self-contradictory action.[6] The Rambam cited these Talmudic regulations to buttress his own decision. According to the decisor, allowing the young man to marry the slave girl after freeing her would not be an *actual* sin, but only "a sort of sin."[7]

In comparison with the scripturally proscribed, severe iniquity of living with her as a non-Jewish slave, the rabbinically forbidden marriage appears to be the lesser of two evils and therefore permissible.

When Maimonides compared this grave iniquity of continuing to live with her in her Gentile state with the alternative of a valid and lasting marriage with the freed slave, now a full-fledged Jew, he knew that violating the prohibition was merely "a kind of sin."

He was, in fact, confronted by a conflict between two laws codified in his *Mishneh Torah.* According to the first, the young man suspected of having had intercourse with the slave girl was forbidden to marry her after freeing her. The talmudic rationale for prohibiting the union was that their marriage might confirm the rumor that he had been sleeping with her while she was still a slave. The rabbinic prohibition is concerned with the public credibility of the original rumor.[8] Once freed, however, she became a full-fledged Jew, and their marriage, although forbidden *ab initio,* would be valid and they need not be divorced. It is clear that a statute that gives post factum recognition to the forbidden marriage and is founded on the believability of gossip can hardly be considered a stringent law. Hence, transgressing it would be only a "sort of sin."

On the other hand, a man is forbidden to make a mistress of his slave.[9] Maimonides admonished his readers not to dismiss this iniquity *(avon)*[10] as inconsequential:

> Do not think that this is a minor sin because the Torah did not prescribe flogging for one who violates the prohibition; for this liaison also causes the son to turn away from the Lord, in that a son born to a maidservant is a slave and not an Israelite. The result is that holy seed is profaned by becoming slaves.[11]

When Maimonides compared this grave iniquity with the alternative of a valid and lasting marriage with the freed slave, now a full-fledged Jew, he knew that violating the prohibition was merely "a sort of sin." In comparison with the severe "iniquity" of living with her as a non-Jewish slave, the forbidden marriage appears to be the better of two bad alternatives and therefore permissible. He had no doubt as to which was the lesser evil, for he had so decided in a number of similar cases.

RELEASE FROM LEVIRATE MARRIAGE

Rabbi Moses Galante, who became the rabbi of Safed in 1580, ruled on an unusual case of the deception and coercion of an intractable brother-in-law who refused to give *halitzah* (release from levirate marriage). Rabbi Galante describes the unusual case as follows:[12]

> In his time there was a case of a sister-in-law who [waited for] *yibbum* (levirate marriage) for two years, and a fire raged among them every day on account of the various claims and quarrels between the relatives of the brother-in-law and the relatives of the sister-in-law; for the brother-in-law said that he wanted to perform *yibbum*....One day the sister-in-law's relatives advised

> her to enter the synagogue, go over to where the brother-in-law was sitting during the reading of the Torah, and spit at him. So it was. She entered on Monday during the reading of the Torah, stood in front of the brother-in-law, and spat at him three times before the entire congregation. Each time she said: "I do not want this brother-in-law who wishes to marry me," as was attested by three members of the congregation who stood nearby and constituted themselves a *beit din,* as they wrote.

Rabbi Galante was asked whether the woman had become forbidden to her brother-in-law and *halitzah* must be performed. Rabbi Galante replied with a long responsum using innumerable rabbinical precedents, concluding that the interplay between the woman and her brother-in-law in the synagogue did not constitute *halitzah.* Nevertheless, the partial and invalid rite did render *yibbum* impossible. Galante ruled that since the sister-in-law is unsuitable for *yibbum,* she must, instead, "be released." In this way Rabbi Galante gave sanction, after the fact, to the woman's desperate and dramatic act, which, by making it impossible for her brother-in-law to marry her, forced him to release her from the bonds of levirate marriage.

These three rabbinical verdicts, covering a period of more than 1500 years, all used radical methods to reach lenient decisions. Hillel used the "Language of Common Folk" of the marriage contracts of the Alexandrian women as if it were a rabbinic legal condition. This blatant legal fiction saved their offspring from becoming *mamzerim.* Now they could marry the partners of their choice.

Maimonides applied his own halakhic innovation of choosing the lesser evil to allow a Jewish man to marry his manumitted slave.

The Rambam chose a number of regulations and precedents to support his revolutionary decision.

In the sixteenth century, Rabbi Galante accepted the "play-acting" *halitzah* forced upon a *yavam* by trickery as a barrier to effectuating *yibbum.* Then he ruled a concatenation of verdicts evolving from the bogus *halitzah:* Even though this was not a valid *halitzah,* it prevented her brother-in-law from taking her in *yibbum;* he must therefore release her, and we may therefore force him to release her. Now she is free to marry a partner of her choice.

NINETEENTH-CENTURY REMEDIES BY RESOLUTION

The newly founded nineteenth-century Reform Synagogues in Germany began their first ideological steps with the publication of halakhic responsa. These polemical Reform responsa, written in the classical style of *shealot u'teshuvot,* were published in the wake of the controversy over the founding of the Hamburg Temple in 1817.[13] They dealt with ritual matters related to the new synagogue and its liturgy. They include halakhic arguments to justify the use of the organ and to permit Ashkenazic Jews to worship with the Sefardic pronunciation. In all these issues the Reform decisors not only were guiding their congregants, but also were polemicizing with such Orthodox sages as the Hatam Sofer. The principal author and editor of responsa books was a layman, Eliezer Liebermann, who enlisted a Hungarian rabbi, Aaron Chorin, and two Italian rabbis, Yaakov Hai Rekanati and Shem Tov Samun. None of these *shealot u'tshuvot* dealt with marriage matters that were less crucial to the early Reformers than were problems of liturgy and worship.

Later in the nineteenth century, Reform Judaism dealt with marriage impediments, but in a manner much different from that of the authors of the early reform responsa. These problems were solved by rabbinical conferences pronouncing declarations and resolutions by fiat, without any halakhic argument or justification by reference to rabbinical sources.

In 1869, the Philadelphia Rabbinical Conference resolved the problem of the marriage of a *cohen* to a divorcee or convert without referring to any halakhic precedents. This was accomplished by repudiating the status of *cohen:* "The priestly marriage laws, which are predicated upon the sanctity of the Aaronites, have lost all significance and are no longer to be respected."[14]

The technique of "solution by resolution" for marriage impediments such as *halitzah* and the status of converts was adopted by rabbinic conferences in Leipzig and Augsberg.

The Second Synod of Rabbis at Augsberg in 1871 resolved the problem of the remarriage of a childless widow in the following way:

> The Biblical precept concerning the Chaliza has lost its importance since the circumstances which made the necessary levirate marriage and Chaliza no longer exist. The idea underlying this observance has become estranged from our religious and social views. The non-performance of the Chaliza is no impediment to the widow's remarriage.[15]

After this absolute declaration, which appears to obviate any ceremony of release, the resolution concludes with a surprising provision unknown in any other Reform decision related to a halakhic matter: "In the interest of liberty of conscience, however, no rabbi, if requested by the parties, will refuse to conduct the act of *Chaliza* in an appropriate form."[16]

We are not told if there was a case in which a widow and her brother-in-law actually requested a Reform rabbi to conduct such a ceremony. Did a non-Orthodox rabbi actually officiate at this archaic ritual? What was its "appropriate form"? The sources are silent.

The second synod in Augsburg also used a nonhalakhic method to resolve the halakhic marriage impediment of a convert who could not marry a *cohen.* She was prohibited by traditional *halakhah* because she was born a Gentile and was therefore under the presumption of having had illicit sexual intercourse, even as an infant.[17] The Augsburg conference declared that

> The ordinances of the Christian Church and the modern States, are in regard to the prohibited degrees of affinity, almost still more rigorous than the Jewish Marital Law;...Therefore, the Jewish Synod declares: "that the Talmudical Marriage Law in reference to proselytes of heathen origin does apply to such persons as are converted to Judaism from Christianity."[18]

TWENTIETH-CENTURY REFORM RESPONSA

It was only in the twentieth century, with the establishment of the Responsa Committee of the Central Conference of American Rabbis (CCAR), that responsa based on halakhic principles were propounded to find solutions to marital impediments. Why were no Reform responsa published from the German *shealot u'teshuvot* of 1818–1820 in defense of the Hamburg Temple until the first responsa were printed in the CCAR *Yearbook* in 1911?[19] What was the reason for this hiatus of almost 90 years?

Walter Jacob explains this phenomenon in his introduction to American *Reform Responsa:*

> The writing of responsa was halted because of the pace of the Reform Revolution. The life of our people was changing rapidly, and it became impossible to argue about each detail.... The path then taken was akin to that of all revolutions: it began rather brusquely, pushed much aside, but always with the understanding that these areas were valuable and needed attention after the main struggle was won. That task could not be accomplished by the revolutionary generation; in such a grand effort, minute details did not have to be justified.[20]

This is an original explanation based on historical and sociological constructs. It may be complemented by another important element in nineteenth-century Reform Judaism; namely, antinomianism. This phenomenon is illustrated in the following guide written in 1842 by Dr. M. Frankel for the editorial board of the Hamburg Temple:

> This Synagogue of the Spirit follows principles different from those of a formal and fixed rabbinism, which happily, forms only a small fraction of our modern Judaism. In such rabbis we see a hierarchical authority which we reject as error. Hence we must hold up to obloquy all these apostles of regression.[21]

Shortly thereafter, Samuel Holdheim, the foremost radical reformer of the period, contended:

> Reform must avoid as much as possible to press the banner of progress into the rigid hands of the Talmud. The time has to come when one feels strong enough vis-à-vis the Talmud to oppose it, in the knowledge of having gone far beyond it.... The

Talmud speaks with the ideology of its own time, and for that time it was right. I speak from the higher ideology of my time, and for this age I am right.[22]

TWENTIETH-CENTURY REFORM RESPONSA

Great scholars have led the CCAR Responsa Committee from its founding in 1906 until today. Chairmen of the Committee include Kaufman Kohler, Jacob Lauterbach, Jacob Mann, Israel Bettan, Solomon B. Freehof, Walter Jacob, W. Gunther Plaut, and Mark Washofsky. Each brought his own specialization and authority to the work of the Committee. The influence of the Responsa Committee expanded greatly under Freehof, who published a series of Reform Responsa in addition to those of the Committee. Walter Jacob has published more reform responsa than all other Progressive respondents together.[23]

Rabbi Israel Bettan, chairman of the CCAR Responsa Committee, was asked whether a young man, who was a Cohen, could marry a divorcee. Professor Bettan's approach was to bring a series of halakhic verdicts that questioned the authenticity of the priestly pedigree in modern times. He quoted Ribash, Rabbi Isaac ben Sheshet of the fourteenth century, who claimed that the Cohen of his time, lacking any documentary evidence of his rightful claim to the priestly title, owed his special privileges and obligations, not to the express mandate of the law, but rather to the force of custom or common usage: How much the more so with *cohanim* for our generation, who have no documented lineage but are considered to have their status only by presumption.[24]

He quotes Rabbi Solomon Luria, the well-known sixteenth-century authority, who asserts that because of the frequent persecutions and expulsions of the Jews, most of the original priestly families failed to preserve the purity of their descent:

> Because of our sins and the unending exile, edicts and expulsions the cohanim have been mixed with others. Would that the holy seed had not been mixed with the profane [of the Gentiles]. But the descendants of priests and levites has almost certainly been commingled, at least for the most part.[25]

Likewise, Rabbi Abraham Gumbiner, author of the *Magen Avraham,* assumes the impurity of the modern Cohen's descent when he seeks to account for the doubtful status accorded him in the law: "he is not considered to be a certain *cohen,* since it is likely that an ancestress was defiled as the descendant of a *cohen,* who had taken a wife who was forbidden to him.[26]

Finally, Bettan quotes Rabbi Jacob Emden's ruling that a *cohen* that receives a sum of money for the redemption of the first born should return the amount. There is a danger that he might be guilty of stealing the sum to which he had no legal claim because of the doubtfulness of his priestly origin.[27]

Bettan bases his *teshuvah* exclusively on halakhic sources, mainly from the responsa literature. By adopting the views of these decisors, he finds justification for Reform practice, as he states:

> When, therefore, Reform Judaism chose to ignore the nominal distinction between the ordinary Israelite and the *cohen*—a distinction which has persisted to this very day—it did not so much depart from tradition as it did display the resolute will to surrender a notion the validity of which eminent Rabbinic authorities had repeatedly called in question.[28]

MARRYING A BROTHER'S WIDOW

The leaders of Reform Judaism debated the question of whether the marriage with a deceased brother's wife should be prohibited by Jewish religious practice.[29] One of the arguments in favor was that the marriage with a deceased wife's sister was permitted. The matter was debated at a number of sessions of the CCAR between 1915 and 1925.

The discussion, which involved many learned rabbis, dealt with biblical, rabbinical, historical and anthropological sources. The major halakhic issue dealt with the possibility of applying the principle of levirate marriage. The precedent of Rabbi Isaac M. Wise, who officiated in 1872 at the marriage of a childless widow with her late husband's brother, was considered proof that this is permissible. Rabbi Schulman stated at the 1925 conference that Wise changed his mind some years later. Wise wrote to Schulman stating that he upheld the younger rabbi's position not to officiate at such marriages.

Professor Samuel S. Cohon, who wrote the opening and major responsum, concluded:

> The feeling of repugnance toward the marriage of the deceased brother's wife has helped to safeguard the integrity of the family. Nothing has occurred in modern times to warrant the removal of this safeguard. The prohibition works hardship on comparatively few people, whereas through upholding a high standard of chastity, its moral benefits are considerable.[30]

The Responsa Committee reviewed this decision in 1980 and commented that the discussion, based on traditional interpretation of *halakhah* affirms the conclusion of the traditional rabbis that there is a prohibition against the marriage of a man to his deceased brother's widow.

MARRYING HIS DIVORCED WIFE'S SISTER

One of the most recent responsa, published in the latest collection of modern reform *teshuvot,* deals with a most stringent impediment to marriage. In 1991 a question was asked whether a man that has divorced his wife may now marry her sister. Although the traditional law of consanguinity forbids it, is it appropriate in our age to continue being strict regarding this particular relationship?[31]

Responsum:

> The biblical prohibition regarding marrying one's ex-wife's sister (Lev. 18:18) states: "Do not marry a woman as a rival to her sister...in her lifetime." The objective of the prohibition is clearly not consanguinity but peace between the sisters. Note that the Hebrew literally says that the marriage is prohibited because its effect would be *litsror ale'hah,* to make life narrow and mean for the first wife. Thus, the purpose of the law is to avoid sibling discord.
>
> The Talmud already posits the question whether the relationship is allowed if the first wife has been divorced, and answers that the addition "in her lifetime" prohibits this. Thus, the reason for the biblical stricture is seen not as permanently inherent in the relationship itself...[and] rests on plain inter-personal considerations, which disappear once the first wife is dead, but not before....This configuration has not lost its potency in our

> time, and our Rabbi's Manual maintains the prohibition. We therefore urge that the rabbi not officiate at the marriage.

Reform Responsa are often lenient in removing legal barriers to marriage, such as in the cases of a *cohen* and a divorcee or convert, allowing a childless widow to remarry without *halitzah*. Most of these cases involve violation of negative precepts that, although they are prohibited either by the Torah or by rabbinic law, are nevertheless valid marriages post factum.

Accusations against Reform Judaism that it is always permissive, especially in matters of marriage, are proved false in the above responsa. The long debate whether a man may marry his brother's widow as well as the modern *teshuvah* about marrying the sister of an ex-wife, were both concluded with prohibitive answers. On the basis of deep halakhic research and modern studies in the social sciences, the members of the Responsa Committee in 1925 rejected the marriage of the wife of a deceased brother. Almost seventy years later, the Responsa Committee of 1991 prohibited a man from marrying his ex-wife's sister. Both decisions emphasized the greater stringency of consanguinity relating back to the forbidden decrees of marital relation, whose roots are in biblical laws of incest.

In removing halakhic impediments to marriage, Reform does not attempt to find the easy path. It bases its decisions on principles of *pesikah* and applied ethics.[32]

MOSHE ZEMER

MAMZERUT (HALAKHIC ILLEGITIMACY)

Surprisingly, of all the impediments to marriage, one of the most serious does not appear in any of the known collections of Reform responsa. Only one known responsum has been written by a Reform rabbi on *mamzerut,* or halakhic illegitimacy, to allow a *mamzer* or *mamzeret* to marry his or her beloved.[33] The Conservative Movement's Committee on Jewish Law and Standards has published no halakhic literature on this subject. On the other hand, there are scores of responsa on the subject in traditional and Orthodox literature.

Why have the non-Orthodox decisors not dealt with the issue? It is apparent that in most Western countries, almost no young Jews are prevented from marrying because of this taint. Non-Orthodox rabbis, for the most part, no longer consider *mamzerut* as a forbidden category. Even Orthodox rabbis in the Diaspora show a lesser tendency to seek out and interrogate prospective marriage partners who had adulterous or incestuous ancestors. According to Louis Jacobs's claim, the norm in the United States is to avoid revealing the identity of *mamzerim.*[34]

The one exception is in the State of Israel. The Chief Orthodox Rabbinate, with its power over marriage and divorce, keeps computerized records of all suspected of being the offspring of an adulterous or incestuous relationship. Of course, then the mark is placed on the forehead of all their descendants.

When these persons come to the *beit din* of the Israel Council of Progressive Rabbis two tasks usually have to be accomplished: (1) to purify them of the taint of *mamzerut* and (2) to permit them to marry their beloved and enter the Congregation of the Lord.

In the Diaspora, the second task of marrying the couple is usually sufficient. In Israel, it is no less important to remove the stain of halakhic illegitimacy, which, with the aid of computers, passes on to the next generations.

How does Progressive *halakhah* depurate the individual and his offspring of this blemish of illegitimacy? Progressive *halakhah* investigates the history of halakhic rulings related to *mamzerut* to find precedents for purifying halakhic illegitimacy.

In essence, in Israel our *beit din* must deal with two kinds of cases when purifying this blemish. The easier one is where the court can empirically show that the suspected individual is not the offspring of an adulterous or incestuous relationship. Two such cases came before our court in the last few years. In one instance the uncle of the bridegroom lied to the Chief Rabbinate of Beersheba that his sister had had an adulterous affair before her son was born. Later, he admitted in an affidavit that he had lied to spite the groom's mother because of their dispute over a family inheritance. The Chief Rabbinate believed his first accusation, but not his recantation. Our Court was convinced that he told the truth when he admitted that he had falsely charged his sister and cast a suspicion on his nephew.

A well-known and publicized case in which the official rabbinic court declared the seven children of a man to be *mamzerim* because he had married his brother's divorced wife. The accused man claimed that the man that was previously married to his wife was not his biological brother. DNA tests conducted by two professors, the foremost experts in the Near East, proved this to be empirically true. The Tel Aviv District Rabbinic Court unfortunately refused to accept the conclusions of the professors.

It is impossible in most cases, to obtain positive proof of a blemish of which the Rabbinate accuses the person involved. Here we focus on probable halakhic solutions, which the official Rabbinate had left unexamined. We must now turn therefore to rabbinic precedents to discover how great rabbis solved similarly difficult situations.

MODERN RESPONSA ON THE PURIFICATION OF *MAMZERIM*

Human nature and sexual behavior seem to have changed little over the centuries, with the all-too-frequent consequence that innocent persons are condemned to suffer. Not only the Sages and medieval decisors had the moral courage to resolve the problem; rabbinic authorities of the last two centuries searched the halakhic literature for practical solutions to their plight and found bold and innovative methods to release such Jews from the chains of *mamzerut*. A review of several cases from this period will exhibit ingenious halakhic methods for purifying *mamzerim*.

Rabbi Shalom Mordecai Schwadron was questioned about the case of a man who had abandoned his wife in Odessa and was later declared dead. Twelve years later his wife remarried. While she was pregnant by her second husband, news arrived that her first husband was still alive. The local rabbis ruled that she was an adulteress and the fetus she was carrying would be a *mamzer*. Schwadron advised effectuating a retroactive annulment of the first marriage by means of a legal fiction. Thus, she would not have been an adulteress and her child would not be a *mamzer*. Unfortunately, Schwadron's ruling could not be carried out because her first husband had already given the woman a valid divorce. Hence, the recommended solution was theoretically valid but not applicable in practice.[35] It was, nevertheless, a halakhic tool that could be used to purify *mamzerim* in similar cases in the future.

Rabbi Jacob Saul Elyashar (1817–1906), the chief rabbi of Jerusalem, made an independent inquiry into the case of a young man, Israel, the son of Rachel, of Corfu, born in 1807, who together with three generations of his offspring were considered to be *mamzerim*. Elyashar and the members of his rabbinic team from Jerusalem reviewed testimony given in 1830 about his mother's alleged adulterous relationship before Israel's birth.

They concluded that the testimony given sixty years previously was halakhically unacceptable and cleansed Israel and his offspring of the blemish of *mamzerut* ninety years after his birth, as well as three generations of his descendants.[36]

Rabbi Abraham Palache (1809–1899), the chief rabbi of Uzmir, was asked to investigate the case of a congenital eunuch whose wife was accused of having adulterous and incestuous relationships. The child she bore was declared a *mamzer*. Rabbi Palache convened a special *beit din* that included two Jerusalem rabbis and reached the following conclusions: Since the husband had never been examined by a physician, it was impossible to state with certainty that he was a eunuch. Rabbi Eliezer ruled in the Mishnah that a congenital eunuch, unlike a castrated man, could be healed

(Yevamot 8:4). Thus even had the man been a eunuch as an infant, he might have become potent by the time he was married.

Given these doubts concerning his diagnosis as a congenital eunuch and the relevant halakhic precedents, Rabbi Palache's *beit din* ruled that the presumed eunuch was the father of his wife's son. His sons and grandsons were thereby fully cleared of the stigma of *mamzerut.*[37]

Chief Rabbi Yitzhak Isaac Herzog was consulted with regard to a Yemenite Jew who had betrothed his minor daughter to a Jew in Asmara, in Eritrea. He failed to inform his daughter or the rest of the family of the alliance. When she reached maturity she married another Jew and bore him a son. When they came to Israel on *aliyah,* the son was declared a *mamzer.*

Rabbi Herzog proposed two avenues for resolving this problem:[38]

(1) We might cast doubt on the validity of the betrothal in Asmara, because the groom's relatives were mixed in among the bystanders and the groom had not designated specific witnesses.[39]

(2) Instead, he suggested adopting the aforementioned solution of Rabbi Schwadron; that is, to have the first husband send a *get* by messenger and then cancel it without notice, thereby retroactively annulling the betrothal. Ultimately, however, Rabbi Reuven Katz of Petah Tikvah discovered that one of the witnesses in Asmara was married to a non-Jewish woman, which disqualified him, invalidated the betrothal, and cleared the child of the stigma of *mamzerut.*

Rabbi Joseph Zussmanovich of Lithuania and Chief Rabbi Abraham Isaac Kook wrote similar rulings concerning separate cases of women who had a civil marriage and a civil divorce and whether they could remarry without a *get*. Both ruled that a couple that has only a civil marriage does not consider their sexual intercourse as a means of *kiddushin* and halakhic marriage. The Lithuanian rabbi ruled: "It is clear and true that any woman who was married only by civil authorities,...even if she was divorced only by civil decree is permitted to marry another man [without a get].[40]

The various responsa and cases cited above provide us with four ways to clear Jews of the stain of *mamzerut*—two based on a determination of paternity and two on nullification of the mother's first marriage: (1) ascribing paternity of the child to the mother's (first) husband; (2) ascribing paternity of the child to a non-Jew; (3) retroactively annulling the mother's first marriage; and (4) determining that the first marriage had never been halakhically contracted.

Underlying all these solutions advanced by eminent rabbis of the recent past and present is an understanding of the injustice done to children who cannot raise Jewish families through no fault of their own. These rabbis found solid halakhic methods and, just as important, the courage to clear *mamzerim* and permit them, not only to be "admitted to the congregation," but also to be fully cleansed of the stain of *mamzerut*. Sometimes they employed a legal stratagem and ruled that the child was fathered by the woman's husband or by a non-Jew; in other cases they found ways to retroactively annul the mother's first marriage or determined that there had been no first marriage, halakhically speaking. In these seemingly insoluble cases bold and learned rabbis found ways to purify the children. We may infer that today, too, it is possible to find halakhic solutions, in the spirit of these responsa, that can clear virtually every *mamzer*. Such halakhic means have in fact served Progressive and Conservative rabbinic courts to remove the taint of *mamzerut*.

Thus, we have seen solutions to marriage impediments by radical means in talmudic and early rabbinic eras, by resolution in the nineteenth century, and by sophisticated halakhic rulings in the twentieth century. Through analysis of the decisions of the centuries and insight gained from the responsa literature, we can indeed find remedies for almost all impediments to marriage.

Notes

1. See Yitzhak Gilat, "Halakhah's Link to Reality," *Studies in Problems of Culture, Education, and Society*, 4, p. 106.

2. Based on Mishnah Yebamot 2:8 and BT Yebamot 24b. The marriage might confirm the rumor that he had had sexual intercourse with her while she was forbidden to him as a Gentile. This rabbinic ruling is concerned with what people might think and say. See Rashi, s.v. *ha-nittan*. More than three centuries later, Joseph Caro codified the punishment for this offense in much harsher tones: "If one is caught with his female slave, they take her away from him, sell her, and distribute the same price among the poor of Israel. The man is flogged, his head is shaved, and he is placed under the ban for thirty days" *Shulhan Arukh, E.H.* 16:14).

3. BT Gittin 55a.

4. As we shall see, this is a composite statement, composed of two talmudic rulings.

5. BT Berakhot 54a.

6. "Choosing the Lesser Evil: A Maimonidean Hermeneutic for Leniency," to be published in Mark Statman (ed.), *A Festschrift in Honor of Walter Jacob*, 1999.

7. "A sort of sin" renders the Hebrew *ke-'ein 'aveirah*, which was Professor Jehoshua Blau's literal translation from Maimonides' original Judeo-Arabic. I would like to thank Professor Blau for clarifying this and other aspects of the responsum.

8. Laws of Divorce 10:14, based on Mishnah Yebamot 2:8 and BT Yebamot 24b.

9. Maimonides, *Responsa,* 353 and 372.

10. Although Maimonides does not always distinguish between the Hebrew terms *'aveirah* and *'avon,* the latter is generally reserved for a more severe category of wrongdoing (Introduction to the Mishneh Torah, s.v. *"u-devarim halalu"*). He uses *'avon* to categorize shaming a person in public (Laws of Beliefs 6:8), tale-bearing (termed "a great *'avon";* ibid 7:1), slander (ibid 7:2), and so on.

11. Maimonides, *Laws of Forbidden Intercourse* 12:11, 13.

12. Responsa Moses ben Mordecai Galante (Venice 1608), Responsum 80.

13. Reform responsa collections entitled *Brit Emet, Nogah Zedek,* and *Herev Kokemet HaBrit* were published in Dessau from 1818 to 1820.

14. *Yearbook of the CCAR,* Vol. 1, 1891, p. 119.

15. *Yearbook of the CCAR,* Vol. 1, 1891, p. 112. See ibid., pp. 106–107, regarding *the* first Leipzig synod, held in 1869, which decided that *"Chalizah* should be dispensed with, being antiquated and superfluous....The neglect of chalizah is no impediment to the marriage of the widow."

16. Ibid.

17. Maimonides, *Hilkhot Issurei Biah* 18:3, based on b. Yebamot 60b and Tosefot ad loc s.v. *v'ta 'ama.*

18. Moses Mielziner, *The Jewish Law of Marriage and Divorce* (New York, Cincinnati, 1901), p. 60. See above n. 2 regarding this Synod.

19. See Walter Jacob, ed., *American Reform Responsa* (New York, 1983), Introduction, p. xvi. The Responsa Committee was established in 1906, but its first responsa were published only five years later.

20. Ibid.

21. Gunther Plaut, *The Rise of Reform Judaism* (New York, 1963), p. 42.

22. Ibid., p. 123.

23. See n. 20 above.

24. *Sefer Bar Sheshet,* Responsum 94 (Lemburg, 1805).

25. *Yam Shel Shelomo,* B.K., chap. 5, sec. 35.

26. Magen Avraham Orach Chayim, Hil. Pesach, sec. 457.

27. *She-elot Ya-avets,* Part I, Responsum 155.

28. Jacob, *American Reform Responsa,* pp. 435–36.

29. Ibid., pp. 419–36.

30. Ibid., p. 427.

31. W. Gunther Plaut and Mark Washowsky, *Teshuvot for the Nineties* (New York, 1997), No. 5751.12, pp. 197–98.

32. "Principles and Criteria for Halakhic Decision," *Halakhah Shefuyah,* Tel Aviv, 46–55.

33. Ibid., pp. 83–89; See Moshe Zemer, "Purifying Mamzerim," *The Jewish Law Annual* 10 (1992), 9–114.

34. Louis Jacobs, *A Tree of Life* (Oxford, 1984), 257–75.

35. Sholomo Mordecai Schwadron, *Responsa of the Maharsham,* 1:9. For an explanation of the legal fiction involved, see J. David Bleich, *Contemporary Halakhic Problems* (New York, 1977), 1, 162ff.

36. Jacob Saul Elyashar, *Responsa Olat Ish, E.H,* Laws of Personal Status, 1a–6b. Eliyahu Hazzan, *Ta'alumot Lev* 3: 1.

37. Hayyim Palache, *'Einei kol Hai,* 135a ff; Jacob Saul Elyashar, *Responsa Simhah la 'ish,* No. 3; Shalom Moshe Hai Gagin, *Responsa Yismah Lev,* No. 13. See also Julian H. Barth and Moshe Zemer, "The Congenital Eunuch, A Medical-Halakhic Study," *Assia Jewish Medical Ethics* 2: 2, pp. 44–50.

38. Yitzhak Isaac Halevy Herzog, *Responsa Heikhal Yitzhak,* Vol. 2, *E.H.,* Nos. 17–19.

39. The witnesses to the marriage are a necessary condition and must be specifically designated as such by the groom: "In a marriage it is the witnesses who validate the act. Accordingly if there are both valid and invalid witnesses present, or relatives, and witnesses to the marriage were not specifically designated, the testimony of all of them is nullified and the woman has not been married" (Herzog, Heikhal Yitzhak, §19). Rabbi Herzog relies on the statement by Rabbi Yomtov ben

Abraham Ishbili (the Ritba), *Novellae,* on Kiddushin 43a and Gittin 18b, in the name of Rabbi Solomon ben Abraham Adret (the Rashba).

40. Joseph Zussmanovich, Responsa *Zera' Hayyim,* No. 11, pp. 308–309. Abraham Isaac Hakohen Kook, *Responsa Ezrat Kohen,* Laws of Marriage, Nos. 38–39.

MARRIAGE WITH SECTARIANS THE CASE OF THE KARAITES

Ariel Stone

To clearly understand the possible range of halakhic obstacles to marriage let us consider the strange case of the Karaites. Defined by various halakhic decisors and Jewish historians as a "sect," they are neither quite Jew nor non-Jew in the eyes of the majority Rabbanite "sect" from which they distinguish themselves. The permitting or prohibiting of marriage between Karaite and Rabbanite Jews occupies a gray area not easily defined. During the last six centuries at least, halakhic reasoning has varied and opinions have diverged. As Rabbi Ben Zion Meir Hai Ouziel, late Rishon le-Zion, stated in a responsum:

> Both earlier and later authorities prohibited and permitted; these and those were both to be considered as words of the living God. Who am I that I shall come later and interpret their words![1]

The institutionalization of Jewish rejection of the Rabbanite approach to Jewish law and life that came to be called Karaism traces its genesis to its eighth-century founder, Anan ben David, and the ninth- and tenth-century codifiers Benjamin al-Nah'awendi and Daniel al-Kumisi. A review of the history shared by Rabbanite Jews with, as they called them, "our brothers the Karaites"[2] over the past millennium indicates a mutually ambivalent stance and a complex and changing attitude marked by periods of both amicable coexistence and hostile estrangement. The relationship between the two sects in the tenth century, Hasd Gisah, was marked by the polemical writings of Saadiah Gaon and Jacob al-Kirkisani; but in the thirteenth century, Idakh Gisah, the Rabbanite philosopher Sa'd ibn Kammuna could serve as *mufti* for both Karaite and Rabbanite communities in Egypt "and write a treatise...in some respects, defending both points of view."[3]

MARRIAGE WITH SECTARIANS

Though no less an authority than Maimonides averred that "one may associate with them, may enter their homes, circumcise their children, bury their dead, and comfort their mourners,"[4] and leaders of both sects did sometimes declare personal respect for the learning of the other, bans and counterbans on the part of Karaites and Rabbanites have been the norms that characterized the relationship.

Today, at least in the State of Israel, the two communities do not intermarry, but this was not always the case. Under what conditions did *halakhah* accept or reject intersectarian marriage of Karaite and Rabbanite Jews, and why? Under what conditions are such marriages considered unacceptable? In other words, in the view of Rabbanite *halakhah,* when is a sectarian not a sectarian, and, finally, what might we possibly extrapolate for our own day?

REVIEW OF HISTORICAL LITERATURE: SOCIAL, POLITICAL, AND THEOLOGICAL CONSIDERATIONS

Israel did not go into exile until it had split into twenty-four sects.[5] Where did the Karaites originate? What were their beginnings? Historians such as Mann, Lasker, and Korman have all pointed out that the Karaites, who appear on the historical scene in the tenth century, are not a singular manifestation of disagreement with the institution of Rabbanite Oral Law but are, more precisely, simply the most successful of all those Jewish groups that rejected Rabbanite leadership after the destruction of the Second Temple.

The Karaites' advocacy of individual religious understanding of sacred texts was contrary to the Rabbanite reliance on the interpretive prism of Oral Law for normative and accepted understanding of the written law (at least as far as the masses are concerned). This caused the sect to be known as and named *Karaim*—those who "read" for themselves, following a dictum attributed to Anan ben David by Binyamin ben Moshe: "Search well in the Torah, and do not rely on my opinion."[6] It also caused the sect to be proclaimed heretical. Many Rabbanite sources consider the Karaites to represent a continuation of the Second Temple period Sadducean sect; thus, Saadiah Gaon's explanation of the emergence of Karaism:[7] "Anan gathered together under [a] date palm every evil man and brigand who remained from the righteous destruction..." Lasker points our that many anti-Rabbanite Jewish sects that appear in the eighth and ninth centuries, sectarians and informers, do bear a resemblance in their teachings to dissenters of the Second Temple period. At the very least we can assume that, in the intervening centuries for which we have no records yet discovered, Jewish political and theological unity did not obtain. Various Jewish sects, united only in their opposition to Rabbanism, seem to sporadically appear and disappear.

Karaism, however, did not disappear. Instead, between the ninth and twelfth centuries, it grew to become a large and influential community of Jews—living, studying Torah, instituting some different ritual practices, and engaging in a lively philosophical debate about those practices with the representatives of Rabbanite Judaism throughout the Byzantine Empire. Their insistence that individuals might legitimately interpret the Scriptures differently and, therefore, that legitimate differences in belief and practice might exist in some places, apparently appealed to many Jews. These were perhaps those antinomians that resented the power of the rabbis and their all-encompassing Oral Law, which had become the required intermediary between Jew and Jewish revelation. If so, those free-thinkers thus drawn to Anan ben David and his followers would have found themselves disappointed, for Karaism was in some ways much stricter in its understanding of God's commands as received through Divine revelation of Torah. Also, like any politically coherent body, the Karaites would expect conformity to their own internal norms.

KARAITE THEOLOGY

Karaite scholars influenced, as scholars agree, by the highly rationalist Islamic Kalam philosophy, disagreed with Rabbanite belief and practice as it centered around two concepts. One was the rejection of the nonrationalistic and mystical tendencies they saw inherent in the anthropomorphisms and anthropopathisms of popular Rabbanite *Midrash*. Regarding themselves as the *maskilim* of their day, they ridiculed works like the highly anthropomorphic Shi'ur Komah and the mystical *Hekhalot* writings. Among other rituals to which Karaism objected may be counted the chanting of *Kol Nidre,* as contrary to the third commandment, and the visiting of the graves of renowned sages and leaders. The Karaite Sahl ibn Mazliah wrote:

> How shall I be silent while the ways of idolaters prevail among some Jews? They dwell at graves and seek out the dead. They say: "Ya Rabbi Yose Hagelili, heal me, give me offspring." They kindle lights on the tombs of the Tzadikkim and burn incense in front of them.... [They] make vows to the dead saints and call upon them to fulfill their needs.[8]

The second, more crucial Karaite objection to Rabbanism, of course, is found in its opposition to the institution of the Oral Law. The founders and codifiers of Karaism held that it was the Rabbanites—not themselves as it was charged—that understood and applied Torah law incorrectly; for, according to the Karaites, their interpretations had led the Rabbanites away form the original intent of the sacred texts. Anan is quoted as explaining:

> The religion of my brother employs a calendar based upon calculation of the time of the new moon and intercalation of leap years by cycles, whereas mine depends upon actual observation of the new moon, and intercalation regulated by the ripening of new grain.[9]

By rejecting Rabbanite mathematical calculation of the month and demanding actual, ritually witnessed observation of each new moon, with data regarding leap-year adjustments dependent on word from *Eretz Yisrael,* the Karaites held that they were restoring the calendar to its proper biblical form.

Another calendrical divergence from Rabbanism concerned the date of Shavuot: the text of Vayikra 23.15–16 specifies that on the first day of Pesach

> You shall count unto you from the morrow after the day of rest, from the day that you brought the sheaf of the waving; seven weeks shall there be complete; even unto the morrow after the seventh week shall you number fifty days; and you shall present a new meal offering unto the Lord.

We are to count the "morrow after the day of rest," seven full *shabbatot,* and on the day that is "the morrow after the seventh week" we are to observe Shavuot. The argument is over whether the term "shabbat" is to be understood as meaning "week," as the Rabbanites understood it; counting seven weeks from the first day of Pesach and the day after the seven weeks, or the fiftieth day, was declared to be the festival of Shavuot. For the Karaites *Shabbat* literally meant the *Sabath day*, and for them, therefore, *Shavuot* can fall only on a Sunday.

Shabbat itself is a very different kind of day among the Karaites, whose understanding of the Torah led them to avoid kindling light at all on Shabbat. Thus, until the fourteenth century, when reforms were instituted, Shabbat was a day on which Karaites would sit in the dark and eat cold food. Sex was prohibited, as was leaving one's house except to attend synagogue. Differences also included the rejection of *tefillin* as not dictated *mi-d'oraita,* and certain variations in the observance of *kashrut:* the chicken was classified as an impure bird, and one cause of "great animosity between the two factions of Jewry in eleventh-century Palestine" was the Karaite legislation permitting the eating of fowl with milk.[10]

Despite their ritual differences and their sometimes heated arguments, Karaite Jews did not seek to separate themselves from the rest of the Jewish people, and neither they nor the Rabbanites with whom they co-existed considered them non-Jews. Much united the two sects. Ankori cites Mahler's description of the early Karaite community's social structure was basically no different from that of the Rabbanites; there was no a social protest, per se, in the origin of the movement.[11] Further, the core beliefs of Karaism, codified by Elijah Bashyazi in 1490 in his book, are very nearly indistinguishable from those of Rabbanism:

1. The physical world was created.
2. It was created by a Creator who did not create Himself but is eternal.
3. The Creator has no likeness and is unique in all respects.
4. He sent the prophet Moses.

5. He sent, along with Moses, His perfect Torah.
6. It is a duty of the believer to understand the original language of the Torah.
7. God inspired the other prophets.
8. God will resurrect humans on the Day of Judgment.
9. God requites each person according to his ways and the fruits of his deeds.
10. God has not forsaken the people of the Dispersion; rather, they are suffering the Lord's punishment, and they should hope every day for His salvation at the hands of the Messiah. the descendent of David.[12]

Unlike some of the major heresies against which the Rabbanites fought in the Second Temple period and after (including the belief system of the Sadducees), Karaite dogma includes the standard Jewish elements of resurrection, reward and punishment, and the coming of a Messiah of the Davidic line. Karaism differs from Rabbanism most significantly in its insistence on the diversity of opinion its philosophy expects among its adherents, since each Jew will understand the Torah from his or her own unique perspective.

INTERSECTARIAN RELATIONS

Regardless of their basic theological affinity, from time to time the leaders of each group proclaimed the other outside the pale. Natronai bar Hilai asserted that Anan ben David had told his followers he would write a Talmud for them, and for that effrontery the Gaon recommended that the Karaites

> be banished, not allowed to pray with Jews in the synagogue and be segregated until they mend their ways and pledge themselves to observe the customs of the two academies.[13]

Lasker described a tenth-century conversation between the Karaite Jacob al-Kirkisani and the Rabbanite Jacob ben Ephraim al-Shami that reveals the ironic underpinnings of the issue dividing the two sects. Kirkisani asks why the Rabbanites allowed intermarriage with the heretical Isunian Jewish sect, which differs markedly from the Rabbanites in theological beliefs but not from the Karaites. Ben Ephraim tells him it is because the Isunians do not disagree with the Rabbanite fixing of the ritual calendar. Because his own Karaites, who do differ in calendrical matters but not in theological ones, were unacceptable marriage partners at the time. Kirkisani deduces from ben Ephraim's answer that, for the Rabbanites, theological heresy is pardonable, but observance of Passover on a different day was not.[14]

Early in the energetically and enthusiastically waged intellectual battle between Karaite and Rabbanite, propagandists of the two sects missionized each other even in each other's places of prayer, despite the bans each placed on contact with the other. The Karaite leader Sahl ibn Mazliah ha-Kohen, "even complained that the Rabbanites introduced the Sabbath illumination of their houses of worship for no other reason than to keep out Karaite speakers to whom Sabbath lights were an abomination."[15]

Polemics, bans, and other antisocial behaviors among the leadership apparently did not bother the average Jew of either sect or abrogate the essential unity of the two groups, either in their own eyes or in the eyes of others. According to a contemporary source in the tenth century many "half-converts" "celebrated two holidays, one according to the observation of the moon, the other according to their previous practice." According to Salo Baron, in Babylonia and Byzantium, Karaite Jews living in an overwhelmingly Rabbanite area observed Rabbanite customs, and Rabbanite Jews living in predominantly Karaite communities similarly followed Karaite norms.

Moving between the two groups "appears to have been no more difficult than is change of membership from a Reform to a Conservative or an Orthodox congregation today."[16] Neither did enemies see any essential differences: in 1099, when the Crusader Godfrey of Bouillon conquered Jerusalem and began to massacre its inhabitants, he did not hesitate to count Karaite and Rabbanite Jews together. On July 15 he and his men crowded them all into a synagogue and burned it down.[17]

Even Saadiah Gaon, whom scholars considered the era's great intellectual opponent of the Karaites, was not an implacable foe; in his conflict with the exilarch he "welcomed the support of the Karaite chieftains in Jerusalem."[18] Lasker notes that his major work of philosophy, *Emunot vDe'ot,* the Gaon "surprisingly has almost nothing to say about Karaism."[19] Baron describes a letter from the Gaon Shlomo ben Yehudah, written at a time in which Karaites enjoyed great power and wealth in Egypt, in which the Gaon "actually wished the Karaite chief in the Holy City, of whom he speaks with great respect, full success on his political mission to Cairo"; he adds to this the account of another letter from the elders of a community in Palestine in which they "unconcernedly addressed themselves to the two communities, Rabbanite and Karaite, in Cairo and requested, in particular, the intervention of 'our elders, the elders of the Karaites'."[20]

EVIDENCE OF KARAITE-RABBANITE INTERMARRIAGE

In the centuries following the destruction of the Karaite spiritual and theological center in Jerusalem, Karaism experienced a decline in the East. Egypt was a notable exception: there the community flourished alongside the Rabbanite community. Some Jews were apparently comfortable following precepts of both sects simultaneously, and the evidence of the Cairo Genizah would seem to indicate that this tolerance of ideological differences extended to marriage arrangements between the two sects. How many instances of intermarriage were there? Baron comments that intermarriage was neither "frequent nor in any way encouraged by the leaders," but Mann speaks of "numerous cases,"[21] and Maimonides, who certainly knew of such marriages, did not prohibit them, as we shall soon see.

These intersectarian marriages were demonstrably contracted between mutually respectful religious equals. Mann's study of *ketubot* from Fostat and Jerusalem legalizing marriage between Rabbanites and Karaites in the eleventh and twelfth centuries demonstrates that each document details conditions meant to safeguard the religious freedom of both the Karaite and the Rabbanite spouses. Indeed, they include a clause that explicitly avers "mutual respect for their different religious practices."[22] Interestingly, at least as far as the evidence of these *ketubot* indicates, neither sect felt the recognition of the other's legitimacy—the recognition that the phrase "these and those are the words of the living God"—presented an inordinate threat to itself.

In the case of the Fostat marriage of the Nasi David, son of the Palestinian Gaon Daniel ben Azaryah, to the daughter of the "wealthy and influential" Karaite Moses Hakkohen ben Aaron in 1082 C.E., each side made concessions to the other's religious sensibilities. On the Karaite side, the usual rule that the husband might not inherit his wife, was abrogated; on the Rabbanite side, the bride was promised that, to accommodate her beliefs, she was

> not to have to keep her husband company on Friday nights in a room lit by the Sabbath candles, nor to partake of the fat-tail (prohibited by Karaite legalism) and not to desecrate the Festivals according to the Karaite calendar, while she had also to observe the Rabbanite festivals.[23]

In another example, a Karaite groom promises to observe the festivals in accordance with his Rabbanite spouses's custom. In a third *ketubah,* the safeguarding of Karaite practices dictated the exclusion of "the meat of a pregnant animal, [the] bread and wine of non-Jews" and further stipulated "no light on Friday nights...no heat on Sabbath, and also the absence of sexual intercourse, the latter prohibition extending also to the Festivals." In this examination of Genizah materials, Mann also includes a *ketubah* of the fourteenth century that mentions the Rabbanite leaders, the Nagid Abraham ben David ben Abraham Maimuni, as well as the Karaite Nasi of the time.[24] The *ketubah* formalizing the intermarriage of Karaite and Rabbanite in the year 1107 C.E. lists as the legal essentials *mohar,* documentation, sexual intercourse, witnesses, and *kiddushin.*[25] In these ketubot we are confronted with the fact that in the course of marriages contracted between Karaite and Rabbanite, both sides repeatedly seem quite ready to lay aside very ideological issues that had originally divided them into two distinct Jewish sects and that would continue to do so in the future of their relationship.

The ascension of Maimonides to leadership in Cairo in the twelfth century marked the beginning of the end of friendly half-conversions between the two sects. The Rambam's attitude toward his Karaite neighbors seems at times to have been ambivalent: Salo Baron points to his commentary on *Mishnah Hullin* 1.2, in which the Rambam refers to the corrupting influence of the "contemporary heretics" but elsewhere denies that the Karaites are heretics "in the technical meaning of the term." As long as they refrain from speaking mockingly of rabbis and Rabbanite traditions,

> One ought to inquire about their well-being even by visiting their homes, to circumcise their sons even on the Shabbat, to bury their dead, and to comfort their mourners.[26]

Echoing the tolerant attitude of the Genizah *ketubot*, Maimonides does not require that the Karaites turn from their sectarian ways before they may be treated as fellow Jews. He further writes that, although the originators of the error of Karaism are liable for their sin of rejecting the Rabbanite Oral Law,

> The children of these mistaken, and their descendants, who were...born into the Karaite community and raised by them according to their beliefs; one of these is like one...who is coerced. Even though he hears afterward that he is a Jew, and he sees [Rabbanite] Jews, and their beliefs, he is as one coerced, for he was raised in the error of his Karaite ancestors. Therefore it is appropriate to bring them to *teshuvah,* and draw them in kindly, until they return to the true Torah.[27]

Maimonides permits their wine, though he will not allow them to be counted for *minyan* and *zimmun;* this was because the Karaites did not recognize these obligations. In a *teshuvah* he wrote:

"In every matter in which they do believe in the obligation ...we are permitted to join them in it."[28]

The Rambam did not prohibit Karaite-Rabbanite marriage in his responsa that Tzvi Zohar notes on his study *Ben Nekhur L'ahuvah.*[29] In one such *teshuvah* Maimonides states unequivocally that "[w]hen anyone married a Karaite woman, she was to be considered his wife and for divorce needed a *get.*" He goes on to specify, however, that the *get* must be written.[30]

For the Rambam a marriage conducted according to Karaite practices is considered binding for the Rabbanite halakhist: a woman married to a man by such a rite is considered married. A woman divorced by Karaite practice, however, is not divorced in the eyes of Rabbanite *halakhah.* Schochtman notes the curious absence of the issue of Karaite-Rabbanite intermarriage in the Rambam's writings; it does not appear in the *Mishneh Torah,* and it is not addressed in his responsa other than in the specific instance cited above.[31]

THE QUESTION OF DOUBTFUL BASTARDY

Although the Rambam pronounced a Karaite *kiddushin* valid and a Karaite *get* invalid, he seems not to have carried the opinion forward to the possible conclusion that, in case of a Karaite divorce ending such a Karaite-Rabbanate intermarriage, the status of future offspring of the divorced mother, should she remarry, might be called into question. We might infer from the fact that, writing at the end of the fifteenth century, the Radbaz, Egyptian Rabbi David Ben Zimri, does follow the question to this point, that there were those who did worry about the possibility of such *mamzerut.* It is possible, the Radbaz writes, that in some cases a woman might have been divorced according to Karaite law; but, he points out, it is also quite possible that she never remarried. If she did remarry, he argues, the possibility has to be considered that she had no children. If she did have children, there is a chance that they never married. In other words, he considers the number of such questionable offspring so small that he did not judge the question of possible bastardy among the Karaites to be a concern.[32] In another of his *teshuvot* he muses:

> Still, there are reasons to generalize about the Karaites. They are Israelites and their marriages are valid; however, their divorces are not according to the rabbinic rules, and all, according to the Torah, are not reliable witnesses; and if we investigate this, there is great danger if many of their families enter into the general community. I do not see any way out of this and it is better to let them sin inadvertently.[33]

The idea is never to rule the Karaites out as Jews; the question was always that of the fine art of delineation between two Jewish sects: just how Jewish are they? Elsewhere, the Radbaz refers to the writings of Hai Gaon, quoted by the Rambam, in which the Gaon rules that Rabbanites should never refrain from involving themselves supportively with the Karaite community (for example, fulfilling the mitzvah *of brit milah* on Shabbat with them), because the aim was always to exploit every opportunity to bring the Karaites back into the Rabbanite fold. Even though the Karaites are, demonstrably, deniers of the Oral Law, and he regards them not as *anusim* but as consciously denying Rabbanite truth, ibn Zimra does not rule out the possibility of their return, although he may occasionally despair of it. As he wrote:

> It is obvious that the Gaon wished to permit them to enter the community through this decision. If that was his intention, then it was to permit them to repent. For that is the decision which must be made to deal with this matter. It is absolutely clear that we do not stand in the way of anyone who wishes to repent.[34]

Radbaz drives his point home by writing that, since we are all aware of the ruling of the sages that "a doubtful bastard shall not enter the community," obviously the Rambam therefore, in his silence on the issue and his upholding of Hai Gaon's ruling on seeking to bring the Karaites back to the true Torah, has to have totally dismissed the question of *safek mamzerut* concerning the Karaites.

The Rabbanite ascension to power in Egypt, represented by the Rambam and the bolstering strength his leadership and writings accorded to the Rabbanite Jewish community, no doubt contributed to the decline in the once-predominant Karaite community and its concomitant intellectual activity in Egypt and the East. In the twelfth century and after, the center of Karaite creativity and growth is traced to Europe.[35] The Egyptian Karaite community, however, apparently continued to enjoy a positive and productive relationship with its Rabbanite cousins. The Nagid Avraham, Maimonides' son, continued the official tolerance shown to the Karaites by declaring that one may believe a pious Karaite's oath "that he had not employed a Gentile in the preparation or the transportation of wine."[36] At the beginning of the fourteenth century, a contemporary source relates that in the days of the Nagid Avraham the Second (mentioned in the Karaite *ketubah* documented by Mann, above) "a large group of Egyptian Karaites accepted the Rabbanite way of life, and many of them married. later, into the elite Rabbanite families."[37]

ESTRANGEMENT OF THE TWO SECTS

Ambivalence between the two groups must have taken a toll among the communities of Rabbanites and Karaites living together, for the historian Alamkarizi reports in the thirteenth century on "the great hatred" growing between the two groups: "[T]hey do not marry each other, they do not speak together, one will not show even a foot in the *beit knesset* of his neighbor."[38] Marriages did still take place in other communities, apparently, for *teshuvot* exist that demonstrate the support of the Radbaz as well as other Egyptian rabbis such as Yaakov Birav, Shmuel ha-Levi HaKim, and Yaakov Castro for the general *heter* allowing such intersectarian marriages. Castro held that "if Karaites wish to accept the Oral Law and live like other faithful Israelites," the custom was for them to formally swear on a Torah before a *beit din* that they would henceforth live by the "requirements of the sages." He had complete confidence in such an oath, for it was known that "Karaites do not recognize any absolution of oaths and, hence, even against their will they must adhere to the end of their lives to the belief in Oral Law." But the rabbi Shlomo Gabison is on record at this time as being against such intermarriages (Korman notes that perhaps at his time and in his place the Karaites were different), as was the author of *Leket Hakemah*, Rabbi Moshe Hagiz, who writes, "their marriages are not Jewishly valid."[39] In Damascus and Constantinople, despite friendly relations between the sects, Benjamin of Tudela spoke of a *mehitzah* between them; there was little or no intermarriage between Rabbanite and Karaite Jews.[40]

The possibly compromised future status of the offspring of Karaite-Rabbanite intermarriage does not seem to be part of the growing Rabbanite controversy in Egypt vis-à-vis their Karaite cousins; that is, the question of marriage between Karaite converts and Rabbanite Jews does not seem to center on suspicions of *safek mamzerut*. Rather, the rabbis are apparently divided over whether conversion to Rabbanite doctrine is sufficient to allow a Karaite into the Rabbanite *kahal*. Although some authorities held that it was indeed permissible to marry a Karaite who returned to the "true way," others insisted that even a Karaite who denied the teachings of his sectarian ancestors could not be permitted to marry a Rabbanite and, in so doing, be allowed to enter the congregation. Since the opinion of *poskim* such as Rambam and Radbaz is apparently insufficient to carry this later day, we might perhaps expect the "doubtful bastardy" question to dominate the historical discussion; it does not. This practical issue of *safek mamzerut,* which speaks to the very formation of the basic family unit and Jewish descent, seems to be sublimated to the ideological question of how to treat a heretic that wishes, in Rabbanite eyes, to "return to the fold" of the true believers.

SIXTEENTH THROUGH NINETEENTH CENTURIES

In the sixteenth through the nineteenth centuries, evidence exists in the form of written *teshuvot* that in Egypt rabbis continued to give their permission for Karaite-Rabbanite marriages. Rishon le-Zion Ovadyah Yosef, who had been Chief Rabbi of Egypt, knew of such permissions granted to many Karaites over the years, as he wrote in a responsum: "Generation after generation of Egyptian rabbis acted to permit their entry into the community."[41] The evidence is very sparse that rabbis in any other country of *Sephardi* Jewish residence did so, but so is the evidence to the contrary.

In Europe, however, where by the thirteenth century the Karaite communities had already spread as far as Troki in Lithuania, an apparently full consensus had formed among the *Ashkenazi poskim* of Europe against allowing Karaites to join the Rabbanite fold; they all ruled that the Karaites were under suspicion of being *safek mamzerim.* In their Lithuanian coexistence Rabbanite and Karaite Jews used the same cemetery in Vilna for a time, and later the Rabbanites defended themselves against royal decrees and blood libels by means of the Karaite charters of Troki. Apparently the two groups, however interdependent they were for survival, did not intermarry.[42]

Zohar attributes the trace of a hardening attitude in Egypt at least partly to the emigration to Egypt of European Jews, who brought the *Ashkenazi* ruling of the Rama against the Karaites:

> As far as Karaites are concerned, it is forbidden to marry with them; all are considered *safek mamzerim* and we do not receive them into the community even if they wish to return."[43]

By the midsixteenth century, ambivalence had spread as far as Palestine, where Caro, writing in Safed, reports in his commentary to the *Tur, Beit Yosef:*

> I have read in responsa... as far as Karaites are concerned, it is forbidden to marry with them as their women marry through a monetary transaction or intercourse and their divorces are not in accordance with the law...and they marry others while their husband is still alive, so their children are *safek mamzerim.*[44]

In his gloss, Isserles writes. "If Karaites marry in accordance with Israelite law, although they are sinners, we consider them as Israelites.[45] In contradistinction to his words in the *Mapah* to the *Shulhan*

Arukh, this statement would seem to indicate his willingness to consider accepting Karaites into the *kahal.*

Zohar traces the halakhic locus for *Sephardi* rejection of the possibility of intermarriage with Karaites to the words of the late nineteenth-century rabbi Hayyim Hezekiah Medini, who attributed to the early nineteenth-century Rishon le-Zion Solomon Moshe Suzin the ruling that conclusively prohibits "our brothers the Karaites" from coming into the Rabbanite *kahal:* "Karaites can never be our brothers."[46] The accuracy of that statement and its attribution, however, are in dispute; and the consensus of rabbis and the Jewish *kahal* in Egypt demonstrated more tolerance than did its European counterpart.

THE TWENTIETH CENTURY

1904, BEIT SHE'AN

In 1904 a Rabbanite man emigrated to Beit She'an, Palestine, and, after some years, sought to marry a Karaite woman. They turned to the Tiberias rabbinic authority, which directed them to Rabbi Yitzhak Moshe Abulafia of Damascus. Abulafia ruled the marriage permissible, and the two married; but the rabbinic authorities of Tiberias, enlisting the support of their Jerusalem colleagues, rejected the ruling. As Zohar relates the story, they objected on technical grounds, but most of all on the principle codified by Moshe Isserles in the *Mapah,* which they cite: How in the world shall it be understood that a Karaite has been allowed to come into the *kahal?* The rabbis published a statement citing Susin's dictum and calling upon all rabbis who might encounter the unfortunate couple to force them to divorce, on pain of *herem*. In response to this outcry, Abulafia withdrew his *heter*.

The rabbis of Tiberias and Jerusalem, in their search for widespread support against Abulafia's ruling, had contacted, among others, the Chief Rabbi of Alexandria, Rabbi Eliyahu Hazan. He did not give them the hoped-for response. Hazan took exception to the quoted reliance on Rabbi Suzin, pointing out the absence of any actual quoted evidence that the Rishon le-Zion had ever pronounced the dictum attributed to him; there was only his disciple Rabbi Medini's admitted "childhood memory" of such a proclamation against the Karaites. Hazan went on, in his response, to describe significant distinctions between different Karaite communities and insisted that each case regarding a Karaite should be judged according to that Karaite's uniquely relevant characteristics. The prohibition against admitting Karaites into the *kahal,* he avers, is "not absolute but conditional."[47] The Israeli rabbis responded by excommunicating him, which apparently did not concern him.

Hazan's explanation of his halakhic stance vis-à-vis the Karaites is built on his rejection of the concept of *safek mamzerut*. This is, after all, in agreement with such halakhic giants as Maimonides, who does not address the issue, and Radbaz, who dismisses it. Hazan's analysis, however, goes further than his predecessors. He observes that the Karaites are organized into self-sufficient, independent *kehillot,* which do not turn to Rabbanite Jews for any legal or ritual functions. Hazan held, therefore, that since there was no chance of Rabbanites witnessing or officiating at a Karaite wedding, the ritual had no authenticity in the eyes of Rabbanite *halakhah*. Karaites, he observed, do not follow Rabbanite customs in matters of intimate relationships, and "furthermore, their leader

...who arranges their marriages, instructs them for evil and not for good." Having made the point that, although they are Israel, they are a separate sect that could never be mistaken for Rabbanite, and that Karaite *kiddushin* was no *kiddushin,* there cannot therefore be any possibility of *safek mamzerut;* Hazan therefore ruled that "Egyptian Karaites are permitted, if they wish, 'to enter the community' and so to blend into the local rabbinic community."[48]

1918 Cairo

Zohar cites a rabbinic proclamation issued by the chief rabbis of Cairo in 1918, in which the rabbis Raphael Aharon ben Shimon, Aharon Mendel Hacohen, and Massoud Hai ben Shimon announced that "any Egyptian Karaite is permitted to come into the *kahal* if he will commit himself to the Rabbanite tradition." Recognizing that they themselves were following in the giant halakhic footsteps of such as the Rambam, the Radbaz, Darkhei No'am, and Ginat Veradim, all Egyptian Rabbanite leaders, they pointed out that "all of them accepted Karaites into the community *lekhathilah,* converted them, and allowed them to come into the *kahal.*"[49]

Soliciting the opinion of the Rishon le-Zion Ya'akov Meir, Rabbi Yehudah Masalton later built his case upon theirs, starting with the same four *g'dolei hador:*

> All of them allowed Karaites into the community *lekhathilah,* as explained in their writings; and even more so in the case of Avraham the Nagid, son of the Rambam, who brought an entire Karaite community into the [Rabbanite] *kahal* in one day. The Radbaz testified that these [Karaite converts] married the *g'dolei hador.* If this was so in their time, and they had the power to "stand firm on religious matters," then all the more so in our

> orphaned age! Who will be more *mahmir* than our early *geonim*, and think of the Karaites of Egypt that there is any suspicion in them of *mamzerut*, for then, God forbid, we will come to the position that we must declare *pasul* all the Rabbanite inhabitants of Egypt.[50]

In the writings attributed to Rabbi Aaron Mendel Hacohen, we find a clear example of the ambivalence of an *Ashkenazi* rabbi living and making halakhic decisions in Egypt at the beginning of the twentieth century. Zohar quotes his early attitude toward the other sect in town:

> I, myself, when I first arrived here and heard the name of a Karaite, I would spit and say about him, "Unclean, unclean— he is a *mamzer,*" and I was careful to refrain even from touching the walls of streets upon which they live. And not only I alone behaved in this way, but also all those who are known to fear God were extremely careful not to come in contact with anything associated with the Karaites."[51]

After gaining some local experience and wisdom, he, like Hazan, learned to distinguish between types of Karaites, disallowing those openly hostile to Rabbanite Judaism, but averring that, regarding those Karaites who live in peace and mutual respect with their Rabbanite neighbors, "who do not act rebelliously or treacherously, we shall rely with all our strength on our rishonim," and follow their lead regarding accepting those Karaites into the Rabbanite community.[52]

We can now answer the question of under what circumstances Rabbanite halakhic decisors permit intersectarian marriage. The rabbis that allow intersectarian marriage of Rabbanite and Karaite Jew, such as Rabbi Yehudah Masalton, specifically do so only when all three of the following conditions are met:

1. That the ancestors of the Karaite Jew are Egyptian.
2. That the Karaite party to the marriage swear a solemn and binding oath that s/he will behave according to Rabbanite law, without any deviation: that s/he will immerse in a pure mikvah according to the laws of conversion.
3. That none of the Karaite's ancestors were ever divorced.

In his responsum Rabbi Maselton apparently agrees with Rabbi Hazan's approach. He is careful to state that this *heter* applies only to the Karaites of Egypt,

> who are completely distinguishable from the Rabbanites; there is no suspicion that the witnesses to their marriages are Rabbanite, and that therefore their *kiddushin* is *kiddushin* or at least *safek-kiddushin*. This is in contradistinction to those Karaite communities in which there is social mixing between Karaite and Rabbanite.[53]

MODERN TIMES

Contemporary *Ashkenazi* halakhic literature is very clear that Karaite and Rabbanite Jew do not intermarry. Korman explained that "since the days of the Rambam, the character of the Karaites has changed, and apropos of this, so has the attitude of *halakha* toward them." Thus, the modern *Ashkenazi* attitude is seen as proceeding from the attitude of Isserles—that they are all *safek mamzerim* and are not to be admitted into the *kahal*—and of the *Shulhan Arukh*—that they are not to be considered *anusim*, or coerced, in their behavior or in their marriages"; and one who buys land from them is judged as one who buys from a Gentile."

> It is also forbidden at the present time to circumcise their sons on Shabbat, because they do not uncover the membrane of the corona after the circumcision, and milah without *pri'ah* is not *milah,* and this constitutes a *hillul Shabbat b'lo mitzvah.*[54]

Rabbi Isaac Klein discussed the question of intermarriage of Karaites and Rabbanites in his *Guide to Jewish Religious Practice,* noting that "the codes are very explicit about the Karaites." After quoting the Rema and the reiteration of his *Mapah* ruling "in a decision of the Chief Rabbanite of Israel" (by which we may perhaps surmise that he meant the Chief *Ashkenazi* Rabbinate), he continued by giving examples of intersectarian marriages at times when relations between the two sects were friendly, and concludes that,

> [w]hile in the past the Karaites disassociated themselves from *Klal Yisra'el,* today they have reversed the process and have even suffered martyrdom for *Klal Yisra'el.* In Israel, although the official policy has been to forbid such marriages, exceptions have been made that may indicate a new trend.[55]

Scholars are divided as to whether one can attribute sociological and political pressures to changes in halakhic decision-making trends, but we can observe that when the two sects enjoy friendly and mutually respectful relations, marriages occur between them. Similarly, the distancing between the two sects that has occurred over the last several hundred years is clearly indicated by the Karaites' successful suit in the court of Catherine the Great, to be treated in such matters as taxation in a fashion different from that of the Rabbanite Jews. Nemoy ascribes such Karaite efforts to escape the legal and social persecutions of Jews in Poland and Russia, as resulting in "a quiet but profound estrangement." (History, however, gives examples of Rabbanite communities that have similarly sought to gain advantage at the expense of their coreligionists.) Nemoy documents the January 1, 1939, decree of the German Ministry of the Interior which "expressly stipulated that the Karaites did not belong to the Jewish religious community; their 'racial psychology' was considered non-Jewish." In Arab countries, however, when the State of Israel was established, they were the victims of equal-opportunity persecution with their neighbor Rabbanites.[56]

Tzitz Eliezer is among those whose rulings seem to echo the bitterness of the past or at least to steadfastly uphold the modern Orthodox ban on intermarriage of Karaite and Rabbanite Jews. In a *teshuvah* Rabbi Eliezer Waldenburg describes how the Jewish Agency approached him for a decision on whether Karaite Jews should be considered for *aliyah* to Israel from the Soviet Union. In his response he takes a very strong line, quoting Isserles, and, because they deny the *Torah she-ba 'al peh,* proclaiming the Karaites "worse than idolaters." "When I think about our fellow Jews, out there in the Golah without a roof over their heads," he writes," the Karaites are not to be compared with them."

> The Karaites are forbidden forever, and they shall not enter the God-fearing community....[57]

In his *Yabbia 'Omer* Ovadyah Yosef specifically replies to Tzitz Eliezer in a prolonged and somewhat more measured discussion of the status of Karaite Jews. He notes that the bread, the cooked food, and the wine of a *mamzer* are acceptable, so is it with a Karaite. He reviews the history of the *halakha,* writing that "the prohibition against allowing Karaites into the *kahal* is not from the

Sages, but rather *mi-de-oraita.*" He points out that the Rambam never issued any prohibition against marrying them, and that "there are many *gedolei olam* who allow the Karaites."[58]

In 1984 the American Conservative Movement's Committee on Jewish Law and Standards adopted a *teshuvah* written by David H. Lincoln regarding the attitude of the movement toward accepting Egyptian Karaites into the *kahal.* Lincoln notes the reluctance of several halakhists to take a stand on the question, including Ouziel (quoted above, p. 21) and Abraham Zevi Hirsch Eisenstadt, rabbi in nineteenth-century Lithuania, who was concerned about *safek mamzerut,* since the majority of them have not been divorced. Although we can draw a line of reasoning from the Radbaz through Masalton, both of whom permitted such intersectarian marriages, to Eisenstadt, he is not ready to declare himself with them and, rather, concludes:

> As so many of the earlier authorities were willing to accept them even in established communities...therefore I am not willing to prohibit or permit.[59]

In adopting Lincoln's *teshuvah,* the Conservative Committee on Laws and Standards agreed with his statement that "their 'Jewish descent' is not really in question." Like Aaron Mendel HaCohen and Hazan before him, Lincoln distinguishes between Karaite communities, but draws the opposite halakhic conclusions in so doing. The European Karaites, those found in Russia, Poland, and Lithuania, Lincoln writes, were "mostly a strange community with Tatar-like features, speaking a Tatar dialect and distancing themselves from the Rabbanite Jews...It was hardly possible for a Polish Jew to marry such a person." Thus, the Rema's ruling and the *Ashkenazi* attitudes on the subject. The Karaites of the Middle

East, however, were much like their neighbor Rabbanites in appearance and manner, and thus the closer relations and the possibility of marriage. Lincoln concludes by dismissing the question of *safek mamzerut* and, to counter the possible assimilation of the small group of Karaites that can be found in the United States today, advocates accepting them "without reservation."[60]

Solomon B. Freehof, in his 1965 responsum on the subject of marriage with Karaites, also dismisses the question of *safek mamzerut* for the Reform Movement on the grounds that Reform Judaism accepts civil divorce. Further, since a Reform ritual divorce would have no more standing in the eyes of Orthodoxy than that of the Karaites, by that standard Reform rabbis marry people who are of doubtful halakhic status comparable to that of the Karaites on a regular basis, "without hesitation":

> Since the authorities agree that Karaite marriages are valid and Karaites are of Jewish descent, and since the only objection is the validity of their divorce and the consequence drawn from it, we should have no hesitation in officiating at the marriage of a Karaite and a Jew.

Freehof did specify, however, that "we might ask" the Karaite to make a declaration of full loyalty to the Jewish community. Taking the ruling of the Radbaz as his precedent, he avers that the Karaite "will not need conversion, but merely a statement of *Haverut*."[61]

For Rabbanite—that is, halakhic Judaism—the sine qua non of Jewish individual identification and communal belonging is the acceptance of *Torah she-bikhtav* through the interpretative prism of Torah *she-be'al peh.* According to Rabbanite dogma, the acceptance of the double Torah was never a question or an issue open to a vote but, rather, a matter of a covenant entered into by the Jews who were at Sinai and incumbent upon all their descendants. On that level, then, it is astonishing that throughout the centuries of Rabbanite halakhic sources, we find conflicting decisions, contradictory attitudes, and lasting ambivalence toward the Karaites, a Jewish sect that completely rejects Torah *she-be'al peh harabbanim.* Why were the Karaites not simply labeled heretics and declared off limits to the self-defined national Jewish identity, which was the Rabbanite community? How is it conceivable that relations between the two groups might be so amicable that marriages would be contracted between them in the past and in recent times as well?

The traditional litany of Jewish identity and survival—is it good for the Jews?—is the litmus test that informs the historical attitude of Rabbanites toward Karaites. Jack J. Cohen of the Hebrew University suggests that "the discouragement of racial mixture, whenever it was felt necessary in biblical times, involved considerations of religiocultural loyalty rather than concern about the biological purity of the Hebrews and Israelites." Group survival required a high degree of "conscious commitment to historically evolved group norms."[62] In order to control and proscribe racial and ideological mixture in the Jewish nation, the Rabbis had to define the requirements for group belonging; once again, the question is, "Who is a Jew?"

The question that might be inferred by the evidence consiered above is that, as so much else in life, the question of how Rabbanites and Karaites interact has to do with power and who has it. Where the Karaite community is large, wealthy, and powerful, Rabbanites contract marriages with them, appeal for their intercession in difficult times, and call them "our brothers." In the

Middle Ages the Karaite movement waned in power and size, and their European communities were shunned by the more powerful Rabbanites of Europe. Thus it is that the Karaites always considered themselves Jews and always shared the fate of the Jewish people (with one notable exception).

Issues of religiocultural loyalty did not apparently trouble Hai Gaon who encouraged tolerance and Rabbanite readiness to accept Karaites into the *kahal.* Rabbanite Jewish concern with biological purity vis-à-vis the Karaites was evident only in Europe, where the predominant *Ashkenazi* Rabbanites reject the entire group as *safek mamzerut,* but in Egypt the Karaites were considered to be just like their *Sephardi* Rabbanite neighbors in talk, in characteristics, and in communal living habits; and the biological purity issue is one that an authority as prominent as the Radbaz considers an unnecessary complication of the halakhic status of the Karaites.

Is this a coincidence or a legacy of equally powerful communities in relationship and, as well, the mutuality of their relationships? As for a "conscious commitment to group norms, this is an important issue to those mostly European rabbis who deny the Karaites the possibility of "return" to the *kahal;* but it is not to those other, Egyptian *poskim,* who point to the *gedolim* that came before us and that accepted Karaites: who are we to do otherwise?

Many words have been written, but if actions speak louder than words, the Fostat and Jerusalem *ketubot* of the eleventh and twelfth centuries speak volumes. The mutual respect that characterized these documents indicates a Rabbanite willingness to see Karaites as Jews—Jews living a Jewish life with integrity, with an interpretative tradition regarding *Torah*-law that is different from that of the Rabbanites, but valid. The attitude of Maimonides, who rules that we may join with the Karaites in *mitzvot* that are authoritative for them as well as us, seems to reach beyond mere tolerance to a kind of acceptance of these coreligionists. It is as if some of the Rabbanites of our own day discovered our brother and sister Jews in Ethiopia, the movement's *Beta Israel,* and refrained from expecting their leaders to pass exams set by the Chief Rabbinate of Israel, as if they had restrained themselves from a show of political power, as if they had not pushed away the Ethiopians' own ritual garments in the Rabbanite rush to put a *kipah* on every male Jewish head.

The Karaites, in their development of a different system of *Torah* interpretation, defined themselves as a Jewish community that took itself and its relation to Jewish history and Jewish law seriously. The Karaite movement produced scholars and codifiers as well as charismatic leaders; they were never a sect of mere rejecters of the Rabbanite approach to the *Torah.* Like any self-sufficient religious sect, they defined their own self-contained and internally coherent system of belief and praxis. Their approach asserts the right of the individual to "search well in the Torah" and not to rely on another's ruling above one's own *seikhel* and yet, for the sake of group identity and preservation, establishes group norms to which they demand conformity.

When is a sectarian not a sectarian? The Karaites were and are, according to some rabbis, heretics. But depending on the time, the place, and the rabbi, *alfheinu haKara'im* were and are considered acceptable companions with Rabbanites on the Jewish journey and, often enough, cobuilders of that most vital religious unit, the family. A cynic might expect the eternal dominance of a religious *realpolitik.* We can learn from this study the eternal potential for a flexible, diverse, and creative corpus of Rabbanite Jewish law and of Rabbanite Jewish legal decisors that, like Rabbi Maselton, look carefully at an individual case or person and consider the social and legal context of a question equally crucial, or maybe more so, than looking over the shoulder to see what other rabbis are ruling. Such a decisor would, as the Radbaz and Rabbi Hazan, be open to conflicting views on the subject and would note differences in communities and in individuals. Then, such a one might add a healthy dose of realism about the everchanging world in which we live and, in the end, like Rabbi Hacohen, choose to "rely with all our strength on the *rishonim*" and decide to behave tolerantly toward those with whom they disagree or perhaps even accept the other as a Jew of integrity, deserving of the mutual respect of Jews, all of whom care for the tradition, live by the Torah as they study, understand and interact with it, and, in so doing, seek the presence of God.

What might we learn from all this for our day and time? The case of the Karaites does not inform a modern-day discussion of intermarriage of Jews and non-Jews, for only the most extreme of halakhists would call a Karaite a non-Jew. This exploration has more to say to the historically uninformed about the nature of Judaism, to those that believe that the only *Ashkenazi* heritage is sacred, and to the apologists of Reform Judaism that would deny its sacred tenets—such as egalitarianism and autonomy—because of a belief that only the Orthodox Jew is a *Torah*-true Jew and that the rest of us are lazy, ignorant, and without principles. Interestingly enough, the story of the Karaites seems to teach that a Jewish movement with self-respect might actually be treated by other Jewish communities with respect.

Notes

1. David H. Lincoln, "Accepting Egyptian Karaites into Our Communities." *Proceedings of the Committee on Jewish Law and Standards of the Conservative Movement, 1980–1985.* New York, The Rabbinical Assembly, 1988, p. 263.

2. Jacob Mann, "New Studies in Karaism," *CCAR Yearbook,* p. 222.

3. Salo Baron, "Karaite Schism," *A Social and Religious History of the Jews,"* Vol. 5 (Philadelphia: Jewish Publication Society, 1957), p. 274.

4. Leon Nemoy, "Karaites," *Encyclopaedia Judaica* (Jerusalem: Keter, 1972), p. 781.

5. Louis Ginzburg, *An Unknown Jewish Sect* (New York: Jewish Theological Seminary, 1976), p. 1.

6. Leon Nemoy, "Karaites," p. 765.

7. Abraham Korman, *Zeramim Vekitut Beyahadut* (Tel Aviv: Safiti, 1966), p. 230.

8. Quoted in Mann, *New Studies,* p. 231ff.

9. Daniel J. Lasker, "Rabbanism and Karaism: The Contest for Supremacy," *Great Schisms in Jewish History,* ed. by Raphael Jospe and Stanley M. Wagner (New York: Center for Judaic Studies, University of Denver, and KTAV Publishing House, Inc., 1981), p. 49.

10. Nemoy, "Karaites," p. 766; Tzvi Ankori, *Some Aspects of Karaite-Rabbanite Relations in Byzantium on the Eve of the First Crusade,* Part 1 (New York:Jewish Theological Seminary, 1959), p. 24.

11. Ankori, *Karaite-Rabbanite Relations,* p. 2, fn. 2.

12. Quoted in Lasker, "Rabbanism and Karaism," pp. 56ff.

13. Amram Gaon, *Seder,* II, 206f., quoted in Baron, "Karaite Schism," p. 276.

14. Lasker, "Rabbanism and Karaism," p. 47.

15. Baron, "Karaite Schism," pp. 270–74.

16. Ibid.

17. Heinrich Graetz, *History of the Jews,* Vol. 3 (Philadelphia: Jewish Publication Society, 1894), p. 308.

18. Cited by Baron, "Karaite Schism," p. 278.

19. Lasker, "Rabbanism and Karaism," p. 57.

20. Quoted in Baron," Karaite Schism," p. 280; Other signs of such recognition also existed.

21. Baron, Ibid., p. 266; Mann, *New Studies*, p. 222.

22. Jacob Mann, "Karaite Legal Documents," *Texts and Studies in Jewish History and Literature,* Vol. 2, *Karaitica* (New York: KTAV, 1972), p. 160.

23. Mann, Ibid., p. 158.

24. Mann, Ibid., pp. 159-161.

25. Mann, Ibid., p. 160.

26. Baron, "Karaite Schism," pp. 280-91.

27. Maimonides, Hil Yad, *Mamrim* 3.3; Korman, *Zeramim Vekitut,* p. 237.

28. Maimonides, Responsa 351, in Schochtman, *Zeramim Vekitut,* p. 41.

29. Tzvi Zohar, *Ben Nekhur L'ahuvah,* p. 21.

30. Maimonides, Responsa 351, in Schochtman, *Zeramim Vekitut.*

31. Maimonides, Ibid., p. 42.

32. Maimonides, Ibid., p. 43: also, see Lincoln, "Accepting Egyptian Karaites," p. 266 and solomon B. Freehof, "Report of the Committee on Responsa," CCAR *Yearbook* (New York, 1965), p. 98.

33. Radbaz, *Responsa* 4:219, 7:351.

34. Schochtman, *Zeramim Vekitut,* p. 44; see also Samuel Morell, "The Halakhic Status of non-Halakhic Jews," *Judaism* 18:4 (Fall 1969), p. 452.

35. Nemoy, "Karaites," p. 770.

36. Quoted in Zohar, *Ben Nekhur,* p. 22.

37. Ibid., p. 21; Baron dated this episode at 1312–1313.

38. Ibid.

39. Cited in Baron, "Karaite Schism," p. 274; *"Leket Hakemah, Even Haezer,"* in Korman, *Zeramim Vekitut,* p. 237.

40. Cited in Baron, "Karaite Schism," pp. 266ff.

41. Schochtman, *Zeramim Vekitut,* pp. 31–32.

42. Mann, *New Studies,* p. 236.

43. Isserles to *Shulhan Arukh, Even Haezer* (end) 4; Zohar, *Ben Nekhur,* p. 22; Schochtman, *Zeramim Vekitut,* p. 49.

44. *Beit Yosef, Even Haezer, Hil. Periyah Ureviya* 4, 5, 15.

45. *Tur, Even Haezer,* 4, 5, 14.

46. Zohar, *Ben Nekhur,* p. 22.

47. This story is related by Zohar, Ibid., pp. 23–25ff.

48. Cited in Zohar, Ibid., p. 24.

49. Ibid., p. 25; cited in *Hazon Ish,* p. 14b.

50. Ibid., *Ben Nekhur,* p. 28.

51. *Vezot Leayahdut,* p. 145a; Schochtman, *Zeramim Vekitut,* p. 36.

52. Zohar, *Ben Nekhur,* p. 25, in *Hacohen,* p. 112.

53. *Yad Ram,* p. 114, in Schochtman, *Zeramim Vekitut,* p. 45.

54. Schochtman, Ibid., p. 37.

55. Isaac Klein, *A Guide to Jewish Religious Practices* (New York: Jewish Theological Seminary, 1979), p. 411.

56. Nemoy, "Karaites," p. 776; Mann, *New Studies,* p. 223.

57. Eliezer Waldberg, "Tzitz Eliezer," Vol. 2, (65) p. 187.

58. Responsa Yabiah Omer, Vol. 5, *Yoreh Deah* 10; 4 and 7.

59. Quoted in Lincoln, "Accepting Egyptian Karaites," p. 264.

60. Ibid.

61. Freehof, "Report of the Committee on Responsa," p. 98.

62. Jack J. Cohen, "Toward a Reasonable Future for the Jewish People," *Judaism* 4: 133, pp 20–23.

SELECTED REFORM RESPONSA

These responsa are a representative selection from more than one thousand American Reform responsa published in the twentieth century. We are grateful to the Central Conference of American Rabbis and the Hebrew Union College Press for permission to reproduce them.

THE TABLE OF CONSANGUINITY

Walter Jacob

QUESTION: The Table of Consanguinity currently used by the Reform Movement is male-centered, and clearly discriminates against women. Should we change the Table to reflect our equal treatment of men and women?

ANSWER: The Table of Consanguinity as produced in the *Rabbis' Manual* is based largely upon Biblical law (Lev. 18:11-21; Deut. 23:3, 27:20-23; Kid. 67b; Yoma 67b; Maimonides, *Yad, Hil. Ishut* IV, *Isurei Bi-a* II; *Shulhan Arukh, Even Ha-ezer* 15:44.6). The Biblical laws were somewhat modified and expanded by the Talmud. A full discussion of those modifications may be found in Mielziner, *Jewish Marriage Laws,* 1897. Each of these statements has approached the entire matter from a male point of view. It would, of course, be possible to rewrite these statements so that they would reflect the views of the current feminist movement. This, however, would add a number of prohibitions, if we simply paralleled masculine prohibitions which exist already. It would be unwise and unrealistic to follow this path for the following reasons: (1) The last major change in Jewish marriage laws was made in the eleventh century through the decree of Rabbenu Gershom, which prohibited polygamy. This decree was effective because polygamy had largely ceased in practice by Ashkenazic Jews, as the general population among whom they lived did not practice it either. The decree, however, was not followed by the remainder of world Jewry, and polygamy continued to be practiced up to modern times by Jews in various Eastern countries. In other words, the decree was effective only because it fitted into the mood of the time and place. Such additional restrictions would, however, not evoke a similar response in our age. The decree of Rabbenu Gershom had long been completely accepted by Ashkenazic Jewry. (2) The presumption of inequality for women has led Judaism to adopt the most lenient definition of bastardy in the Western world. Only the off-spring of those prohibited from marrying by the laws of consanguinity and adultery on the part of the married woman are considered *mamzerim*. Any change would also alter this definition to the disadvantage of infant children. (3) It is extremely doubtful whether our rabbis or our laymen would follow any additional restrictions in the field of marriage. It is difficult enough to enforce some strictures which we have now, much less impose others. In other words, any restrictive decision on the part of our committee in this matter would represent a mere gesture toward the feminist movement rather than an effective effort. Anyhow, one should not legislate when it is obvious that no one will follow what has been decreed (Yev. 65b, Shabbat 148b)

In addition, our Reform Movement has made some changes: (1) We have recognized the marriage of divorcees to those of priestly descent. This permissive change was made as we no longer recognize priestly privileges. (2) We have accepted civil divorce as sufficient for remarriage. The reliance on civil divorce is, *ipso facto, an* effective and realistic measure toward equality of both sexes, since women can and do institute divorce proceedings in their own right under State laws. Both changes have gained complete acceptance by Reform Jews and also by a large percentage of the American Jewish community.

The existing Table could be rewritten in a more permissive way That also does not seem appropriate for us for the following reasons: (1) We are continuing to try to work out distinctive, but naturally agreeable approaches to family law along with our Conservative and Orthodox co-religionists in order to avoid conflict over family matters in the Land of Israel. A decision such as this on our part would increase the difficulties of this task. (2) Most state legal systems parallel our Table of Consanguinity or are very close to it. Any changes we might make would only raise additional problems. In this case, the abstract notion of complete quality would hinder rather than help us or the feminist movement.

For these reasons the Table of Consanguinity should remain as it now stands.

Walter Jacob (ed.), *American Reform Responsa,* New York, 1983, #129

ORTHODOX ASPERSIONS AGAINST REFORM MARRIAGES

Solomon B. Freehof

QUESTION: This problem is involved in the situation which is described in the letter which follows:
"You may be aware that in Great Britain there seems to be now a more or less concentrated attack on the Reform Movement, especially in connection with the acceptance by Orthodox authorities of marriages conducted in our synagogues It has gone so far as to cast doubts that Orthodox synagogues would accept such marriages as valid, and it has been intimated that the Jewish status of children from such marriage may be in question. I speak of marriages among Jewish persons, excluding proselytes." (Dr. W. Van der Zyl, Senior Minister of the West London Synagogue, London)

ANSWER: There are certain technical differences between Orthodox and Reform marriages as to witnesses, *ketubah,* and so forth. Some Orthodox authorities in England have spoken of declaring marriages performed by Liberal or Reform rabbis invalid. Is such a declaration of invalidity justified by the *halakhah* itself? In general, what is the validity in Orthodox law of marriages in which procedure varies from that which is normally required by Orthodox laws.

Orthodox Jewish marriage requires a *minyan* present at the ceremony, a *ketubah* and kosher witnesses to the declaration of marriage, the giving of the ring the reciting of the seven blessings, and so forth. While all these observances are *required,* are they indispensable? Suppose a marriage takes place without some of them; what is it in Jewish law which makes a marriage valid?

It must be noted that this question has been an important one and a practical one for many centuries: for example, in the case of the Marranos in Spain and Portugal who escaped to Jewish communities and said they had been married in a church, or in the cases of civil marriage in modern times. Are such marriages valid?

It is true that there is a considerable disagreement as to what is the basic requirement for the validity of a Jewish marriage, but the majority of opinion, which is becoming increasingly weighty in modern times with the spread of civil marriage, is that the validity of the marriage is not dependant at all upon most of these ceremonial or ritual requirements.

The basic marriage requisite is that the man speaks of his intention to be married and gives the woman an object of some value - "he says and he gives." And, indeed, the basic ground for marriage is that the man takes the woman into his house and they live together in physical relationship. Now, while this Mishnaic method of marriage *(biah)* was frowned upon in the Middle Ages by Israel Isserlein (*Terumat Hadeshen* 209), nevertheless when it does occur the general attitude of the law is that such a marriage is valid, This is based upon the opinion of Rav (Ketubot 72b to 73a), that if a man takes a woman into his house for the purpose of marriage, she cannot be freed from that marriage without a formal divorce (i.e., this simple marriage is valid). The opinion of Rav is based upon the belief that a man does not generally intend his sexual relationship to be adulterous (*ein adam oseh*, and so on). However, this presumption that the sexual relationship is intended as a marriage relationship, and not as an adulterous one, broke down in later years and was no longer held to be valid; as, for example, in the case of certain Marrano marriages about which some authorities said that, since they could have escaped and did not escape, we no longer apply to them the presumption which we grant to righteous people, that their sexual relationship was meant to be a marriage relationship.

However, suppose the couple thus informally married stay together as husband and wife, and this is public knowledge. Then the fact that they are known to live together as husband and wife proves retroactively their original intention, and the presumption *(hazakah) is* thus reestablished and their marriage, therefore, is valid. This attitude is increasingly held by Orthodox authorities, namely, that they follow Rav in the Talmud, that the very bringing of the woman into his house constitutes proof of proper intention and therefore of the validity of the marriage. Thus, for example, Isaiah Trani (Riaz), quoted as part of *Shiltei Hageborim* to Alfasi to *Kiddushin* 3, says definitely: "Although there are no witnesses of the marriage itself, or even witnesses that they secluded themselves (*yihud*), nevertheless it is presumed in their locality that they are man and wife. This presumption is equivalent to clear and perfect testimony."

This, too, is the basis of the famous responsum of Isaac Elchanan Spektor of Kovno in his responsa (*Ein Yitzhak*, vol. I, *Even Haezer* 47, especially paragraph 12). He discusses the case of a Jewish soldier who lived with a Jewish woman without formality of marriage, and then the man deserted the woman. Is she married to him or not? Spektor, on the basis of the above-mentioned laws, says that if they were known as man and wife for thirty days in the city where they lived, the marriage is valid and cannot be broken without a *get*. *So* also the late Orthodox authority Yechiel Epstein (*Arukh Ha shulhan Kiddushin* 26.11) says that if a Jew and a Jewess live together and say that their living together is meant to be a marriage - if it is known to all that they live together the marriage cannot be broken except by a *get*. The most recent authority is Joseph Henkin, of New York (*Perushei Ibra*, chapters 3 and 4) proves the general thesis that if a man takes a woman for the purpose of marriage and they just live together (under that intention) this is an absolutely valid marriage. Their physical relationship (known in the Jewish neighborhood) makes the marriage as valid as if there were all the necessary witnesses. This source *(Perushei Ibra)* gives the fullest discussion of the laws involved. Rabbi Henkin returns to give a briefer statement of the law (*Hapardes*, XXXIII, no. 10, p. 12), in which he simply says that if a man lives with a woman and the Jews of the neighborhood know it, it is a full marriage.

Of course, the opposite opinion is also held in the law, that such free unions or, for that matter, civil marriages are not Jewishly legal. However, the opinions cited above that such marriages are legal are sufficiently important that they must be given considerable weight and certainly cannot be brushed aside. Furthermore, the tendency of the law among recent Orthodox scholars is to consider such marriages as Jewishly legal (Abraham Haim Freiman, *Seder Kiddushin Unissuin*, p. 362).

Now let us assume that Reform or Liberal marriages lack many of the observances which Orthodox law considers necessary to marriage, kosher witnesses (i.e., those who do not violate the Sabbath and other ritual observances), a properly written *ketubah*, and so forth; nevertheless none of these defects can possibly invalidate the marriage, for the couple live together as man and wife in the knowledge of the community. Add to this the fact that in Reform marriages the *intention* clearly is to be according to the laws of Moses and Israel as the contracting parties understand it; then even the objection which some scholars made against the Marrano marriages falls to the ground. Here, in Reform marriages, there is the clear intention of marriage, of *Jewish* marriage. There is also the living together in the knowledge of the community. In that case, the wedding ceremony may be objected to by the Orthodox, but the *marriage* itself is absolutely valid according to Orthodox law.

This being the case, any Orthodox official who casts doubt on the validity of such marriage is not only callous to human considerations, but ignores the main development and tendency of Orthodox law.

There is a much more serious aspect to the whole question than the technical implications of the *halakhah* itself. It involves the unity and the integrity of the Jewish people, and also raises the problem of what should be the mutual relationship of Jewish groups who differ from each other in religious matters.

First of all, it must he realized that the Jewish legal tradition on marriage is so complicated and is such a melange of laws and customs that it is only too easy to cast aspersions on the validity or at least the propriety of almost any marriage. For instance, the marriages conducted in Orthodox synagogues in the United States and in England have been subject to bitter attack by those who are more extreme in their Orthodoxy or who give special weight to specific customs. As an example, though Maharil, of the fourteenth century in Mainz, conducted marriages in the synagogue, the overwhelming opinion of Orthodox authorities of the last century has been that it is absolutely forbidden to have marriages within the synagogue; they must be conducted elsewhere, preferably out of doors, or at least under an open skylight in order to fulfill Isserles' suggestion that marriages should be under the stars as a sign of blessing. Most of the marriages taking place in Orthodox synagogues in England and in America are thus open to serious objection.

Then further, modern Orthodox weddings generally take place in the presence of men and women sitting too "ether. This has been strongly denounced by many Orthodox authorities. Some rabbis turn over the task of reciting the seven blessings to some bystander in order not to recite them in a mixed company. What about the witnesses at these Orthodox marriages? Is the rabbi sure that they are valid witnesses, truly kosher witness, and not violators of the Sabbath, and so on (*Hoshen Mishpat* 34, 2, 3, 17 ff.)? If the mood of belligerence is permitted to hold sway, as it does in some quarters, then perhaps fifty percent of the Orthodox marriage in England and in America can be deemed improper.

In this regard Orthodoxy is indeed more vulnerable than we are, for to Orthodoxy no commandment is minor and all established customs have their importance. Ben Zion Uziel and also Hillel Posek, of Tel Aviv, both bitterly objected to the mood surrounding the breaking of the glass at weddings (*Mishptei Uziel* II, *Even Haezer*, p. 431; *Omer Hillel, Even Haezer* 59). But both indicated that they dared not abolish this aged custom. How, then, can Orthodox rabbis permit the modern custom of holding marriages in the synagogue or in the midst of a mixed company of men and women, and with witnesses of dubious eligibility

Our own attitude to these variations of observance in both Orthodox and Reform Judaism is based on our general attitude to Jewish tradition. We respect the spirit of both Bible and *halakhah*, but we seek to find this spirit according to our conscience and judgment, rather than to be bound by specific enactment. We ask ourselves, therefore: What is the spirit of Jewish law in relation to variant types of marriage and the families derived from such variant marriages?

To discover the basic mood of Jewish law, it is not sufficient to study one enactment or another; we must cover whole sections of the law to see if there is one prevalent mood, or a tendency toward a certain consistency. Let us consider, for example, an extreme case, the case of the Karaites. These people, unlike ourselves, are a separate sect, a separate community with no communal cooperation or fellowship with the rest of Israel They reject outright the entire rabbinic tradition. They have been hostile and have been met with hostility since the days of the Gaon Saadia almost down to our day. One would therefore think that this hostile sect, the occasion of so much controversy, would be rejected outright as a potential part of the Jewish people, that their marriages would be declared invalid and that any intermarriage with them would be prohibited unless after conversion. Certainly this would seem to be the case if one merely judges by the statement of Moses Isserles (*Even Haezer* IV, 37) in which he says it is forbidden to enter into marriage with Karaites because all of them are under suspicion of bastardy and we do not even accept them if they wish to return. Actually this statement of Isserles is based upon one opinion, cited by Joseph Caro in his *Bet Joseph* from a responsum of Rabbi Samson. But this opinion of Rabbi Samson is only one opinion. There are contrary opinions of such various shades that the law of the marital status of Karaites is a vast confusion.

The fullest discussion of the question is found in the responsa of Jacob Castro, of Egypt (died 1610), who was greatly honored by Joseph Caro. In his response (*Ohalei Yaakov* 33)he quotes the various opinions of the great authorities on both sides of the question. An analysis of his large and complete responsum essay will reveal something of the spirit of the *halakhah* in this regard. It becomes clearly evident that the rabbis on both sides of the question are eager to find some way in which the Karaites might not be rejected. Those rabbis who say that Karaite marriage is not valid conclude from that statement that therefore their wives are not actually wives, that therefore there is no bastardy among them (since in Jewish law a bastard is the offspring of a *married* woman and a man not her husband), and that therefore we *may marry with them.* But those rabbis who say that we may not marry with them base it on the interesting ground that there *is* the suspicion of bastardy since their mothers *are* married women, in as much as Karaite marriages are *valid marriages,* if not by rabbinic law and custom, at least by Biblical law. In other words, both sides in dealing with this ancient enemy want in some way to continue the bond with them, either by permitting us to marry them or by declaring their marriages Biblically valid.

This reluctance to exclude Jews from the family fellowship of Israel is basic to the *halakhah* It can be seen still more clearly from the relationship of the law to an apostate (*mumar*). A *mumar* (which would include a public violator of the Sabbath) is ineligible as a witness, cannot be counted to a *minyan,* and so forth. He loses all his Jewish rights except one basic one, namely, his marital status. "His marriage is marriage and his divorce is divorce." This inalienable marital and family status of the apostate (whatever else he has lost) has in clearest expression in the resonsum of Saadia (*Otzar Hageonim, Yevamot,* pp. 1-7), in which he says that a man's status with regard to his trustworthiness as witness, and so on, depends upon his observance of the commandments, but his marriage rights and status depend upon his birth. Saadia ends his statement by saying firmly, “This is the law and one may not change it." In other words, whether a man is obedient or disobedient to the commandments can never invalidate his marriage and family rights.

This reluctance of Jewish legal tradition to invalidate marriages when such will break up the unity of our people has its august precedent in the relations of the school of Hillel and the school of Shammai to each other. They disagreed as to the permissibility of a certain form of levirate marriage. Then the Mishnah says, after stating the disagreement (*Yevamot* 1.4): "Although these forbade and those permitted these declared unfit and those declared eligible, nevertheless, the school of Shammai never hesitated to marry women from the school of Hillel nor did the school of Hillel hesitate to marry women from the school of Shammai." Bertenoro, to make the situation unmistakable, says, "Even though, according to the interpretation of one school the children of the marriages which they prohibited would be deemed *mamzerim*, the two groups nevertheless intermarried."

To sum up: If we keep from getting lost in the maze of separate enactments and customs and look for the basic spirit of our *halahic* tradition, we find from the days of the schools of Hillel and Shammai, through the Talmudic and Gaonic laws pertaining to apostates, and in all the complicated laws in regard to the hostile sect of Karaites, that the ruling spirit of the tradition was to maintain as much as possible the unity of our people.

Clearly, then, anybody or any group which seeks to declare another group of Jews unfit to marry with according to Jewish law is violating the basic tendency of the law. Even though certain specific requirements can serve to bolster their opinion, they themselves are not free from similar accusations upon the ground of their own violation of certain other enactments.

But the practical question is, how shall we react to thos embittered people who, in the heat of controversy, would break the family unity of our people there is no answer to this. Those who want to exclude will find reasons for it. We may face them, however, in the confidence that they will not succeed. We are part of the Jewish people. We share its destiny. We join in every great Jewish cause. No legalists will succeed in persuading the majority of Jews - Orthodox, Conservative, or Refom - that we must cease marrying one with another. We may leave the decision as to "Who is a Jew?" to the sound instinct of our people, which has expressed itself magnificently in the spirit of the *halakhah*: "Let the people of Israel alone [they will find their way]. If they are not prophets, they are certainly the children of prophets." (*Pesahim* 66a)

Solomon B. Freehof, *Recent Reform Responsa*, Cincinnati, 1963 # 42.

JEWISH MARRIAGE WITHOUT CHILDREN

Walter Jacob

QUESTION: Is it possible to have a valid Jewish marriage without children? Should a rabbi perform such a marriage when a couple specifically states that they plan to have no children? (Michael A. Robinson, Croton-on-Hudson, New York)

ANSWER: First, we should address the validity of a marriage without children. There is no doubt that procreation, companionship, joy, unity of the family, etc., are basic elements of marriage as seen by the Jewish tradition (Ket. 8a). Procreation was considered essential as already stated by the *Mishnah*: "A man may not desist from the duty of procreation unless he already has children." (Yev. 6.6) The Gemara to this concluded that a man may marry a barren woman if he has fulfilled this *mitzvah* of procreation, *as* in any case he should not remain unmarried (Yev. 61b). If the parties marry beyond the years when child-bearing is possible, or if one of them is sterile the same wedding blessings are, nevertheless, recited (Abudraham, *Birkhot Erusin* 98a) There was a difference between the schools of Hillel and Shammai about what was required to fulfill the *mitzvah* of procreation. The tradition followed Hillel, who minimally required a son and daughter, yet the codes all emphasize the need to produce children beyond that number (Tos. Yev. 8; *Yad, Hil. Ishut*, 15.6; *Shulhan Arukh, Even Ha-ezer* 1.5).

Tradition emphasized the need for a greater number of children as the fulfillment of two Biblical verses: Is. 45:18, "He created the world for habitation *(lashevet)*," and Eccl. 11:6, the obligation to sow seed in the evening *(la-erev)* as well as in he morning. In other words, one should constantly expand the Jewish population (Yev. 62a,b) This was also in keeping with the thought that before the Messiah could come, all the souls waiting for bodies will have to be placed into the world *(ibid.;* Nidda 13b) During our entire history, persecution and natural disaster have decimated our people, and so repopulation has always been emphasized. Lack of children was considered grounds for divorce after a decade of childless marriage, but Isserles indicated that nowadays we do not force the issue and permit the couple to remain together (Isserles to *Shulkhan Arukh, Even Ha-ezer* 1.3 and 8; also Isserles to 154.10) This was particularly true if the man had already had children by a previous marriage. All of this makes it clear that children were considered essential to a marriage, and it was considered desirable to have a large number of children, but a marriage without them was also condoned (Abraham di Boton, *Lechem Mishneh* to *Yad, Hil. Ishut* 4.10; Yair Hayyim Baharach, *Havat Yair,* #221)

The strictest interpretation of the traditional *halakhah* which makes a distinction between the obligations of men and women (a distinction not accepted by Reform Jews) would allow a woman to marry a sterile male, since the obligation of procreation was not incumbent upon her. When the husband or wife was sterile and it was not possible to have children, the marriage was always considered valid *(bedi-avad);* i.e., since it had been entered in good faith, it need not be terminated as mentioned earlier This was stressed by Maimonides who considered such a marriage valid under any circumstances *(Yad, Hil. Ishut* 4.10), whether the individual was born sterile or was sterilized later. Later authorities went somewhat further, and Yair Hayyim Bacharach stated that as long a the prospective wife realized that her prospective husband was infertile, though sexually potent, and she had agreed to the marriage, it was valid and acceptable *(Havat Yair,* #221). Isaac b. Sheshet *(Responsa,* #15) permitted a couple who knew that they would not have children to become married As long as both were fully aware of the situation, it was permissible, even *lehat-hilah*

In sum, the traditional attitude was as follows: Our tradition encourages marriage for the purpose of procreation and would strongly urge all couples to have children. However, if they enter the marriage fully aware of the refusal of one or the other to have children - either because of a physical defect or because of an attitude - the marriage can be considered valid, either *lehat-hilah* or *bedi-vad.* Nothing should prevent a rabbi from conducting such a marriage; although some rabbis would refuse to officiate. In light of the Holocaust and the current diminution of the world Jewish population, it is incumbent upon each of us to urge Jewish couples to have two or more children. Although young people may marry reluctantly and late, the marriage at least represents a step in the direction of children.

In Jewish law, the marriage is valid, yet given the Reform emphasis on the underlying spirit of the law as a guide to modern practice, marriage without children is very distant from the Jewish ideal of marriage. The letter of the law may permit it, but we must encourage every couple to have at least two children.

Walter Jacob, *American Reform Responsa*, New York, 1982, #132 permitted [illegible] who know [illegible] would not have [illegible] become married. As long as [illegible] fully aware of the situation [illegible] was permissible [illegible]

In [illegible] Sanhedrin [illegible] allows [illegible] encourage[illegible] marriage for the purpose of procreation [illegible] strongly [illegible] couples to have children. However, if [illegible] marriage [illegible] of the refusal or [illegible] either because of a physical defect [illegible] marriage can be considered valid [illegible] Nothing should prevent a rabbi [illegible] would [illegible] In light of [illegible] current dim[illegible] world Jewish population, it is incumbent upon each of us to [illegible] couples to have [illegible] more children [illegible] young people [illegible] reluctantly and [illegible] the marriage at least represents a step [illegible]

In Jewish law, the marriage [illegible] given the [illegible] emphasis on the underlying spirit [illegible] guide [illegible]

MARRIAGE AFTER A SEX-CHANGE OPERATION

Walter Jacob

QUESTION: May a rabbi officiate at a marriage of two Jews, one of whom has undergone a surgical operation which has changed his/her sex?

ANSWER: Our responsum will deal with an individual who has undergone an operation for sexual change for physical or psychological reasons. We will presume (a) that the operation is done for valid, serious reasons, and not frivolously; (b) that the best available medical tests (chromosome analysis, etc.) will be utilized as aids; and (c) that this in no way constitutes a homosexual marriage.

There is some discussion in traditional literature about the propriety of this kind of operation. In addition, we must recall that tradition sought to avoid any operation which would seriously endanger life (*Yoreh De-ah* 116; Hulin 10a). The *Mishnah* dealt with the problem of individuals whose sex was undetermined. It divided them into two separate categories, *tumtum* and *androginos*. A *tumtum* is a person whose genitals are hidden or undeveloped and whose sex, therefore, is unknown. R. Ammi recorded an operation on one such individual who was found to be male and who then fathered seven children (Yev. 83b). Solomon B. Freehof has discussed such operations most recently; he permits such an operation for a *tumtum*, but not for an *androginos* (*Modern Reform Responsa*, pp.128ff). The *androginos* is a hermaphrodite and clearly carries characteristics of both sexes (M. Bik. IV. 5). The former was a condition which could be corrected and the latter, as far as the ancients were concerned, could not, so the *Mishnah* and later tradition treated the *androginos* sometimes as a male, sometimes as a female, and sometimes as a separate category. However, with regard to marriage, the *Mishnah* (Bik. IV.2) stated unequivocally: "He can take a wife, but not be taken as a wife like men." If married, they were free from the obligation of bearing children (*Yad, Hil. Yibum Vahalitzah* 6.2), but some doubted the validity of their marriages (Yev. 81a; *Yad, Hil. Ishut* 4.11; also *Sh.A., Even Ha-ezer* 44.6). The Talmud has also dealt with *ailonit*, a masculine woman, who was barren (*Yad, Hil. Ishut* 2.4; Nid. 47b; Yev. 80b). If she married and her husband was aware of her condition, then this was a valid marriage (Yad, *Hil. Ishut* 4.11); although the ancient authorities felt that such a marriage would only be permitted if the prospective husband had children by a previous marriage, otherwise, he could divorce her in order to have children (Yev. 61 a; M. Yev. 24.1). Later authorities would simply permit such a marriage to stand.

We, however, are dealing either with a situation in which the lack of sexual development has been corrected and the individual has been provided with a sexual identity, or with a situation in which the psychological makeup of the individual clashed with the physical characteristics, and this was corrected through surgery. In other words, our question deals with an individual who now possesses definite physical characteristics of a man or a woman, but has obtained them through surgical procedure, and whose status is recognized by the civil government. The problem before us is that such an individual is sterile, and the question is whether under such circumstances he or she may be married. Our question, therefore, must deal with the nature of marriage for such individuals. Can a Jewish marriage be conducted under these circumstances?

There is no doubt that both procreation and sexual satisfaction are basic elements of marriage as seen by Jewish tradition. Procreation was considered essential, as is already stated in the *Mishnah*: "A man may not desist from the duty of procreation unless he already has children," The *Gemara* to this concluded that he may marry a barren woman if he has fulfilled this *mitzvah*; in any case, he should not remain unmarried (Yev. 61b). There was a difference between the Schools of Hillel and Shammai about what was required to fulfill the *mitzvah* of procreation. Tradition followed Hillel, who minimally required a son and a daughter, yet the codes all emphasize the need to produce children beyond that number (Tos., Yev. 8; *Yad, Hil. Ishut*

15.16, etc.). The sources also clearly indicate that this *mitzvah* is only incumbent upon the male (Tos., Yev. 8), although some later authorities would include women in the obligation, perhaps in a secondary sense (*Arukh Hashulkhan, Even Ha-ezer* 1.4; *Hatam Sofer, Even Ha-ezer*, #20). Abraham Hirsh (*Noam*, vol.16, pp.152ff) has recently discussed the matter of granting a divorce when one spouse has had a transsexual operation. Aside from opposing the operation generally, he also states that no essential biological changes have taken place and that the operation, therefore, was akin to sterilization (which is prohibited) and cosmetic surgery.

Hirsh also mentions a case related to our situation. A male in the time of R. Hananel added an orifice to his body, and R. Hananel decided that a male having intercourse with this individual has committed a homosexual act. This statement is quoted by Ibn Ezra in his commentary on Lev. 18:22. We, however, are not dealing with this kind of situation, but with a complete sexual change operation.

Despite the strong emphasis on procreation, companionship and joy also played a major role in the Jewish concept of marriage. Thus, the seven marriage blessings deal with joy, companionship, the unity of family, restoration of Zion, etc., as well as with children (Ket. 8a). These same blessings were to be recited for those beyond child-bearing age, or those who were sterile (Abudarham, *Birkhot Erusin* 98a).

Most traditional authorities who discussed childless marriages were considering a marriage already in existence (*bedi-avad*) and not the entrance into such a union. Under such circumstances the marriage would be considered valid and need not result in divorce for the sake of procreation, although that possibility existed (*Shulkhan Arukh, Even Ha-ezer* 23; see Isserles' note on 154.10). This was the only alternative solution, since bigamy was no longer even theoretically possible after the decree of Rabbenu Gershom in the 11th century in those countries where this decree was accepted. (Oriental Jews did not accept the *Herem* of Rabbenu Gershom). Maimonides considered such a marriage valid under any circumstances (*Yad, Hil. Ishut* 4.10), whether this individual was born sterile or was sterilized later. The commentator, Abraham di Boton, emphasized the validity of such a marriage if sterility has been caused by an accident or surgery (*Lehem Mishneh* to *Yad, Hil. Ishut* 4.10). Yair Hayyim Bacharach stated that as long as the prospective wife realized that her prospective husband was infertile though sexually potent, and had agreed to the marriage, it was valid and acceptable (*Havat Yair*, #221). Traditional *halakhah*, which makes a distinction between the obligations of men and women (a distinction not accepted by Reform Judaism) would allow a woman to marry a sterile male, since the obligation of procreation did not affect her (as mentioned earlier).

There was some difference of opinion when a change of status in the male member of a wedded couple had taken place. R. Asher discussed this, but came to no conclusion, though he felt that a male whose sexual organs had been removed could not contract a valid marriage (*Besamim Rosh*, #340 - attributed to R. Asher). The contemporary Orthodox R. Waldenberg assumed that a sexual change has occurred, and terminated the marriage without a divorce (*Tzitz Eliezer* X, #25). Joseph Pellagi came to a similar conclusion earlier (*Ahav Et Yosef* 3.5).

Perhaps the clearest statement about entering into such a marriage was made by Isaac bar Sheshet, who felt that the couple was permitted to marry and then be left alone, although they entered the marriage with full awareness of the situation (*Ribash*, #15; *Sh.A., Even Ha-ezer* 1.3; see Isserles' note). Similarly, traditional authorities who usually oppose contraception permitted it to a couple if one partner was in ill health. The permission was granted so that the couple could remain happily married, a solution favored over abstinence (Moses Feinstein, *Igerot Mosheh, Even Haezer*, #63 and #67, where he permits marriage under these circumstances).

Our discussion clearly indicates that individuals whose sex has been changed by a surgical procedure and who are now sterile may be married according to Jewish tradition. We agree with this conclusion. Both partners should be aware of each other's condition. The ceremony need not be changed in any way for the sake of these individuals.

Walter Jacob (ed.), *American Reform Responsa*, New York, 1983, # 137.

MARRIAGE OF A COHEN TO A DIVORCEE

Israel Bettan

QUESTION: There is a problem which I am trying to help a young couple solve. The young woman is a divorcee; the boy is a *kohen*. The man's father objects to the marriage. I wonder: Is there any argument, based on Jewish law, which I can use with the father to keep him from making his son's life miserable because of this marriage?

ANSWER: The status of the modern *kohen* has long been questioned by leading authorities in Jewish law. As early as the 14th century, Isaac ben Sheshet differentiated between the ancient priest and the modern *kohen* in no uncertain terms. He contended that the *kohen* of his time, lacking any documentary evidence of his rightful claim to the priestly title, owed his special privileges and obligations, not to the express mandate of the law, but rather to the force of custom or common usage: *"Kol sheken kohanim shebedorenu she-ein lahem ketav hayachas ela mipenei chezkatan nahagu hayom likro rishon batorah. Kohen afilu am ha-arets lifnei chacham gadol shebeYisrael" (Sefer Bar Sheshet, Responsum* 94, Lemberg, 1805).

Solomon Luria, the well-known 16th century authority, states it categorically that because of the frequent persecutions and expulsions of the Jews, the original priestly families, in most instances, failed to preserve the purity of their descent: *"Uva-avonoteinu, merov arichut hagalut, gezerot vegerushim, nitbalbelu. Vehalevai shelo yehe nitbalhel zera kodesh bechol, aval zera kohanim uleviyim karov levadai shenitbalbelu, ve-im lo kulo, harov nitbalbel" (Yam Shel Shelomo,* B.K., ch. 5, sec. 35).

Likewise, the author of the *Magen Avraham* assumes the impurity of the modern *kohen's* descent when he seeks to account for the doubtful status accorded him in the law: *"She-ein machazikin oto kechohen vadai dedilema nitchalela achat me-imotav" (Magen Avraham, Orakh Hayim, Hil. Pesah,* sec. 457).

Jacob Emden was so impressed with the questionable character of the *kohen's* claims that, while hesitating to invoke the power of the law, he urged upon the *kohen* the wisdom to refund the sum given him for the redemption of the first-born, and thus preserve his own moral integrity. Since he could not be sure of his priestly origin, Emden declared, the *kohen,* in keeping the redemption fee, ran the risk of pocketing money to which he had no legal claim: *"Nir-eh she-ein kohen yafeh lehafkia mamon bechezkato hageru-a. Vechim-at she-ani omer demidina tserichin lehachzir, ulefachot kol kohen yachush la-a tsmo lifrosh misafek gadol shems eino kohen" (She-elot Ya-avets,* part I, *Responsum* 155).

When, therefore, Reform Judaism chose to ignore the nominal distinction between the ordinary Israelite and the *kohen* - a distinction which has persisted to this very day - it did not so much depart from tradition as it did display the resolute will to surrender a notion the validity of which eminent Rabbinic authorities had repeatedly called in question.

Walter Jacob (ed.), *American Reform Responsa,* New York, 1983, #133.

ADULTERY AND MARRIAGE
Walter Jacob

QUESTION: One of the partners in a marriage has engaged in an adulterous relationship, and the marriage has terminated in acrimonious divorce. Subsequently, the adulterous party has asked the rabbi to officiate at the marriage to "the other person." Should the rabbi comply with the request?

ANSWER: The sources are clear in their prohibition of adultery (Ex. 20.13) and of marriage between the adulterous party and her lover (Sot. 27b; *Shulhan Arukh Even Haezer* 11.1, 178.17). The traditional statements, of course, deal primarily with the adulterous woman and her lover. They are very strict in this regard and even prohibit remarriage to her former husband, though she may not have been married to anyone else subsequent to the divorce *(Shulhan Arukh Even Haezer* 11.1). The prohibition against marrying her lover holds true not only after divorce but even after the death of her former husband (Yev. 24b *Shulhan Arukh Even Haezer* 11.1).

Despite these strictures the reality of the situation, which usually led the adulterous parties to live together and possibly to marry, brought rabbinic recognition of this status. Tradition gives its grudging consent by stating that if, nevertheless, the adulterous parties marry, they are not compelled to divorce *(Shulhan Arukh Even Haezer* 11.2 ff and commentaries, 159.3; *Otzar Haposqim Even Haezer* 11.1, 44).

A rabbi may, in this instance, find herself/himself in a difficult position as she is duty-bound to strengthen family life and defend the sanctity of marriage. If he/she, however, refuses to marry this couple, they may simply opt to live together, as is frequent in our time, that will not help their situation or the general attitude towards family life. Therefore, the rabbi should officiate at such a marriage, while at the same time discussing her own hesitation in keeping the tradition.

She/he may insist on some special counseling before the ceremony. He/she should insist that it be a simple ceremony and one which places special emphasis on the seriousness and sanctity of marriage.

Walter Jacob, *Contemporary American Reform Responsa*, New York, 1987, # 192.

CONCUBINAGE AS AN ALTERNATIVE TO MARRIAGE

Walter Jacob

QUESTION: Does Reform Judaism recognize concubinage as an alternative to formal marriage? If a man cannot or does not wish to divorce his disabled wife may his "arrangements" with another woman be formalized? Can formal Jewish status be give to two retired individuals living together without marriage? Can these "arrangements" be formalized in a manner akin to the ancient form of concubinage? (CCAR Family Life Committee)

ANSWER: Each of the arrangements suggested by the question is clearly illegal and violates the laws of all the states within he United States and of the provinces of Canada. Therefore, no rabbi can formalize such an arrangement through a Jewish ceremony. Since the Paris Sanhedrin of 1807, we have recognized the supremacy of State in matter of marriage (See M.D. Tama, *Transactions of the Parisian Sanhedrin*, pp 133ff). This has been accepted by most modern Jews. It would be helpful, however, to discuss briefly the forms of marriage and concubinage. We should understand that concubinage in Biblical times seems to have referred solely to wives in addition to the primary wife. From the Hellenistic period on, a concubine could be any wife of lower status. As is well known, rabbinic tradition recognized three forms of entering a full marriage. Consent was, of course, always necessary *(Shulhan Arukh, Even Haezer* 42.1), and all three forms were combined in the Jewish concept of marriage as developed during the Middle Age.

The three ways of effecting a marriage cited by the *Talmud* are:through a document, through money, or by intercourse (Kid. 2a; *Shulhan Arukh, Even Ha-ezer* 25.4)

(a) The most common form featured a deed witnessed by two competent individuals and handed by the groom to the bride (Kid. 9a; *Shulhan Arukh, Even Ha-ezer* 32.14) This has remained the essential covenant of the modern wedding. The deed is the modern *ketubah* signed by two witnesses.

(b) In addition, it was possible to effect a marriage through the transfer of an item of value *(kesef)* in the presence of two competent witnesses. This remains as part of the modern wedding in the form of presenting a ring or for us exchanging rings with the formula *"Harei at mekudeshet....."* (Kid. 2a,b; *Shulkhan Arukh, Even Haezer* 27.1)

(c) Finally, marriage can be effected through intercourse *(bi-a)* preceded by a statement indicating the wish to take this woman as wife and with two witnesses who saw the couple leave for a private place (Kid. 9b; *Shulhan Arukh, Even Ha-ezer* 33.1). This last method was severely frowned upon by the Rabbis, but *bedi-avad* it was valid. Marriage simply through intercourse with proper intent would be akin to "common law" marriage.

There is an additional form of marriage - the concubinage *(pilegesh) -which* needs to be discussed. Concubines were mentioned fairly frequently in the Biblical literature, especially for kings (II Sam. 3:7, 21:8ff, 5:13; I Kings 11:3; II Chron. 11:21, etc.). These references dealt with women who possessed the status of an inferior wife. We should remember that the nature of concubinage changed radically from the Biblical period to the Greco-Roman period (Louis Epstein, "The Institution of Concubinage Among Jews," *Proceedings of the American Academy for Jewish Research,* vol. 6, pp. 153ff) Epstein has pointed out that the status of the Biblical concubine was determined by the ancient Near Eastern corporate family with the head of the household *(ba-al)* possibly consorting with wives at various levels, from his main wife to a slave girl. The legal relationship of the half-dozen subsidiary wives is no longer clear to us. According to some ancient codes, the *pilegesh* was second to the main wife and had definite rights as did her children. This was also her status in ancient Israel. The custom of concubinage died out during the late Biblical period, according to Epstein, and was then reintroduced among the Hellenistic Jews of the Roman Empire into a family structure which was no longer corporate, but monogamous. Among the Romans and Greco-Roman Jews, the *pilegesh* became a mistress of doubtful legal status, and in Roman law had no legal status. Nevertheless, concubinage became an accepted institution during this period, and was carried over into the Christian era; concubines were, frequently found among the ruling and upper classes well as among Christian priests. This was the form of concubinage known to the Talmud and the medieval Jewish literature, and it was read back into the Biblical period.

In the Talmud, according to R. Judah, quoting Rav the difference between a wife and a concubine was that the latter had neither *kiddushin* nor *ketubah* (San. 21a Maimonides, *Yad, Melakhim* 4.4, and commentaries to this section) However, according to the Palestinian Talmud a concubine had *kiddushin,* but no *ketubah* (Yerushalmi Ket. 5.2; 29b) The former, not the latter, definition was generally followed by most of the authorities (Caro to *Yad, Melakhim* 4.4; de Boton to *Yad, Melakhim;* Radbaz *Responsa,* vol. IV, #225, V1. VII, #33; Adret, *Responsa* vol;. IV, #314). However, Rashi, Ribash, *Maggid Mishnah,* and others followed the latter. The two definitions may refer to two levels of concubinage, as will be discussed later, or they may reflect errors in the original Talmudic text (G. Ellinson, *Nisu-in Shelo Kedat Mosheh VeYisra-el, pp.* 40ff) The sources clearly indicated that we are dealing with an individual of intermediate status who did not have all the rights of a married wife, but on the other hand was not to be considered as a prostitute either.

Maimonides protested vigorously against concubinage, and sought to eliminate it by claiming that it was a right limited to royalty and not permitted to ordinary Jews *(Yad, Melakhim* 4.4) The woman was, therefore, to be considered a prostitute *(zona),* and both she and the male involved could be whipped *(Yad, Ishut* 1.4). Jacob b. Asher and Caro later also prohibited concubines *(Tur* and *Shulhan Arukh, Evan Ha-ezer,* 26.1 and 2.6) This prohibition was accepted by most Jews, but not all. Concubines were permitted by many Spanish and Provencal authorities - such as Abraham ben David, Abulafia, R. Jonah, A. Nissim, R. Adret, R Asher Meiri, etc. (Ellinson, *Op. Cit.*, p. 54) - although they disagreed of their precise status. Nahmanides also accepted concubines *(Responsa,* #284; commentary to Gen. 25:6), although he warned against the moral evil involved Concubines were discussed in the Middle Ages among both Sefardic and Ashkenazic Jews, and were often considered outside the *herem* of R. Gershom *(Tzeida Laderekh* III, #1, 2; Adret, *Responsa,* vol. I, #1205, IV, #314; Rabbenu Nissim, #68; Asheri, #37.1; Meir of Padua, #19; *Shulhan Arukh, Even Ha-ezer* 13.7; *Otzar Haposkim, Even Ha-ezer* 26.3ff). Isserles permitted concubines as long as they were careful about *mikveh* (Isserles to *Shulhan Arukh, Even Ha-ezer* 26.1). Most authorities previously cited based their prohibition and cautions on the Deuteronomic law prohibiting prostitution in Israel (Deut. 23:19ff; Lev. 19:29, 21:9)

The general mood of the Rabbinic authorities was to prohibit concubines or accept them only reluctantly. The latter position was partially the result of embarrassment about Biblical concubines. Concubinage was further restricted by the *herem* of Rabbenu Gershom *(Shulhan Arukh, Even Haezer* 1.10; *Arukh Hashulhan* 1.23) This ordinance prohibited the individual from marrying an additional wife, unless special permissions were provided by one hundred rabbis from three districts. It also prohibited a husband from divorcing a wife against her will. This ordinance has continued in force for Ashkenazic Jews, but was not made universally effective among Sephardic Jews until 1950 (Ben Zion Schereschewsky, *Dinei Mishpahah,* pp. 72ff) These decrees and their legal interpretations virtually eliminated concubinage. An exception to the general prohibition of concubinage was the 18th century Jacob Emden, who favored the institution as a way of increasing the population of the Jewish community (Emden, *She-elot Ya-avetz* II, 16)

The status of a concubine with *kiddushin,* but no *ketubah,* was as follows: Regarding adultery and incest, she was considered a wife; in financial matters, her consort's responsibility was limited, and he was obligated for neither maintenance nor ransom, but, if he became tired of her, he had to divorce her (Adret, *Responsa* V, #242).

A concubine actually needed no formal divorce (*get*), but some felt hat tor the sake of public appearance, she should have a *get.* If the man with whom she lived did not wish it, or had simply disappeared, she could remarry without a *get* (*Shulhan Arukh, Even Ha-ezer* 26, 26.1). The children of a concubine bore no blemish and possessed all the rights of other children, i.e., inheritances etc. (Adret, *Responsa,* vol. IV, #14, 315) A concubine who entered the relationship without *kiddushin* or *ketubah* needed no divorce when the relationship ended; in fact, a man could simply give her to his son (Asheri, #32.1; Ribash, #395). This woman was simply a mistress; she could not be charged with adultery, although she could be flogged for lewd conduct, and she had no legal or financial standing.

All this would show that two forms of concubinage have existed in Jewish tradition till the beginning of the 19th century. Both of them were accepted only reluctantly *(bedi-avad).* The practice of concubinage was rare in northern Europe and became infrequent even in the Mediterranean basin after the 16th century. It continued to be discussed in the codes and in occasional responsa.

This discussion has clearly shown us that Judaism sought to remove the practice of concubinage and various authorities prohibited it. Only the Biblical example made it difficult to eliminate it entirely as a recognized form of marriage We cannot validate this form of marriage, as it violates our ideals of marriage and the laws of the states or provinces in which we live. It is contrary to the general development of Jewish law in the last eight hundred years.

Walter Jacob (ed.), *American Reform Responsa*, New York, 1983, # 133.

REFORM JUDAISM AND MIXED MARRIAGE
Walter Jacob

QUESTION: May a Reform rabbi officiate at a marriage between a Jew and a non-Jew? What is the attitude of Reform Judaism generally to such a marriage?

ANSWER: Reform Judaism has been firmly opposed to mixed marriages. This was true in the last century and in this century. At its New York meeting in 1909, the Central Conference of American Rabbis passed the following resolution: "The Central Conference of American Rabbis declares that mixed marriages are contrary to the tradition of the Jewish religion and should, therefore, be discouraged by the American rabbinate" (CCAR Yearbook, vol. 19, p. 170). This resolution was reaffirmed as part of a lengthy report in 1947 (CCAR Yearbook, vol. 57, p. 161). A considerably stronger resolution was passed in Atlanta in 1973. Its text reads as follows:

The Central Conference of American Rabbis, recalling its stand adopted in 1909 "that mixed marriage is contrary to the Jewish tradition and should be discouraged," now declares its opposition to participation by its members in any ceremony which solemnizes a mixed marriage.

The Central Conference of American Rabbis recognizes that historically its members have held and continue to hold divergent interpretations of Jewish tradition. In order to keep open every channel to Judaism and *K'lal Yisrael* for who have already entered into mixed marriage, the CCAR calls upon its members:

1. to assist fully in educating children of such mixed marriage as Jews;

2. to provide the opportunity for conversion of the non-Jewish spouse; and

3. to encourage a creative and consistent cultivation of involvements in the Jewish community and the synagogue. (*CCAR Yearbook*, vol. 83, p. 97)

These resolutions clearly state the position of the Reform

rabbinate in this matter. They reflect only the latest steps in the long struggle against mixed marriage which began in Biblical times and will now be traced as background for this resolution.

The Bible and Mixed Marriage

If we review the marriages of the Patriarchs, we can see that they went to considerable trouble to obtain wives within the family circle, presumably with individuals who would be friendly to the religious ideals which the Patriarchs held. It is clear that endogamous marriages were preferred to exogamous marriages: Abraham married his half-sister (Gen. 20:12); Isaac married Rebecca, the granddaughter of Abraham's brother and niece, his double first cousin once removed (Gen. 24:5); Jacob married Leah and Rachel, who also were his first cousins, the daughters of his mother's brother (Gen. 29:12); and Esau married Mahalat the daughter of Ishmael, his uncle, also a first cousin (Gen. 28:9). It is quite clear that Abraham wished Isaac to marry someone not a Canaanite; later Esau understood that the daughters of Canaan would not please his father, Isaac. There were many instances which demonstrated that endogamous marriages were preferred for religious, family, and national reasons.

It would be appropriate to look at the Biblical legislation against mixed marriage more closely. A prohibition against marriage with Edomites and Egyptians appeared in Deuteronomy 23:8-9. Children of such unions were not to be admitted into the congregation until the third generation. The Bible reported no marriages with Edomites, but mentioned a number of marriages with Egyptians and two involved problems. Leviticus 24:10-11 dealt with the son of an Israelite woman and an Egyptian father who became a blasphemer. Solomon married many foreign wives for the purpose of political alliance, and among them was a daughter of Pharaoh (I King 3:1, 9:16, 11:1). The Book of Kings specifically warned against these foreign wives: "You shall not enter into marriage with them, neither shall they with you, for surely they will turn away your heart after their gods (I Kings 11:2), which happened in the case of Solomon. Finally, there is a reference to Sheshan who married his daughter to Jarha, an Egyptian slave (I Chronicles 2:34). These three isolated incidents indicate that such marriages involved both male and female Egyptians.

Moabite and Ammonites were prohibited from being "admitted to the congregation of the Lord.....even in the tenth generation (Deut. 23:4). This statement contains no reference to mixed marriages. Negative references connected with mixed marriages to Ammonites were associated with Rehoboam, who was considered an evil king and his mother was Ammonite (II Chronicles 12:13); in addition, Joash was slain by assassins whose mothers were Ammonite and Moabite (II Chronicles 24:26). While the Israelites were in the desert, they consorted with Moabite women and were led astray after their gods (Num. 25:1ff)). In that same section we have a report of an Israelite who brought a Midianite woman into camp and was slain by a zealot. In both these instances the danger of other religious was decried. Ruth, a Moabite woman, demonstrated an opposing point of view as she became the antecedent of David (Ruth 4:18).

The most thorough Biblical injunctions were directly against mixed marriages with the seven Canaanite nations; so the Hittites, Girgashites Amorites, Canaanites Perizzites, Hivites, and Jebusites (Deut. 7:1; also Exodus 34:11) were prohibited. "You shall not intermarry with them and not give your daughters to their sons or take their daughters for your sons: (Deut. 7:3). A clear exception was made for a woman taken as prisoner of war (Deut. 21:11ff). After a period of delay, her captor could marry her; and the legislation made no comments of a religious nature, nor did it mention conversion. The Bible contains few references to proselytes (Is. 14:1; Esther 10:27).

When the Israelites entered Canaan, they intermarried with the local inhabitants and served other gods (Judges 3:6). The most striking example of such a mixed marriage was that of Samson and Delilah (Judges 14:1). She was a Philistine, and became responsible for his downfall. Later Solomon married many foreign women as part of royal alliances (I Kings 11:1ff), and they, too, led him astray in his old age. If we look at the subsequent record of the kings of Judah and Israel we may be surprised at the paucity of mixed marriages. Among the nineteen kings of Israel who ruled for two hundred forty-one years we find only Ahab, who was married to Jezebel (I Kings 16:31). Among the twenty kings of Judea who ruled for three hundred ninety-three years we have only Jehoram (II Chronicles 21:6), and possibly Jehosaphat (II Chronicles 18:1), whose mother's name may have been omitted because she was not an Israelite (Leopold Loew, "Eherechtliche Studien," *Gesammelte Schriften*, vol. 3, pp. 138ff.).

The Book of Proverbs contains a number of references against associating with loose or foreign women (Prov. 2:16-17, 5:3-20, 7:5-27). These are horatory statements, not prohibitions. The prophet Malachi denounced such marriages (Mal. 2:11).

The clearest statements against mixed marriage appeared at the end of the Biblical period in the days of Ezra and Nehemiah, when we find specific legislation prohibiting such marriages and demanding that Israelites separate themselves from foreign wives (Ezra 9:12, 10:10ff). Ezra scrutinized the marriages of the citizens of Jerusalem and neighboring villages. Considerable time was taken to complete this task against some opposition. A list of priests, Levites, and other Israelites who had intermarried and relinquished their foreign wives was provided (Ezra 10:18ff). Among those listed by Ezra as having engaged in intermarriage we find priests, ten Levites and eighty-six Judeans. The problem was not entirely solved as the same difficulty arose again in the days of Nehemiah, who railed against those who had taken wives from Ashdod, Ammon, and Moab. Nehemiah did not advocate the dissolution of these marriages, although he removed the son of a High Priest who had entered such an alliance.

Each of these statements prohibiting mixed marriage was subjected to detailed Talmudic discussion, which provided a totally different interpretation. We should remember that all of these Biblical statements which dealt with mixed marriage or prohibited it, did not declare such a marriage invalid. That thought was foreign to the Bible and did not appear until a later period.

Hasmonean and Hellenistic Period

Mixed marriages were discussed by the *Book of Jubilees,* which opposed them with the same vigor as Ezra and Nehemiah earlier. In it, Abraham, and later Rebeccah, condemn marriages between Israelites and Canaanites (Jub. 20:4, 25:1). This theme also continued in later portions of the book (Jub. 22:16ff) Those who permitted their daughters to marry Gentiles were to die through stoning and the daughters through fire (Jub. 30:7ff). There could be no atonement for this sin, and the act was considered akin to presenting the child to Moloch.

The *Book of Maccabees* reported mixed marriages as part. of the general pattern of assimilation to the Hellenistic culture and condemned them (I Macc. 1:5, 11:18). The *Prayer of Esther,* an interpolation to the Biblical Esther, stressed her detestation "of the bed of the uncircumcised and of any alien." It was only necessity which brought her into the palace and into her position *(Prayer of Esther*, 115f). Charles considered this and other additions as dating from the first century of our era or earlier.

The same reluctance to engage in public intercourse or

marriage with non-Jews was reflected in Josephus' tale of Joseph, who loved a pagan actress (Josephus, *Antiquities* XII, 4.6); he was eventually tricked into marrying the Jewish daughter of his own brother. Further evidence of mixed marriage is provided by some of the papyri (Tcherikover, *Hellenistic Civilization and the Jews*, p. 70). Those who left Judaism and probably were motivated by the desire to marry Gentiles were also vigorously denounced in Egypt by Philo (*Moses* I, 147) and by the author of *III Maccabees* (7:10ff).

Talmudic Period

The vast literature of the Talmud contains few discussions concerning mixed marriage. Each of the Biblical statements cited in the earlier section provided a basis for further development Every effort was made to create a protective wall against the outer pagan world and to shield Jews from contact with non-Jews. During the most restrictive periods, non-Jewish bread, wine, and oil were prohibited, and anything cooked by non-Jews could not be consumed by a Jew (Avoda Zara 35b-38a); virtually all contact with non-Jews was prohibited (Nid. 34a; Shab 16b; Avoda Zara 36b). Naturally, this prohibition extended to casual sexual contact, and those who violated this injunction faced punishment without trial in the same fashion as imposed by Phinehas (Num. 25:7f; Avoda Zara 36b). If the parties involved went further and actually married, they were subject to whipping (Avoda Zara 36b; Kid. 6b; *Yad, Isurei Bi-a* 12.1).

Not all the Talmudic authorities and not all periods were as restrictive as those previously cited and, and the exchange of food, as well as social intercourse, with non-Jews was allowed but the basic wall of separation remained (Avoda Zara 57a, 58b, and 59a).

The most significant change made during this period was the declaration of invalidity of mixed marriages. This remained a dictum of rabbinic literature (Mishna, Kid. 6b, 68b). This Talmudic tractate provides a long list of marriages which are null and void as no *kiddushin* is possible. This new view may have reflected an internal Jewish development, or it may have been influenced by Roman law (Boaz Cohen, *Jewish and Roman Law*, vol. I, pp. 339f).

The Biblical laws against intermarriage were reinterpreted sometimes more strictly, and on other occasions leniently. The Schools of Hillel and Shammai expanded the list of nations excluded from intermarriage beyond the seven peoples of Canaan, to include all pagans. Simeon ben Yochai agreed with this interpretation (Avoda Zara 36b).

A very strict view was taken by Rava, who felt that the prohibition against the seven nations continued after their conversion. This was one of the many attempts to maintain absolute family purity. It meant that intercourse or marriage with pagans was seen as prohibited from a biological or racial point of view; it was *zenut*, and would be punished through whipping (Yev. 76a; *Yad, Isurei Bi-ah* 12.1).

Part of the strong feeling against mixed marriages was reflected in a general emphasis on family purity. It existed from the time of Ezra and Nehemiah to the destruction of the Temple. The loss of records at that time and in the later revolt of Bar Kochba made such genealogical practices difficult. The long genealogical lists in *Chronicles* reflected the mood, as did the Mishnaic concern with *mamzerim* and *netinim*. Degrees of family purity were established for various Israelites (Kid. 71b, 75aff). Such laws of purity were especially enforced for the priesthood (Kid. 66a, 76a, 77a).

The Tannaitic interpretation of the prohibition against marrying Ammonites and Moabites was limited to males, and did not extend to females - provided that they converted to Judaism. They could marry a native Israelite in the third generation (M., Yev. 8.3; Yev. 76bf). Rabbi Simeon sought to apply the same principle to Egyptians. Another *mishnah* simply declared that Ammonites could no longer be clearly identified since the days of Sennacherib (M.,Yadayim 4.4; Ber. 28a; *Yad, Isurei Bi-a* 12.25)

Deuteronomy had prohibited Egyptians and Edomites until the third generation, and in this case there was no tradition to make marriages with females possible after conversion, while excluding males. Although Rabbi Simeon sought to establish such a practice (M. Yev. 8.3; Yev. 76b, 77b), but his view was not accepted. If the Egyptians and Edomites converted, they were not permitted to marry born Jews until the third generation (*Yad, Isurei Bi-ah* 12.19).

Others rejected these interpretations, so Rav Asi stated that the century-long mingling of pagans and Jews in Babylonia meant that many might be descendants of the ten lost tribes. One could marry them without conversion or any other step, as they were Jews of doubtful status (Yev. 16b, 17a).

Similarly, Sennacherib so mixed the nations that it was no longer possible to tell who belonged to the seven prohibited peoples. This meant that they were eligible for conversion and acceptance as Jews (M. , Yadayim 4.4). Rabbi Judah and Rabbi Johanan simply stated that Gentiles outside of the land of Israel were not idolaters, but bIndly followed the habits af their fathers, so matters of belief were no longer at issue, nor was there a danger of being led astray by them (Avoda Zara 65a; Hulin 13b). The principle of population mixture could be applied to Egyptians and Edomites also, and there was some Talmudic discussion about this (M., Yadayim 4.4; Tos., Kid. 5.5; *Yad, lsurei Bi-a*h 12.25).

In general, the Talmudic period expanded the prohibition

against intermarriage so that it included all pagan people. Restrictions against specific nations were eliminated. This meant that they, as well, as any other pagan, could convert to Judaism and thus become part of the Jewish people. If this occurred without ulterior motive, but simply because of an attraction to Judaism, then the convert - no matter what his national origin - was treated as any other Jew.

The Talmudic invalidation of all mixed marriages meant that an insurmountable wall had been erected between the Jewish and pagan communities. As marriage to a pagan was simply not recognized (*einan tofsin*), that family unit did not exist as far as the Jewish community was concerned, and was effectively excluded from the community. The union had no Jewish legal status in the various Christian communities. It was then unlikely that such unions would occured with any degree of frequency.

The Middle Ages

The discussion of mixed marriage continued into the Gaonic period. The responsa of the Gaonim show some incidence of mixed marriage. The prohibitions of the Talmudic period were extended with further discussion about their implications but without substantial changes (B. Lewin, *Otzar Haga-onim*; Yev. 48b; Kid. 22b, 66b, 68b, etc.). In these instances both casual intercourse and long-term relations with servants, concubines, or wives were contemplated. We should recall that interdictions toward mixed marriage were expressed with equal vigor by Christians; this occurred frequently during the Middle Ages. The statements generally followed the pattern of those of the Council of Orleans, adopted in 538 C.E., which declared:

Christians quoque omnibus inerdicimus, ne Judaeorum

conjugiis misceantur: quod si, fecerint, usque ad sequestrationem, quisquis ille est, communione pellatur. Item Christianis convivia interdicimus Judaeorum; in quibus si, forte fuisse probantur, annuali excommunicationi pro hujusmodi contumacia subjacebunt. (Ephraim Feldman, "Intermarriage Historically Considered," *CCAR Yearbook*, vol. 19, p. 300).

Similar prohibitions can be found expressed by Church Councils throughout the Middle Ages (Toledo, 589; Rome, 793; etc.). Their constant renewal may point to a continuing series of mixed marriages, or it may indicate the Church's desire to reemphasize its hostility toward Jews and Judaism.

The highest rate of mixed marriage in the Middle Ages occurred in Spain, and we find reports of Gentile wives and concubines. Such relations were already reported in Visigoth Spain in the fifth, sixth, and seventh centuries. The Arian Christian Church did its best to halt them and frequently adopted statements of Church Councils, most to no avail (Georg Caro, *Sozial und Wirtschaftsgeschichte der Juden*, vol. I, 85ff, II, 225ff). Various forms of illicit relationships between Jews and Christians were reported (Adret, *Responsa* I, 1187, IV, 257; Asher, *Responsa* VIII, 10; Baer, *Die Juden im Christlichen Spanien*, "Urkunden und Regesten" I, 171, 442). We should remember that stiff penalties for such illicit intercourse were also imposed by Christians; it could mean death by fire (Baer, *Die Juden im Christlichen Spanien*, "Urkunden und Regesten" II, 125, no. 72; Asher, *Responsa* VIII, 10; Baer, *Ibid.*, I, 456, 1037-1038, II, 63, p. 48). As such transgressions could endanger the entire Jewish community, they were dealt with severely by Jewish authorities (*Zikhron Yehudah*, #80, 91). A considerable number of cases of adultery and intercourse between Gentiles and Jewish women was reported in the responsa literature (*Adret,* I, 1187, 1250, IV, 257; Asher, *Responsa* VIII, 10, XVIII, 113). We also find occasions of intercourse between master and slave, presumably non-

Jewish (Adret, *Responsa* I, 7.10, 6.28, 12.05, IV 3.14; Asher, *Responsa* XXXII, 13, 15). The medieval authorities, like their Talmudic predecessors, made some distinction between relationships with Gentile men or women. Although they prohibited such relationships with both, they tended to be a little more lenient if it was between a Gentile and a Jewess, as the possible offspring of such a union would be Jewish (Rashba to Kid. 21a in *Otzar Haposkim*, p. 253). An anonymous Spanish rabbi commanded, "You should proclaim a ban with the sounding of a horn against anyone who would have intercourse with a Gentile woman. He that is found to have done so should be severely punished, since many children have been born to Jews by their non-Jewish maid-servants." (*Zikhron Yehudah*, #91) Zakuta reported that some Jews killed during the persecution of 1391 were actually slain by their own Christian sons born to Christian women (*Yohasin*, ed. Filiopowski, 225a). These conditions were endemic to Spanish Jewry and continued after the expulsion in the lands to which Jews fled (David ben Zimri, *Responsa* I, 48, 409, III, 443, 520). Moses of Coucy succeeded in getting a number of Spanish coreligionists (about 1236) to set aside their Christian or Moslem wives (*Semag, Lo Ta-aseh* 112). Loew has suggested that these marriages probably referred to concubines (Loew, *Op. Cit.*, vol. III, p. 176). Isaac Aramah (*Akedat Yitzhak*, #120, etc.) denounced irregular sexual unions in his sermons. He may have painted an excessively gloomy picture, but was certainly dealing with a real problem.

Among the Spanish authorities we should also mention Simon of Duran, who dealt with Jews who had more casual relationships with Gentile women (Radbaz, *Responsa* III, 158), and Solomon Adret, who reported relationships and concubinage with Moslem women (*Responsa* V, #242) with some frequency.

Medieval Egypt seems to have been an exception to the continuing problem of mixed marriage. S.D. Goitein (*A Mediterranean Society,* vol. II, pp. 277f) reported no such marriages in the Geniza material without conversion. Marriages between Karaites and Jews were mentioned, but none between Moslems and Jews.

Mixed marriages also occurred in Northern Europe although there less data is available (G. Caro, *Op. Cit.*, I, 57, 70, 94, II, 224). In contrast numerous instances of mixed marriage and sexual relationships with non-Jews were reported during the Renaissance in Italy (Cecil Roth, *The Jews and the Renaissance*, pp. 45ff, 344ff).

The *halakhic* literature of the Middle Ages which prohibited mixed marriage had to concern itself with the status of Moslems and Christians, who were not pagans. The pattern for a new attitude toward these monotheistic religions had already been set by R. Johanan (third century) , who stated that Gentiles outside the Land of Israel were not to be considered as idolaters, but merely as people who followed the practices of their ancestors (Hul. 13b). Non-Jews could, therefore, be subdivided into three categories: (a) idol worshipers, (b) Gentiles outside of Israel, who simply continued the habits of their ancestors, and (c) Gentiles who observed the seven Noahide commandments, which included the prohibition of idol worship. Maimonides considered Christians and Moslems in the second of the above categories (Commentary on M., Avoda Zara 1.3; Zimmels, *Op. Cit.*, p. 208. On other occasions he went even further and categorized Christians and Moslems as *benei noah*. In that category they assisted the preparation for the Messianic era (*Yad Hil. Melakhim* 11.4). The Tosafists of Northern Europe generally included Christians among the *benei noah* (Tos. to Avoda Zara 2a), but occasionally also saw them as simply following the practices of their ancestors (responsum by Gershom b. Judah Meor Hagola). Rashi had come to a similar conclusion, quoting the Gaonim (Tos.,

Avoda Zara 2a, 57b). There were some variations in the outlook adopted toward Christians or Moslems, depending on the economic and social circumstances of the Jewish communities, as well as on the distinction between Ashkenazim and Sephardim.

This new and friendlier outlook towards Christians and Moslems had definite limits, both in commenrcial transactions and in communal festivities. (Tos. to Avoda Zara 57b; *Yak, Hil. Ma-akhalot Asurot* 40.7; Ribash, *Responsa,* 255, 256; Moses Schick, *Responsa, Yoreh Deah* 15). The restrictions definitely prohibited both sexual relations with non-Jews and mixed marriage. Marriages of Jews with Christians or Moslems were clearly prohibited by Maimonides and others (*Yak, Hil. Ishut* 4.15; *Hil. Isurei Bi-ah* 12.1; *Hil. Melakhim* 8.7; *Tur, Even Ha-ezer* 16.1; *Shulhan Arukh, Even Ha-ezer* 16.1, 44.9).

All the medieval codes contain the Talmudic prohibition against mixed marriage. The codes differed in their interpretation as to whether the prohibition represented a Biblical or Rabbinic ordinance (based on Yev. 76a) . Maimonides considered it Biblical, while Jacob ben Asher in his *Tur* invalidated such marriages on Rabbinic rounds. The codes, like the Talmud, indicate definite punishment for intercourse with Christians or for mixed marriages. Thirty-nine lashes were prescribed for such intercourse, and if a man lived with a Gentile concubine, then the punishment was to be tripled (*Shulhan Arukh, Even Haezer* 16.1-2). In addition, the sinner was also to suffer divine punishment. Maimonides' code mentioned the Talmudic teaching that the slayer of a Jew engaged in intercourse with a non-Jew was not liable for punishment (*Yad Hil. Sanh.* 18.6).

Rabbi Simon of Duran reported that the government permitted the Jewish community to stone Jews who had illicit sexual relations with a non-Jewess (*Responsa* III, 158). The responsa not only reported a variety of forms of such relationships, but also tried to discover solutions. So, when unions between Jewish masters and Gentile slaves were reported (*Zikhron Yehudah*, 91, p. 44a; Baer, *Die Juden im Christlichen Spanien*, "Urkunden und Regesten," I, 164; #6), this was sometimes used to compel a master to liberate such a slave and convert her to Judaism. In those instances, she may have become his Jewish concubine (Adret, *Responsa* I, 12.19).

In the 18th century, when social barriers between Jews and non-Jews decreased in England, intermarriage increased. Coversions to Judaism were rarely permitted, so such individuals usually were married in the church. Intermarriage did not necessarily mean that the party wished to leave the Jewish community, but they had little choice, as they were inevitably expelled from the synagogue. Sometimes the children of such unions later converted to Judaism, and were brought back into the community. Although no numbers were provided, there were enough to be worth noting. (Albert M. Hyamson, *The Sephardim of England*, pp. 176ff). We find a similar phenomenon in France before and during the French Revolution (Z. Szajkowski, "Marriage, Mixed Marriages and Conversions among French Jews During the Revolution of 1789," *Jews and the French Revolutions of 1789, 1830 and 1848*, pp. 826ff). We can see from this essay that a goodly number of individuals who entered mixed marriages subsequently converted to Catholicism. All of these incidents have been cited to demonstrate the reality of the problem throughout the medieval period. The codes and legal literature attempted to halt the process, and generally succeeded, but never completely.

Conversion for the Sake of Marriage

Many non-Jews joined the Jewish community in the Biblical and early post-Biblical periods. However, formal conversion was first discussed by the Talmud, which required sincere motivation as a prerequisite. Sincere converts could, of course, marry Jews (*Shulhan Arukh, Even Ha-ezer* 4, 8-10). Those who converted for the sake of marriage or for the sake of wealth or power, or those who were prompted by greed, were not considered proper proselytes (Yev. 24b, 76a; *Shulhan Arukh, Yoreh De-ah* 268.12), but the matter is not quite as clear cut as it might seem, since various Biblical texts were interpreted as referring to conversion for the sake of marriage. This is how the captive woman (Deut. 21:13) was seen (Kid. 68b; Yev. 48a). Furthermore, prohibition against marriage with the Ammonite or a Moabite was limited to males, while females were permitted to be married immediately after conversion (Yev. 76b). Another statement in the same tractate held that we do not question the motivation of converts if they joined us during persecution or if they could gain no improvement of status by doing so (Yev. 24b). Others went even further; thus Hillel converted a Gentile who sought to become a High Priest (Shab. 31a), while Rabbi Hiya converted a woman who simply wished to marry a Jew (Men. 44a).

In the Middle Ages a major distinction concerning converts developed between the Spanish authorities and the Franco-German rabbis (B.Z. Wacholder, "Proselytizing in the Classical Halakhah," *Historia Judaica,* Vol. 20, 77ff). The form represented chiefly by Alfas and Maimonides, emphasized purity of purpose, and did not recognize any injunction to seek proselytes, a matter questioned by Simon ben Zemah of Duran (*Encyclopedia Talmudit* VI, p. 426). Therefore, only those who came with noble and lofty purposes were to be accepted (*Yak, Hil. Isurei Bi-a* 13.14ff). The Tosafists, on the other hand, stressed the commandment of seeking converts and were willing to do so even if not all the technical requirements could be met (Tosafot to Kid. 62b; Git. 88b, 109b; Yev. 45bff; *Or Zarua* II, 26a, 99). There were a fair number of converts during the Tosafist period despite the Church injunctions against conversions. So, Wacholder found twenty-five converts in the responsa of the 12th and 13th centuries (B. Z. Wacholder, "Cases of Proselytizing in the Tosafist Responsa," *Jewish Quarterly Review*, Vol. 51, pp. 288ff). A number of them were due to mixed marriages and were cited by Rabbenu Tam (Tos. to Ket. 3b; Yoma 82b) and Yehiel of Paris (Mordechai, San. 702; *Toledot Adam Vehava* 23.4). In addition, there were numerous converts among slaves of Jews, which in some cases involved sexual unions and concubinage.Social relationships, mixed marriage, and conversion remained a factor in Jewish life even in the most difficult periods of the Middle Ages. They led to conversions in both directions, with probably a larger number leaving Judaism than joining it. Any conversion could endanger the life of the convert his family, and in some instances the entire Jewish community (Jacob ben Moses, *Maharil*, 86b; J. R. Rosenblum, *Conversion to Judaism*, 74ff).

The issue of convertiong for marriage is discussed at length by Caro and Joshua Falk in their commentaries to the *Tur, Yoreh De-ah* 268). Caro concludes that some proselytes who convert for the sake of marriage may, nevertheless, be sincere; all depended on the judgment of the court (*hakol lefi re-ut beit din*). Falk concludes that such conversion would be accepted *bedi-avad*. There are, therefore, good grounds in tradition for acceptng such converts.

Modern Times

Mixed marriages occurred with increasing frequeny beginning in the latter part of the 18th century. This was true in all lands of Western Europe and in the United States. Szajkowski has shown that such marriages occurred among the obscure and the prominent during the French Revolution (Z. Szajkowski, *Op. Cit.*, pp. 826ff). Mixed marriagrs increased rapidly during the succeeding century as a number of careful studies have indicated (E. Schnurmann, *La Population Juive en Alsace*, pp. 87ff; N. Samter, *Judentaufen im Neunzehnten Jahrhundert*, pp. 86ff).

The largest incidence of mixed marriage and conversion to Christianity, in many cases, was found in the German-speaking lands of Central Europe. This began in the generation after Moses Mendelssohn, and occurred in the fashionable circles of the upper class as well as among those who sought upward mobility. Much has been written about Rachel Varnhagen and her intellectual circle, but we should note that the phenomenon also existed among those further down the social ladder. Eastern European Jews who settled in Central Europe in large numbers throughout the 19th century were equally involved in this phenomenon. If we look at the entire 19th century, we shall find that approximately ten percent of the Jewish population was intermarried (A. Ruppin, *The Jews in the Modern World*, pp. 157ff). The peercentage remaioned fairly stable throughout the century, but increased in the 20th century.

The lands of Eastern Europe and the Balkans were not entirely free from this problem although the numbers involved were smaller (Ruppin, *Op. Cit.*, p. 159).

We should remember that opposition to mixed marriages remained equally strong on the part of Catholics and Protestants granted concessions if the children were raised as Christians. The Catholic Church insisted that such marriages were not valid and that remarriage was necessary after conversion of the non-Catholic partner, although some changes in this view began to occur in 1821 (Leopold Loew, "Eherechtliche Studien," *Gesammelte Schriften*, vol. 3, pp. 194ff). Slowly intermarriage was legalized in modern European states. This occurred in Germany in 1875, in Hungary in 1895, and in Rumania a little later. In 1913 it was still prohibited in Austria, Russia, Spain, Portugal, and Islamic lands. Even within the Jewish community, marriages between sub-groups like Ashkenazim and Sephardim were rare in the 19th century.

Intermarriage was highest in lands where the number of Jews was small and where there was little discrimination, as in Denmark, Italy, Australia (Ruppin, *Op. Cit.*, p. 161). It reached 34.1% in Italy in 1881, while in New York in the same year it was one percent, as most Jews had settled there only recently. The figures in Germany between 1904-1908 were 22.2%. It should be noted that the authorities in pre-World War I Hungary stipulated that those about to "contract a mixed marriage can make an arrangement as to the religion they wish their children to have. In the absence of such an agreement, the sons follow the religion of the father, the daughters that of the mother" (Ruppin, *Op. Cit.*, p. 177).

The pattern of increasing mixed marriage, which was noted for England in the 18th century, grew especially with the establishments of civil marriages in 1837. Before that time Jews who married Christians were forced to do so in the Church (C. Roth, "The Anglo-Jewish Community in the Context of World Jewry," *Jewish Life in Modern Britain*, pp. 83ff; S. J. Prais and M. Schmool, "Statistics of Jewish Marriages in Great Britain," *Jewish Journal of Sociology*, IX, no. 2).

Such marriages were also found with fair frequency in early America (M. Stern, "Jewish Marriage and Intermarriage in the Federal Period 1776-1840," *American Jewish Archives*, vol. 19, pp. 142ff; J. Goldstein, *A Century of Judaism in New York*, pp. 328ff; H. B. Grinstein, *The Rise of the Jewish Community of New York, 1654-1860*, pp. 372ff). Studies for the mid-20th century indicated an increasing rate of mixed marriage, which has now reached approximately thirty-five percent of all Jewish marriages. Accurate broad statistics are not available, but many specialized studies have been undertaken (Erich Rosenthal, "Studies of Jewish Intermarriage in the United States," *American Jewish Yearbook,* 1963, pp. 3ff; B. Kligfeld, "Intermarriage: A Review of the Social Science Literature on the Subject," *CCAR Yearbook*, Vol. 72, pp. 87ff; M. Davis, "Mixed

Marriage in Western Jewry," *Jewish Journal of Sociology* 10, pp. 197 ff; J. Rosenbloom, *Conversion to Judaism,* pp. 121ff).

The issue of mixed marriage was raised in a formal way by the Napoleonic Sanhedrin in 1806. Among the questions posed to this body was the following: "Can a Jewess marry a Christian, or a Jew a Christian woman, or has the law ordered that Jews should only marry among themselves?" As a result of the French Revolution, marriage and divorce had been made a concern of the State. Keenly aware of the implications, the Sanhedrin conducted lengthy discussions, in which reference was made to marriages between Jews and Christians which had taken place in France, Spain, and Germany and which had sometimes been tolerated by the rulers. The final answer stated: "The Great Sanhedrin declared further that marriages between Israelites and Christians, contracted according to the laws of the Code Civil, are civilly binding, and that, although they cannot be invested with religious forms, they shall not result in anathema." (Tama, *Transaction of the Parisian Sanhedrin*, transl. F. Kirwan, p. 155; G. Plaut, *The Rise of Reform Judaism*, pp. 71ff). The French text here simply declared civil marriages between a Jew and a non-Jew valid, but avoided the issue of religious marriage; the Hebrew text deemed such marriage religiously invalid (E. Feldheim, "Intermarriage Historically Considered," *CCAR Yearbook*, vol. 19, p. 296). The Napoleonic Sanhedrin here applied the legal principle *dina demalchuta dina* to civil marriage, without granting religious status. This Talmudic principle was constantly used for civil and criminal law, but never previously in matters of personal status. Some modern Orthodox authorities recognize such marriages, while others do not and therefore require no religious divorce for them (Abraham Freimann, *Seder Kiddushin Venisu-in*, pp. 362 ff; C. Ellinson, *Nisu-in Shelo Kedat Mosheh Veyisra-el*, pp. 170ff).

The Rabbinical Conference of Braunschweig in 1844 intended to endorse the statements of the Napoleonic Sanhedrin, but as no one possessed a copy of the resolution, it actually went further by stating: "The intermarriage of Jews and Christians and in general, the intermarriage of Jews with adherents to any of the monotheistic religions is not forbidden provided that the parents are permitted by the law of the state to bring up the offspring of such marriage in the Jewish faith." A motion was also made to permit rabbis to officiate at such marriages, but that was rejected, and so no Jewish authority was authorized to conduct such marriages. (For a summary of the debate, see W. G. Plaut, *The Rise of Reform Judaism*, pp. 220ff). The author of the general resolution, Ludwig Philipson, later changed his mind on this question (L. Philipson, *Israelitische Religionslehre*, vol. III, p. 350; Moses Mielziner, *The Jewish Law of Marriage and Divorce*, p. 48). Abraham Geiger similarly opposed mixed marriages (A. Geiger, *Referat ueber die der ersten Israelitischen Synode ueberreichten Antraege*, pp. 187ff). At the conference held in Breslau in 1846, Samuel Holdheim suggested that rabbis should officiate at mixed marriages, but this motion was rejected (*CCAR Yearbook*, vol. 1, p. 98). Resolutions calling for acceptance of civil marriage and marriages between Jews and Christians were introduced at the Leipzig Synod of 1869, but none were passed. The Synod of Augsburg (1871) stated that civil marriages were to be considered as valid (*CCAR Yearbook*, vol. 1, p. 113). None of the other rabbinical conferences held in Germany or in the United States during the last century passed resolutions on this subject; a number of individual rabbis dealt with the issue in essays and lectures. The radical David Einhorn called mixed marriage "a nail in the coffin of the small Jewish race" (*Jewish Times*, 1870). This citation was frequently quoted by others in the last century and in our own.

The Central Conference of American Rabbis has dealt with the question of mixed marriage extensively from its earliest days. Mendel Silber read a lengthy historical essay on the subject to the Conference in 1908 (Mendel Silber, "Intermarriage," *CCAR Yearbook*, 1908, p. 207). This represented part of the concern over the subject and the desire to establish a policy of the question. The following year a major portion of the Conference was dedicated to this subject with the presentation of two papers (E. Feldman, "Intermarriage Historically Considered," and S. Schulman, "Mixed Marriages in their Relation to the Jewish Religion," *CCAR Yearbook*, 1909). Both cited a considerable number of sources and reviewed the positions taken by various Reform groups in the 19th century. The discussion of the Conference indicated that all the rabbis present opposed mixed marriages, although some were wiling to officiate at them. The debate dealt with the freedom of the individual rabbis versus the power of the Conference and the general force of the rabbinic tradition. The debate on the subject dealt with the question itself and with the issue of rabbis officiating at such marriages. The resolution which was passed read:

"The Central Conference of American Rabbis declares that mixed marriages are contrary to the tradition of the Jewish religion and should, therefore, be discouraged by the American rabbinate."

There was no substantial additional discussion in the following years, but the matter was mentions peripherally in a lengthy paper by Kaufmann Kohler ("The Harmonization of the Jewish and Civil Laws of Marriage and Divorce," *CCAR Yearbook*, 1915, pp. 335ff). This essay made it clear that Reform Judaism accepts civil marriages as valid and does so in the case of mixed marriages as well.

The following decades saw some discussion of this subject in responsa of the Conference ("Forfeiture of Congregational Membership by Intermarriage," *CCAR Yearbook*, 1916, pp. 113ff; "Burial of Gentiles in a Jewish Cemetery," *CCAR Yearbook*, 1963, pp. 85ff), and those of Solomon B. Freehof in his various volumes. Fairly frequent articles in the *CCAR Journal* and elsewhere by Reform rabbis demonstrate continued concern; minor discussions of this question occurred at conferences through the years. It was not brought to the floor of the Conference again until 1947, when a lengthy report of a special committee under the chairmanship of Solomon B. Freehof proposed a set of recommendations with considerable annotations, which were adopted after some debate ("Report on Mixed Marriages and Intermarriage," *CCAR Yearbook*, pp. 158ff). The Conference reaffirmed the 1909 resolution on mixed marriage and then proceeded to deal with the specifics involved in mixed marriage through resolutions embodied in the report. These were as follows:

> II. The CCAR considers all sincere applicants for proselytizing as acceptable whether or not it is the intention of the candidate to marry a Jew.
>
> III. We consider civil marriage to be completely valid but lacking the sanctity which religion can bestow upon it. We recommend that whenever a civil marriage between Jews has taken place, it be followed as soon as possible by a Jewish religious marriage ceremony.
>
> IV. Since it is the point of view of the Conference that all sincere applicants for conversion be accepted whether marriage is involved or not, and since, too, we recognize the validity of civil marriages but urge that they be sanctified by a religious marriage ceremony, we surely would accept such a proselyte and officiate at the religious marriage. However, it should be clear that the fact that the couple is already married by civil law does not obviate the necessity of conversion of the Gentile party before the Jewish marriage service can take place.

V. The Conference may well take the stand that wherever the state acknowledges the validity of common law marriage, we likewise consider them to be valid; but that just as in cases of civil marriage we urge that they be changed to regular marriage by license and religious ceremony.

VI. We cannot take quite the same attitude which traditional law has taken inasmuch as marriage, especially in England and the United States, is not only church marriage; it has also, to some extent, the status of civil marriage, at least to the extent that the license to marry was issued by the state. Nevertheless, in this case, the mood of the traditional attitude must determine our point of view. We cannot declare such a marriage invalid but would consider it highly improper and should endeavor, as much as possible, to persuade the couple to be married subsequently by Jewish ceremony. Likewise, on the basis of the unanimous attitude of traditional law, it would be improper for a rabbi to participate with a Christian minister at such a marriage.

Children of religious school age should likewise not be required to undergo a special ceremony of conversion but should receive instruction as regular students in the school. The ceremony of Confirmation at the end of the school course shall be considered in lieu of a conversion ceremony. Children older than confirmation age should not be converted without their own consent. The Talmudic law likewise gives the child who is converted in infancy by the court the right to reject the conversion when it becomes of religious age. Therefore, the convert should receive regular instruction for that purpose and be converted in the regular conversion ceremony.

Considerable background material for each conclusion was provided. These specific recommendations have gone much farther than any other material in providing an orderly and uniform approach to the questions connected with mixed marriages.

A further recommendation was made by a special committee under the leadership of Eugene Mihaly in 1962 ("Report of the Special Committee on Mixed Marriage," *CCAR Yearbook*, 1962, pp. 86ff). It analyzed the problem and recommended a resolution which would have changed the position of 1909 and permitted rabbis to officiate at mixed marriages. There was considerable debate in which all matters connected with mixed marriage were thoroughly discussed. The substantive portion of the resolution failed, but it was decided to study the matter further and monitor it.

The issue of mixed marriage was raised again in 1971 with a demand for further study which was brought to the floor of the Conference in 1973 through a report under the chairmanship of Herman E. Schaalman ("Report of the Committee on Mixed Marriage," *CCAR Yearbook*, 1973, pp. 59ff). In this instance the majority report was accompanied by several minority statements. The entire matter was then subjected to lengthy discussion. The resolution accompanying the report urged that the 1909 statement be reaffirmed and then proposed a series of detailed statements which sought to restrain rabbis officiating at such marriages and co-officiating with Christian clergy. It also dealt with the question of welcoming those who had already entered a mixed marriage as well as their children. The discussion which followed dealt again with every aspect of mixed marriage as well as the issue of rabbinic freedom. The resolution finally adopted read:

> The Central Conference of American Rabbis, recalling its stand adopted in 1909 that "mixed marriage is contrary to the Jewish tradition and should be discouraged," now declares its opposition to participation by its members in any ceremony which solemnizes a mixed marriage.
>
> The Central Conference of American Rabbis recognizes that historically its members have held and continue to hold divergent interpretations of Jewish tradition. In order to keep open every channel to Judaism and *K'lal Yisrael* for those who have already entered into mixed marriage the CCAR calls upon its members:
>
> 1. to assist fully in educating children of such mixed marriage as Jews;
> 2. to provide the opportunity for conversion of the non-Jewish spouse; and
> 3. to encourage a creative and consistent cultivation of involvement in the Jewish community and the synagogue.

The Conservative Movement felt it necessary to deal with the intermarried Jew and his rights within the synagogue and community at length ("Intermarriage and Membership in a Congregation," *Rabbinical Assembly Annual*, 1958, pp. 110ff). The statement which opposed mixed marriage also sought to deal with the non-Jewish partner in a conciliatory manner. "It should be clearly understood that in frowning upon intermarriage and in voicing opposition to the choice of a non-Jewish mate, neither Judaism at large, nor Conservative Judaism in particular, expresses any judgment about the morality of character of these non-Jewish men and women." A list of fourteen reasons for not accepting the non-Jewish partner into a congregation was provided. Congregational membership could be retained by those already holding it, even after a mixed marriage, but would not be accepted initially. Such an individual would be permitted to worship with the congregation, but could not join it. In either case, it was recommended that synagogue honors be withheld, and the non-Jewish members of the family were not granted burial rights. The statement concluded with a milder injunction considering it "a mistake to permit the unconverted non-Jewish wife to be a member of the women' organization of the congregation." The Law Committee of the Rabbinical Assembly has dealt with the question further, but not in published responsa.

Orthodox Judaism has not changed its approach to this question. Civil marriages are not recognized by most Orthodox authorities. When a civil marriage has united a Jew and a non-Jew and, subsequently, the non-Jew converts to Judaism, some Orthodox authorities have refused to conduct a religious marriage (*Mishnah*, Yev. 11.8), while others have followed a more lenient point of view as did Ben Zion Uziel (*Mishpetei Uzi-el, Yoreh De-ah*, #14; also see B. Schereschewsky, *Dinei Hamishpaha*, pp. 80ff).

There were a number of responsa by David Hoffman (*Melamed Leho-il,* vol. 3, #10, 14, etc.) which dealt with the status of intermarried individuals, especially in cases of a later desire to convert, or where there was some concern about the future of the offspring of such a union. Such converts were refused. Similar responsa are also found in Moses Feinstein's *Igerot Mosheh, Even Ha-ezer*, #73, 44, etc.) and elsewhere. All of them simply reported the incidence of intermarriage and decried it.

Israeli law has followed Orthodox law in matters involving family and personal status. It has, however, recognized civil marriages conducted in other lands in accordance with international law (*Skornik V. Skornik*, 1951, 8:155-156). For Purposes of the Law of Return, a non-Jewish spouse and his/her children possess similar rights of immigration as Jews (*Law of Return*, Amendment, 2, 4a, March, 1970).

Summary

Reform Judaism and the Central Conference of American Rabbis has opposed mixed marriages. We recognize the problem as significant in every period of Jewish history. It has become more severe in 20th-century America, and, therefore we have made provisions for families of mixed marriages and their children. They are welcome in our congregations, and we continue to urge them to convert to Judaism. The Conference resolution of 1973 succinctly summarizes our position:

The Central Conference of American Rabbis, recalling its stand adopted in 1909 that "mixed marriage is contrary to the Jewish tradition and should be discouraged," now declares its opposition to participation by its members in any ceremony which solemnizes a mixed marriage.

The Central Conference of American Rabbis recognizes that historically its members have held and continue to hold divergent interpretations of Jewish tradition. In order to keep open every channel to Judaism and *K'lal Yisrael* for those who have already entered into mixed marriage, the CCAR calls upon its members:

1. to assist fully in educating children of such mixed marriage as Jews;

2. to provide the opportunity for conversion of the non-Jewish spouse; and

3. to encourage a creative and consistent cultivarion of involvement in the Jewish community and the synagogue.

Walter Jacob (ed.), *American Reform Responsa*, New York, 1983, # 146

THREE GENERATIONS OF MIXED MARRIAGE

Walter Jacob

QUESTION: A young man who grew up in the South is the product of three generations of mixed marriage. His great grandfather was Jewish and his great grandmother was Christian. His grandmother was raised as a Christian, but married a few. Both of his parents come from mixed marriages, and have provided him with no formal religious education. He would now like to claim his Jewish heritage and feels that the recent decision of the Central Conference of American Rabbis would make this easier for him. (H. S., Washington, DC)

ANSWER: The resolution of the Central American Rabbis, passed in 1983, has stated:

"The Central Conference of American Rabbis declares that the child of one Jewish parent is under the presumption of Jewish descent. This presumption of the Jewish status of the offspring of any mixed marriage is to be established through appropriate and timely public and formal acts of identification with the Jewish faith and people. The performance of these *mitzvot* serves to commit those who participate in them, both parents and child, to Jewish life.

"Depending on circumstances, *mitzvot* leading toward a positive and exclusive Jewish identity will include entry into the covenant, acquisition of a Hebrew name, Torah study, *Bar/Bat Mitzvah,* and *Kabbalat Torah* (Confirmation). For those beyond childhood claiming Jewish identity, other public acts or declarations may be added or substituted after consultation with their rabbi."

This resolution deals with the current generation and cannot be applied retroactively. In any case, there was no Jewish education or commitment in the previous generations. This young man has been raised in a secular fashion which has been colored by Christian traditions. Although there was very little formal Jewish education for three generations, some Jewish heritage survived. Otherwise, the young man in question, who now lives in a slightly larger town, would not be interested in reclaiming his Jewish identity. From a traditional Jewish point of view, he would not be considered Jewish as the link was broken in the second generation in which the father was Jewish and the mother, non-Jewish. Had this not been the case, traditional Judaism might consider him as a Jew in accordance with the view of Solomon ben Simon of Duran (Rashbash, *Responsa #89)*. He was concerned with the offsprings of Marranos and considered them Jewish indefinitely, if the female Jewish lineage remained unbroken. Most authorities would insist on some form of *haverut* to mark a formal re-entry into the Jewish community *(Shulhan Arukh Yoreh Deah* 268.10 f; Ezekiel Landau, *Noda Biyehudah, #150, etc.)*.

We, however, feel that there must be a strong educational component which will create a positive identity, and so would demand more regardless of matrilineal or patrilineal descent.

As this young man and his forefathers had no Jewish education or contact, we should treat him as a convert to Judaism and welcome him to Judaism. In the process of conversion and the final ceremony, we should stress his links to a Jewish past which he now wishes to establish firmly for himself and for future generations.

Walter Jacob, *Contemporary Reform Responsa*, New York, 1987, # 59.

MARRIAGE WITH A "MESSIANIC JEW"

Walter Jacob

QUESTION: May a Reform rabbi officiate at a marriage between a Jewish girl and a boy who was born a Jew but now considers himself a "Messianic Jew?" Is this in consonance with Reform Judaism? (Rabbi Seymour Prystowsky, Lafayette Hill, Pennsylvania)

ANSWER: Reform Judaism has been firmly opposed to mixed marriages. This was true in the last century and in this century. At its New York meeting in 1909, the Central Conference of American Rabbis passed the resolution, "The Central Conference of American Rabbis declares that mixed marriages are contrary to the tradition of the Jewish religion and should, therefore, be discouraged by the American rabbinate" (*CCAR Yearbook*, vol. 19, p. 170). This resolution was reaffirmed as part of a lengthy report in 1947 *(CCAR Yearbook*, vol. 57, p. 161). A considerably stronger resolution was passed in Atlanta in 1973. Its text reads as follows:

"The Central Conference of American Rabbis, recalling its stand adopted in 1909 that "mixed marriage is contrary to the Jewish tradition and should be discouraged," now declares its opposition to participation by its members in any ceremony which solemnizes a rnixed marriage.

The Central Conference of American Rabbis recognizes that historically its members have held, and continue to hold divergent interpretations of Jewish tradition. In order to keep open every channel to Judaism and *K'lal Yisrael* for those who have already entered into mixed marriage the CCAR calls upon its members:

1. to assist fully in educating children of such mixed marriage as Jews;

2. to provide the opportunity for conversion of the non-Jewish spouse; and

3. to encourage a creative and consistent cultivation of involvements in the Jewish community and synagogue.
(*CCAR Yearbook*, vol. 33,p. 97)

These resolutions clearly state the position of the Reform rabbinate in this matter. They reflect only the latest steps in the long struggle against mixed marriage which began in Biblical times. The Responsa Committee has written a long responsum on this subject.

If we consider a "Messianic Jew" as an apostate Jew, what would his status be for us? Judaism has always considered those who left us as sinners, but still as Jews. They could always return to Judaism through *teshuvah* and the exact response of Judaism depended very much on the conditions of the time. Hai Gaon (as quoted by Adret, *Responsa* VII, #292) felt that an apostate could not be considered as a Jew. Centuries later the rabbis of the Mediterranean lands had to face the problems of the Marranos (*anusim*). Their attitude differed greatly and may be summarized under five headings: (1) Apostates are Jews who sinned but, nevertheless, are considered Jewish (Isaac bar Sheshet; Simon ben Zemah of Duran but on some occasions he did not grant this status; Solomon ben Simon Duran; Zemah ben Solomon). (2) The apostates are considered Jewish only in matters of matrimony (and so their offspring are Jewish), but not in any other area (Samuel de Medina). (3) Marranos (*anusim*) are considered non-Jews in every respect, including matters of marriage; their children are not considered to be Jews (Judah Berab, Jacob Berab, Moses ben Elias Kapsali, etc.). (4) An apostate is worse than a Gentile (ben Veniste, Mercado ben Abraham) (5) Descendants of the Marranos who have been baptized are like Jewish children who have been taken captive by non-Jews and their chldren are Jewish (Samuel ben Abraham Aboab). All of these references and excerpts from the relevant literature may be found in H. J. Zimmels, *Die Marranen in der Rabbinischen Literatur*, 21ff. One extreme position was held by Solomon ben Simon Duran (Rashbash *Responsa*, #89) who felt that not only the apostate, but also the children would continue to be considered Jewish forever into the future as long as the maternal line was Jewish. He also felt that nothing needed to be done by any generation of such apostates when they returned to Judaism. No ritual bath nor any other act was considered necessary or desirable. In fact he emphasized that no attention be given to their previous state for that might discourage their return. Rabbenu Gershom gave a similar view and urged the quiet acceptance of all who returned to Judaism (*Machzor Vitry*, 96 and 97).

The other extreme has been presented by Rashi (in his commentary to Kid. 68b and Lev. 24:10). He felt that any returning apostate, or the children of a Jewish mother who had apostacized, are potentially Jewish, but most undergo a process akin to conversion if they wish to become part of the Jewish continuity. That point of view was rejected by most later scholars, as for example Nahmanides (in his commentary to Leviticus 24: 10; *Shulhan Arukh Yoreh De-ah* 268. l0f, Ezekiel Landau, *Responsa*, #150 etc.). We, therefore, have two extremes in the Rabbinic literature; both, of course, represented reaction to particular historic conditions. Solomon ben Simon of Duran wished to make it easy for a large number of Marranos to return to Judaism; unfortunately, this did not occur. Even when it was possible for Jews to leave Spain, the majority chose to remain. Rashi's harsh attitude probably reflected the small number of apostates who were a thorn in the side of the French community. Normative rabbinic Judaism chose a middle path and encouraged the apostate's return along with some studies, but without a formal conversion process. If an apostate did not wish to return to Judaism he would, nevertheless, be considered as part of the Jewish people (San. 44a). His or her marriage, if performed according to Jewish law as Marranos, and therefore as unwilling apostates, were valid (Yev. 30b; *Shulhan Arukh, Even Ha-*

ezer 44.9); divorce procedures for them are somewhat modified. Such an individual was not considered as reliable witness except in the case of an *aguna*. Penalties may be imposed on his inheritance (Kid. 18a), although he does have the right to inherit (B.B. 108a, 111a). Normal mourning rites should not be observed for such a person (M. San. 6.6; *Shulhan Arukh, Yoreh De-ah* 345.5). It is clear, therefore, that an apostate stands outside the community in all but relatively few matters until he has repented. We cannot officiate at his marriage with a Jewish girl.

We should be much stricter in our relationship with "Messianic Jews" than with other Christians with whom we continually attempt to establish good interfaith relations. The normative Christian churches are known for their beliefs and practices and are easily distinguishable by our people. Although they may continue to seek some converts from Judaism, most churches have not pursued active missionary activities in modern times. Directly the opposite is true of "Messianic Jews." They have established a vigorous missionary presence and often seek to confuse Jews about the nature of their religion. They have frequently presented themselves as Jews rather than Christians through misleading pamphlets, advertisements, and religious services. We should do everything in our power to correct these misconceptions and to maintain a strict separation from anyone connected with this group. We should, of course not officiate at such a marriage.

Walter Jacob (ed.), *American Reform Responsa*, New York, 1983, # 150.

CONTRIBUTORS

Israel Bettan (1889-1957), was Professor of Midrash and Homiletics at the Hebrew Union College, Cincinnati, Ohio. President of the Central Conference of American Rabbis, Chair of its Responsa Committee. Author of *Studies in Jewish Preaching in the Middle Ages* (1939), *The Five Scrolls* (1950).

David Ellenson is I. H and Anna Grancell Professor of Jewish Religious Thought at the Hebrew Union College-Jewish Institute of Religion, Los Angeles, California. His books include *Tradition in Transition* (1989), *Rabbi Esriel Hildesheimer and the Creation of a Modern Jewish Orthodoxy* (1990) and *Between Tradition and Culture: The Dialectics of Modern Jewish Religion and Identity* (1994).

Solomon B. Freehof (1893-1990) was Rabbi of the Rodef Shalom Congregation, Pittsburgh, Pennsylvania, Past President of the Central Conference of American Rabbis, and the World Union for Progressive Judaism; he was past Chair of the Responsa Committee of the Central Conference of American Rabbis, and the author of twenty-six books including eight volumes of responsa, *Reform Jewish Practice* (1947, 1952), The *Responsa Literature* (1955), *A Treasury of Responsa* (1963), *Reform Responsa for our Time (1977), Today's Reform Responsa*, (1990).

Walter Jacob is Senior Scholar of the Rodef Shalom Congregation, Pittsburgh, Pennsylvania, Past President of the Central Conference of American Rabbis, past Chair of the Responsa Committee; President of the Freehof Institute of Progressive *Halakhah* and the Associated American Jewish Museums. Author and editor of twenty-five books including *Questions and Reform Jewish Answers* (1991), *The Healing Past: Pharmaceuticals in the Biblical and Rabbinic World* (1993),

Israel and the Diaspora in Jewish Law (1997), *Aging and the Aged in Jewish Law* (1998), *Die Lehren des Judentums* (1999).

Peter Knobel is rabbi of Beth Emet, Evanston, Illinois. Chair of the Liturgy Committee of the Central Conference of American Rabbis; the author of numerous scholarly articles; he is editor of *Gates of the Season* (1983), *Duties of the Soul, The Role of Commandments in Liberal Judaism* (1999), and of the new American Reform prayer book..

Daniel Schiff is Rabbi of Temple B'nai Israel, McKeesport, Pennsylvania, Community Scholar of the Jewish Education Institute of Pittsburgh. Member of the Responsa Committee of the Central Conference of American Rabbis.

Ariel Stone is Associate Rabbi of Congregation Beth Israel of Portland, Oregon. While serving the Progressive congregation in Kiev, she also led services at the city's Karaite synagogue. Her research has included the Karaites, heresy in Talmudic Judaism, and bioethics.

Moshe Zemer is Director of the Freehof Institute of Progressive *Halakhah*; a founder of Progressive Judaism in Israel; founding rabbi of the Kedem Synagogue-Bet Daniel, Tel Aviv. *Av Bet Din* of the Israel Council of Progressive Rabbis, Senior Lecturer in Rabbinics at the Hebrew Union College, Jerusalem. Contributor of numerous articles on *halakhah* in the Israeli press and scientific journals; he is the author of *The Sane Halakhah* [Hebrew] (1993), with English and German translations in preparation.

www.ingramcontent.com/pod-product-compliance
Lightning Source LLC
Chambersburg PA
CBHW060032030426
42334CB00019B/2294
9780929699103